Death, Diversion, and Departure

There are many explanations for the survival of long-serving political parties, from access to state wealth to the use of excessive violence. A yet unexplored reason, particularly for parties that have survived under extreme conditions, is voter exit. In *Death, Diversion, and Departure*, Chipo Dendere shows that voter exit creates new opportunities for authoritarian regime survival. With an empirical focus on Zimbabwe, Dendere centers two types of voter exit: death and migration. She shows how the exit of young, urban, and working professional voters because of mass death due to the AIDS pandemic and mass migration in the wake of economic decline has increased the resilience of a regime that may have otherwise lost power. With authoritarianism on the rise globally and many citizens considering leaving home, *Death, Diversion, and Departure* provides timely insights into the impact of voter exit.

Chipo Dendere is an assistant professor of political science in the Africana Studies Department at Wellesley College. Her research focuses on African politics, democracy, migration, elections, and the politics of cacao and chocolate. Dendere has previously worked at the World Bank, The Carter Centre, and Oxfam. She regularly shares political commentary on traditional media and social media spaces. She is active on X (formerly Twitter) as @drdendere.

Death, Diversion, and Departure

Voter Exit and the Persistence of Authoritarianism in Zimbabwe

CHIPO DENDERE
Wellesley College

Shaftesbury Road, Cambridge CB2 8EA, United Kingdom

One Liberty Plaza, 20th Floor, New York, NY 10006, USA

477 Williamstown Road, Port Melbourne, VIC 3207, Australia

314–321, 3rd Floor, Plot 3, Splendor Forum, Jasola District Centre, New Delhi – 110025, India

103 Penang Road, #05-06/07, Visioncrest Commercial, Singapore 238467

Cambridge University Press is part of Cambridge University Press & Assessment, a department of the University of Cambridge.

We share the University's mission to contribute to society through the pursuit of education, learning and research at the highest international levels of excellence.

www.cambridge.org
Information on this title: www.cambridge.org/9781009678995

DOI: 10.1017/9781009678988

© Chipo Dendere 2026

This publication is in copyright. Subject to statutory exception and to the provisions of relevant collective licensing agreements, no reproduction of any part may take place without the written permission of Cambridge University Press & Assessment.

When citing this work, please include a reference to the DOI 10.1017/9781009678988

First published 2026

Cover image: Zimbabwe Exit – Barry Lungu

A catalogue record for this publication is available from the British Library

A Cataloging-in-Publication data record for this book is available from the Library of Congress

ISBN 978-1-009-67899-5 Hardback
ISBN 978-1-009-67901-5 Paperback

Cambridge University Press & Assessment has no responsibility for the persistence or accuracy of URLs for external or third-party internet websites referred to in this publication and does not guarantee that any content on such websites is, or will remain, accurate or appropriate.

For EU product safety concerns, contact us at Calle de José Abascal, 56, 1°, 28003 Madrid, Spain, or email eugpsr@cambridge.org

For My Family
Veneka-Alexandra our daughter, my husband Trevor,
my mother Aqueline, and my sisters Pamela and Rowesayi

Contents

List of Figures		*page* ix
List of Tables		xi
Acknowledgments		xiii
Chronology		xv
List of Abbreviations		xvii
1	Introduction	1
2	Theory of Exit and How to Study Exit	33
3	Death and Dearth of Democrats: HIV/AIDS and Voter Exit	74
4	Voting with Our Feet: When Voters Leave, the Regime Survives	115
5	Remittances and ZANU-PF Survival	153
6	Connecting the Dots: Voice, Exit, Loyalty, and Regime Survival	193
References		205
Index		223

Figures

2.1	ZANU-PF durability showing combined opposition votes	page 46
2.2	Support for ZANU-PF and opposition	47
2.3	Electorate lost to migration, 1990–2023	52
3.1	Impact of HIV/AIDS on the effective electorate	87
3.2	Impact of HIV and the population of voters	88
3.3	Cumulative HIV deaths	89
3.4	HIV death rates by province, 1999–2013	90
4.1	Considered emigration, at least a little bit	127
4.2	Total outward migration from Zimbabwe, 1980–2022	144
5.1	Zimbabwe sources of income, 1999–2012: GDP, remittances, and FDI	157
5.2	Zimbabwe personal remittances received	158
5.3	Zimbabwe economy: GDP, remittances, FDI, and agriculture, 1980–2016	159
5.4	Scatterplot of money usually sent	164
5.5	Profile of remittance receivers in 2009	167
5.6	Type of remittances in 2009	168
5.7	Receiving remittances 2014	169
5.8	Receiving remittances 2017	170
5.9	Contacting elected officials or media at least once	171
5.10	Voted in most recent election	172
5.11	Samson	174
5.12	Maria	178
5.13	Vongai	182
5.14	Rudo	186

Tables

2.1	Zimbabwean responses to sensitive questions	*page* 48
2.2	Profile of opposition supporters	50
3.1	Summary of impact	92
3.2	2000 elections	93
3.3	2002 presidential elections	95
3.4	2005 parliamentary elections	97
3.5	2008 presidential election results in harmonized election	98
3.6	2008 parliamentary election results in harmonized election	100
3.7	2013 elections	101
4.1	2000 parliamentary elections	146
4.2	2002 presidential elections	147
4.3	2005 parliamentary elections	148
4.4	2008 presidential election	149
4.5	2013 election	150
6.1	Summary of impact	199

Acknowledgments

Since I began this work, I have looked forward to the day I get to thank everyone who helped propel me forward. This project would never have come to life without my graduate school advisor, Daniel Young. Dr. Young had faith that my multifaceted ideas about exit and regime survival were worth pursuing and encouraging. When I told Dr. Young that I wanted to study the survival of dominant parties in Africa, he helped me find the resources to travel from South Africa to Tanzania. When I returned to Zimbabwe, I emailed him that I had found my voice and argument. Missing from everything I had learned up to that point was the study of the impact of voter exit on party survival. In my travels, I had met and talked to hundreds of people leaving home. I wanted to know what effect that would have on the politics of the sending countries. I am so glad that my advisor gave me the space to pursue this project. Dr. Ryan Carlin and Dr. Carrie Manning served generously on my dissertation committee and have continued to provide me with professional support. My academic mentor, Elisabet Rutstrom, went out of her way to help me secure funding for my extensive field work. I am lucky to have found such a solid network of mentors.

I am grateful to all the academic institutions I have worked at that provided me additional research funds: Gettysburg College, Amherst College, and my current employer, Wellesley College. At Wellesley College, I am especially grateful to our former Provost Andy Shennan, who believed in my work and provided me with additional resources. I am also deeply indebted to my colleagues in the Africana Studies department, Layli Maparyani, Kellie Carter-Jackson, and Liseli Fitzpatrick, for their unwavering support.

I am grateful to the American Association of University Women's sabbatical funding that enabled me to afford childcare, making it easier for me to find time to write. I am indebted to the organization's leaders who understand that it takes a village to get our work done and that mothers face additional challenges.

I feel extremely lucky that I found Tom Mowle of Rampart Professional Solutions, who worked with me for over three years as a developmental editor, writing coach, and my very own writing therapist. Any errors in the book are mine, but I would not have been able to put down my thoughts in a beautifully crafted way without his help and support.

Drafts of this book also benefited from many rounds of feedback at conferences and workshops. I am grateful to my friend and colleague Sara Dorman, who organized a summer workshop for me at Edinburgh University. I am thankful to Farai Chipato, Amy Kaler, and Thabani Mutambarese, who provided me valuable feedback at the workshop. I am also grateful to Jill Kelly, Meghan Healy-Clancy, Wendy Urban-Mead, and Brady G'sell, who have provided me immeasurable support and feedback – all via our WhatsApp group.

I will forever be indebted to hundreds of Zimbabweans, many of them immigrants, who opened their hearts, minds, and doors to me. I asked sensitive and personal questions. Thank you for trusting me with your life stories. I hope when you read my work, you see yourselves reflected with dignity and respect. There are not enough words to express my gratitude Ndinotenda.

I am grateful to my very large network of friends: my high school friends who have cheered me on via WhatsApp, my Linfied College and Georgia State friends, friends I have made along the way who have endured listening to me talk about my book for hours on end, my friends from church, and friends I have made through motherhood. Thank you for encouraging me.

I am also grateful to my late stepfather, Edward Nyandiya, who taught me the joy of reading and never tired of my many questions. I know that if he were still with us, he would be carrying a copy of my book everywhere. To my early educators at Hatfield Junior in Harare and Waddilove in Marondera, who believed that I was smart and encouraged me to take myself seriously, Thank you.

This book is dedicated to our daughter Veneka-Alexandra and to my rock and biggest cheerleader, my husband Trevor. I am very lucky to be born of a strong, kind, and cheerful woman – my mama, Aqueline. I am grateful to my sisters Rowe and Pamela and my brother Henry. I am also grateful to all the children in my life who have provided me much joy and the needed distraction.

Chronology

1965 Unilateral declaration of independence: Southern Rhodesia, led by Ian Smith, declares independence from Britain, which is not recognized internationally.
1979 Lancaster House Agreement: This agreement ended British–Rhodesian colonial rule.
1980 Official independence: Zimbabwe becomes an independent nation on April 18, with Robert Mugabe of the Zimbabwe African National Union (ZANU) becoming prime minister.
1983 The start of the Gukurahundi in Matebelaland
1985 Zimbabwe's first recorded case of HIV
1986 ZAPU and ZANU unify to form ZANU-PF
1987 Constitutional amendment: The constitution is amended to allow Robert Mugabe to become the executive president, consolidating his power.
1997 Major payout to war veterans of ZWD 50,000
1997 Black Friday, the day the Zimbabwean dollar crushed
1997 Tony Blair's UK government pulls out of land reform negotiations
1999 Formation of the Movement for Democratic Change (MDC): The MDC is led by trade unionist Morgan Tsvangirai. It is formed as a primary opposition party to challenge ZANU-PF's dominance.
2000 Fast-track land reform program: A politicized government program for land redistribution from minority White owners to majority Black.
2000 Constitutional referendum: A vote for a new constitution fails
2000 Zimbabwe experiences a massive wave of outward migration

2002 Presidential election: Robert Mugabe wins a disputed election against MDC leader Morgan Tsvangirai, amid reports of electoral fraud and violence.
2005 Operation Murambatsvina: A government program aimed at clearing unpermitted structures leads to the displacement of hundreds of thousands of people.
2008 Zimbabwe inflation reaches 89.7 sextillion percent
2008 Presidential election: Morgan Tsvangirai wins the first round but does not secure an outright victory. A runoff is marred by violence and intimidation, leading to Robert Mugabe being declared the winner.
2009 Formation of a unity government: A power-sharing agreement is reached between ZANU-PF and the MDC, with Morgan Tsvangirai becoming prime minister.
2013 New constitution: A new constitution is adopted, creating presidential term limits.
2017 Military intervention: Robert Mugabe is deposed in a coup after decades in power, leading to Emmerson Mnangagwa becoming president.
2018 General elections: Emmerson Mnangagwa wins the presidential election amid allegations of fraud and political violence.

Abbreviations

AIDS	acquired immunodeficiency syndrome
ANC	African National Congress
ART	antiretroviral therapy
EU	European Union
HIV	human immunodeficiency virus
MDC	Movement for Democratic Change
MDC-M	Movement for Democratic Change – Mutambara
MDC-T	Movement for Democratic Change – Tsvangirai
UN	United Nations
UNAIDS	Joint United Nations Program on HIV/AIDS
ZANU	Zimbabwe African National Union
ZANU-PF	Zimbabwe African National Union – Patriotic Front
ZAPU	Zimbabwe African People's Union
ZEC	Zimbabwe Electoral Commission

I

Introduction

STORY OF THE FIRST MOVEMENT FOR DEMOCRATIC
CHANGE (MDC) ELECTION

A few months before Zimbabwe's 2000 parliamentary elections, the air in the capital of Harare and throughout the country was thick with tension and hope. Two decades after Zimbabwe had gained its independence, the ruling Zimbabwe African National Union – Patriotic Front (ZANU-PF) was facing its first formidable challenger at the polls, the Movement for Democratic Change (MDC). The MDC was led by the young, charismatic trade unionist Morgan Tsvangirai. Initially founded as a worker's party, the MDC gained a loyal following across regional and tribal divides, across classes, and from rural voters and White Zimbabweans. Its symbol of an open palm was a direct contrast to ZANU-PF's closed fist. Hundreds of opposition supporters were arrested every week for wearing red or flashing homemade red cards calling for incumbent Robert Mugabe to go. I was too young to vote, but I remember waiting anxiously as my family spent more than ten hours in line to cast their votes for the MDC. People did not seem to mind the long waits. Vendors were selling food, and people brought camping chairs and blankets to brave the winter chills. Many, especially young first-time voters, had no doubt that it was time for Mugabe to go and that the newcomers would win at the polls. They could be seen brandishing the red cards, sending the message that Mugabe's time was over. They were wrong. Although the MDC held the ruling party to a narrow sixty-three to fifty-seven majority in parliament, it did not send ZANU-PF packing. In 2002, Tsvangirai narrowly lost his bid for the presidency, and Mugabe retained power. Millions have since voted for the opposition, but the ruling party has held on to power even as the economy entered a free fall.

Soon after the 2000 elections, a wave of migration began, and HIV-related deaths reached an all-time high. Since then, an estimated quarter of the Zimbabwean population, about six million people, have either emigrated or died from HIV/AIDS and related causes. I show that their exit provided a lifeline that sustained the illiberal authoritarian in Zimbabwe led by ZANU-PF. Since 1980, Zimbabwe has routinely held elections, but those elections have been neither free nor fair. In 1999, the formation of MDC put pressure on ZANU-PF and ignited people's hopes for change. The MDC was strongest in urban areas and among the young, the educated, and the working and middle classes. The exit of would-be opposition supporters due to death and migration allowed the regime to hang on to power under conditions that have toppled other regimes.

The last two decades have been marked by exit, death, and fatigue for Zimbabweans. Most of them were young, educated, urban professionals, many of whom had supported the opposition or would have voted for it if they had not exited. Black and White Zimbabweans were escaping different forms of violence. Most of the Black Zimbabweans who exited were escaping poverty or violence related to their participation in politics. White Zimbabweans and their farm workers were fleeing violence and the destruction of their property by the regime. About one million Zimbabweans left the country at the peak of land reform between 2001 and 2002 (Crush & Tevera, 2010). Most of them were White farm owners and their workers, who often left their country after violent takeovers of their homes and farms. Another wave of migrants exited after the government displaced over 700,000 urbanites as part of Operation Murambatsvina in 2005 (Tibaijuka, 2005). By 2008, the flow of hundreds of thousands of Zimbabweans into South Africa and other countries had created a regional crisis, as people swam across the crocodile-infested Limpopo River to escape. During the simultaneous health crisis, at least two million died from HIV (Crush et al., 2015). The death rate from HIV peaked in the 2000s, when the virus's prevalence rate reached 32 percent (Mahomva et al., 2006). In the same week, a family might accompany a relative to the airport as they made their escape to the United Kingdom and go to the graveyard to bury relatives who had died from complications related to HIV and AIDS. The puzzle driving this book is ZANU-PF's continued survival despite having governed the country so badly since independence in 1980.

My theory shows that the exit of millions driven by factors related to death and migration helped the electoral authoritarian regime in

Zimbabwe hold on to power from 1999 to 2013.[1] Like other such regimes, Mugabe's ZANU-PF used a mix of violence, patronage, cheating, and cooption to thwart its opposition. This task was made easier by a massive voter exit over a short period of time. I expand and modify Albert Hirschman's "exit, voice, loyalty" to show how exit, even if not voluntary, can help an authoritarian regime sustain its hold on power. A standard reading of Hirschman (1970) is that people have two options for dealing with underperforming institutions or states: They can exit the state by voting with their feet, or they can voice their disappointment by staying put and expressing their views through actions like voting for the opposition or protesting. A mass exodus of people would harm the state, so it either cultivates loyalty or allows voice to prevent people from leaving (other than opposition leaders, whose exile is welcome). In some circumstances, however, exit may help a regime by reducing its need to use standard autocratic tools to maintain power.

Zimbabwe exemplifies this. Exit sometimes was manifest in its standard form – emigration. There have been at least three such waves: first by Whites in the immediate period before and after independence, then by ethnic minorities in the south because of the Gukurahundi genocide, and more recently by young, educated professionals who seek economic opportunity and personal fulfillment. I am interested in the relationship between the third wave of exit and the regime's political survival. Those who have emigrated continue to express loyalty to the nation (not the regime) and to their families left behind by remitting millions into Zimbabwe every year. These remittances have bolstered the regime by providing much-needed investment and depressing the political participation of receivers.

Exit has also taken another form, one not anticipated by Hirschman. The HIV/AIDS pandemic led to the final exit of millions of Zimbabweans. It diverted many more into long-term caretaking, which left them too fatigued to engage in politics. Many orphaned children transitioned from the middle class, who often have higher rates of political participation, to the poor.

This book explains what happens when there is a massive exit of people from a country, whether through migration, death, or fatigue. Based on my calculations of exit via death and migration, a quarter of

---

[1] I stopped in 2013 because the 2008 was the last election before the government of national unity. By 2018, there was a coup; Zimbabwe's government is now more clearly a military dictatorship.

the Zimbabwean electorate exited due to death and migration. Most of them shared traits with opposition supporters who remained in the country and continued to participate. The loss of those who exited thus harmed the opposition more than the ruling party, which took advantage of exit and manipulated the system for its political survival.

Zimbabwe's recent history is an example of an increasing trend: authoritarian states that nevertheless hold elections. Some authoritarian states criminalize opposition parties, as in China, Vietnam, Cuba, North Korea, Syria, and Eritrea. But most are like Zimbabwe. They allow opposition parties to participate in elections because even dictators care about the illusion of legitimacy that they bring (Higashijima, 2022). This regime type has been called illiberal democracy. Zakaria (1997) used the term to refer to countries that have procedural aspects of democracy, such as regularly holding elections, but are weak on liberal aspects such as individual rights and freedoms. When such regimes open political space by expanding liberal rights, they risk losing the election. Exit makes it easier for such regimes to deepen their manipulation strategies and increase their longevity.

This is particularly true when the profiles of those who exit match the profiles of opposition supporters: young, urban, and educated. To win against a long-serving regime, the opposition requires the support and participation of all eligible voters with shared goals. In Zimbabwe, even though the ruling party supporters have also exited, the absence of opposition supporters amplified the difficulty of contending with the repression strategies used by the ruling party. ZANU-PF's strategies were primarily geared at increasing turnout among their supporters by providing patronage and making it easier for them to register and access polling stations on election day. The regime also used violence, a tactic carried over from the liberation struggle, to solidify support among its supporters. Finally, the regime used its control over state resources to reduce turnout for the opposition by making it difficult for them to register to vote or get to polling stations. The mass exodus of voters due to migration, death, fatigue, and fear made this strategy easier to implement, and the government did nothing to alleviate the causes of exit. Instead, the regime manipulated the exit of millions to its benefit.

Remittances, the money those who have exited send to families back home, also play a role in politics. Remittances bolstered ZANU-PF when the regime was broke and internationally isolated. With limited access to foreign investments, remittances provided a financial lifeline. Since 1999, remittances have exceeded most forms of direct investment in the country. The Zimbabwean government has made tax revenue from remittances a core part of its budget. Remittances also affect the political behavior of receivers. Senders often discourage the family members to whom they send money from participating in politics. Receivers are also likely to have less desire to engage in politics because remittances fill the void left by state failure.

Although my arguments are drawn from the Zimbabwean case, it is hardly unique in its form of government and in having experienced a massive exodus of people because of declining political and economic conditions. Today, there are signs of democratic decline or increased authoritarianism in many countries. Challenges brought on by climate change–related disasters are impacting democratic governance, as there has been an increase in conflicts, forced migration, and various insecurities. Thousands of people have drowned at sea trying to escape poverty and conflict in their home countries (Wamsley, 2023). This book helps explain the impact of exit during crises like those in Nigeria, Sudan, and Ukraine, where ongoing wars have displaced millions. Displacement is particularly meaningful when the country denies or limits the right to vote for its citizens once they live abroad, as Zimbabwe has done. If the diaspora can vote, it is sometimes effective at bringing about change. In 2017, French voters living abroad played an important role for Emmanuel Macron against the extreme far-right leader Marine Le Pen in the second round of a tough election (Brunet, 2017).

In the next section of this chapter, I describe my theory and argument in more detail. I then provide the historical context about Zimbabwe and explain why the case matters. Finally, I discuss alternative explanations for the survival of ZANU-PF and similar regimes.

THEORY AND ARGUMENT IN BRIEF

My theory of exit expands and modifies Hirschman (1970) to explain the impact of the peacetime mass exodus of millions of voters from a country that has an electoral authoritarian regime (also known as an illiberal democracy). My theory is that when voters exit, either temporarily via migration or participation fatigue, or permanently because they have died, their exit bolsters the survival of these regimes because they are not available to participate in the voting process. My theory argues that electoral participation is important for the ouster or maintenance of electoral authoritarian regimes. These regimes manipulate the democratic system for their own gain. When there is a massive exodus of the electorate, it is easier for them to retain power.

My theory expands Hirschman (1970) in four important ways. First, I discuss a type of regime that he does not. Second, I expand exit to include death and the diversion of caregivers. Third, I show that voice can still be available even after people exit, although that voice has limited influence on elections. Fourth, I show that emigrants can express loyalty after they leave through remittances and other support to family members. All these factors conspire to help electoral authoritarian regimes retain their hold on power.

Electoral Authoritarian Regimes

Illiberal democracies or electoral authoritarian regimes, as we know them today, did not exist when Hirschman proposed his theory: a regime was either a liberal democracy or fully authoritarian. Electoral authoritarian regimes behave differently than pure dictatorships because they want the legitimacy that comes from elections. But they are not willing to lose power in those elections, so they expend a lot of effort manipulating the electoral system in their favor, violating democratic norms in the process. The massive exodus of those who would have supported the opposition strengthens their position. Anything that reduces turnout for the opposition bolsters the survival of an autocratic regime by reducing the amount of manipulation needed without going as far as banning elections altogether.

Death, Disease, and Exit

My second innovation is expanding exit to include death and disease, which Hirschman did not consider. The death of millions of voters in a short period of time has an impact on electoral outcomes. Dead people have no voice and cannot contribute to political discourse. Nevertheless, their absence has an impact on the politics of the countries they leave behind, especially when their votes could have influenced political outcomes. The HIV/AIDS pandemic came at one such crucial time in Zimbabwean politics, when it looked like the opposition might be able to defeat the ruling party. Furthermore, HIV/AIDS, like other terminal illnesses, demands a lot of attention from caregivers for an extended time. Most caregivers are left with little energy for themselves, let alone for politics. Caring for one individual requires at least two people dedicated to the task. In Zimbabwe, most of these were young women who sometimes had to quit work or school to become full-time caregivers. Fatigued caregivers often found themselves disconnected from the state and exited themselves from participation. Their voices became silent. Nonstrategic exit matters because it still directly impacts political outcomes. As I discuss later, exit from most nondemocracies continues to increase and requires study.

Exit and Voice

Third, while migrants lose their right to vote when they exit, sometimes that revitalizes their ability to use voice. Hirschman and others (Warren, 2011) argued that voters who exit give up the option to use voice, but I argue they can retain their voice by participating in conversations via the internet, radio, or television. They may even have more voice after exit, given that authoritarian regimes work very hard to suppress voice by criminalizing protest and journalism. Citizens who go abroad can renew their use of voice by sharing their thoughts via the internet from places where such actions are not criminalized. The activities of exiled activists are well documented (Kuhlmann, 2010; Mutambasere, 2022; Wellman, 2021). The use of voice encourages opposition supporters in the home country and might even translate to financial support from friendly regimes.

That said, the voices of exiles are not always an effective tool for regime change in illiberal democracies. The regime has no way to stop them from using their voice, but it can influence what exiles say by inducing fear for the safety of their family members who have not exited. It can also make it impossible for migrants to vote from outside the country and introduce laws that would lead to the arrest of those who speak against the government if they return. This might not suppress voice, but it keeps migrants away from political participation. Because the voices of those who have exited are not expressed in actual votes, it does not hurt the electoral chances of the regime.

Loyalty after Exit

My fourth modification to Hirschman is that exit does not mean the end of loyalty to the country. Along with using technology to comment on politics from abroad, those who emigrate can show loyalty and ties to their home country via remittances. However, these expressions of loyalty to the state bolster the regime by reducing the intensity of opposition supporters and by inadvertently funding the regime.

When voters exit by migration, they often do not completely cut their ties to their home country and family; they sometimes express loyalty as remittances. The money they send to family members can benefit the regime. While most remittances do not lead to large-scale development, they do reduce the number of aggrieved citizens who might otherwise protest the government because their basic needs have not been met. Remittances allow receivers to afford food, shelter, healthcare, and education, which are the issues that lead people to take to the streets. Furthermore, senders may also remit fear. This is especially true of mothers – and most Zimbabwean emigrants are women because they tend to work in health care and education, the professions with the most straightforward opportunities for migration (Hlatshwayo, 2019; Makina, 2008). They might encourage their children and other family members to stay out of politics, given that their primary needs have been met. Hirschman (1970) did not consider the loss of voice among those who remain in the country but disagree with the regime.

Authoritarian regimes can also directly benefit from those who have left. The regime might add a fee to receive remittances or even become the money transfer agency. This gives the government direct access to foreign currency, which is often difficult to come by in authoritarian countries. Regimes might also find ways to receive direct payment for the labor of citizens working abroad.

Summary

My theory is that large-scale voter exit provides a lifeline to authoritarian parties that would lose power if free elections were allowed. When voters are not physically present to vote for their preferred party, either because they have moved abroad or have died, their party will receive fewer votes. Authoritarian regimes benefit when the profile of those who exit matches the profile of those who support the opposition. When voters in certain areas exit en masse, it is easier for ruling parties to suppress support for the opposition. Voters who exit can use their voice, but without the right to vote from exile, they are disenfranchised, which benefits the regime. Other forms of exit come without voter choice – death, of course, but people who are sick for a long time or engaged in caregiving responsibilities are also less likely to participate in politics. They have effectively exited the system. Those who do not exit might still be limited in how they use their voice because the regime punishes the use of voice. The support of those who have exited but express loyalty to their families through remittances can also lead to the political exit of those families and offer economic benefits to the regime.

METHODOLOGY

I used both qualitative and quantitative methods for data collection and analysis. First, I used published returns from local and national elections to establish the durability of ZANU-PF from 1980 to 2023. Then, I used Afrobarometer time series and cross-sectional data to create profiles of Zimbabwean opposition supporters over time. The Afrobarometer project completed eleven surveys in Zimbabwe from 1999 to 2022. I analyzed this dataset using regression tools to examine the relationship between party profile, migration, and the impact of the HIV pandemic on various demographics.

I used data from the Joint United Nations Program on HIV/AIDS (UNAIDS) spectrum model to calculate the population that exited because of HIV. The spectrum model pulls together demographic data and other measures of the impact of HIV, including migration, and estimates adult and childhood prevalence. I also drew migration data from the International Organization for Migration, which tracks human movement; from the UN Refugee Agency, which provides global information on Zimbabwean refugees; and from previous regional surveys of Zimbabwean migrants.

These secondary sources allowed me to understand the demographics of those who exited through emigration or death and the voting preferences of Zimbabweans who remained in the country and shared those demographics. I conducted fieldwork in the United States, the United Kingdom, South Africa, and Zimbabwe to understand the political preferences of actual migrants. I used snowball sampling to build a panel of 100 respondents, whom I interviewed in person and remotely using semistructured, open-ended questions (Dendere, 2019). I collected data on over forty topics. The main data points were what influenced individuals to relocate, their political participation in home country politics, their remitting patterns, and their experience with HIV as victims or family members. I then connected with family members in Zimbabwe and asked them similar questions. Most of the data were collected between 2013 and 2015, but I conducted four rounds of follow-up interviews between 2016 and 2022. In 2020, I conducted a survey on remittances using Qualtrics.

I analyzed the interview data in multiple ways. First, I spent a lot of time reading through the interviews, looking for patterns and themes shared across the interviews. Fujii (2017) argued that repeated reading of interviews allows researchers to have a deeper, clearer understanding of the data – especially when they are investigating difficult, complex topics. Multiple readings of the data also helped me determine whether I needed to conduct an immediate follow-up interview with a respondent to clarify comments that might be unclear or to cross-check facts (Read, 2018). I separated respondents by reported party support and analyzed in greater depth their different reasons for exit. Experiencing violence was not always their actual motivation for leaving Zimbabwe, and not all political asylees experienced the same type of violence. I traced differences and similarities across racial and tribal groups' relationships with politics back home. For example, most Shona urbanites showed unwavering support for the opposition, but Ndebele urbanites were more reserved about it. This nuance would have been lost in a survey.

To complement these sources, I drew on news articles, policy documents by government agencies, blog posts, and social media discussions on these topics. Social media platforms like Facebook and Twitter (now X) have created important channels where people in authoritarian regimes can discuss political issues anonymously and without fear of being tracked by the government.

In the next section, I explain why Zimbabwe is a critical case for evaluating the effects of exit on electoral authoritarian regimes. Finally, I provide a brief history of Zimbabwe for context, during which I illustrate steps the ZANU-PF regime took to retain power, steps that seem insufficient to explain its survival while similar regimes fell.

ZIMBABWE AS A CRITICAL CASE

Using the case of Zimbabwe where the ruling party, the ZANU-PF, has been in power since independence in 1980, I provide a theory of how voter exit sustains the survival of long-ruling political parties. ZANU-PF has maintained its hold on power despite years of active citizen protest, a crumbling economy, and an active opposition. Such conditions have toppled more robust regimes in Africa and elsewhere. The difference in Zimbabwe is the outmigration of millions and the death of a million more from HIV/AIDS.

This puzzle is very personal to me, as someone born and raised in Zimbabwe. Robert Mugabe was the only president I had. He ruled from 1980 until 2017, when a coup orchestrated by his own party ousted him. For most of my childhood, nearby countries also retained the same president and political party. Hastings Kamuzu Banda ruled Malawi from 1966 to 1994. Mozambique was led by the Liberation Front of Mozambique (FRELIMO), first under Samora Machel until his death in

1986 and then under Joaquim Alberto Chissano until 2005. Zambia was ruled by Kenneth Kaunda from 1964 until 1991 and then by the United Opposition Movement (MMD) until 2021. Although South Africa and Botswana are considered democracies, even they have been governed by the same political parties since independence. The African National Congress (ANC) has won every South African election since 1994, and the Botswana Democratic Party (BDP) has ruled Botswana since 1963. Because of this lack of change, it was reasonably easy to memorize the names of the ruling parties and their leaders.

While most of my insights are drawn from the case of Zimbabwe, an electoral authoritarian regime, it highlights the impact of voter exit anytime a political system loses many voters. Future researchers could use my theory to study the impact of the loss of millions of lives because of the COVID-19 pandemic, the exit of at least five million middle-class and young voters from Russia at the start of its war in Ukraine, and the impact of death and migration on the future of Ukrainian democracy. In Africa, my theory of exit provides lessons that can be used to understand the impact of mass exodus on Sudan and Ethiopia and the exit of middle-class South Africans who feel disillusioned by the ruling party there.

The Zimbabwe case is ideally suited to contribute more knowledge to the question of why long-serving parties survive and how events that neither the government nor citizens manufacture can drastically shift the course of democracy. Some states with long-serving parties have also experienced high death rates from HIV, such as Botswana, South Africa, Zambia, and Uganda. However, none of these also experienced an extreme economic meltdown and massive outward migration within the same period. Zimbabwe is a critical case because, although the government is very repressive, it is considered an illiberal democracy. Elections have never been suspended, and the opposition has continued with their activities, albeit under challenging conditions. This differentiates it from a one-party state. While very high, violence levels have not escalated to the level of a civil war.

The ruling party in Zimbabwe has survived economic hardship that is unmatched in contemporary times. Zimbabwe's year-on-year inflation rate peaked at 89.7 sextillion percent in mid-November 2008. Viral images of children carrying bricks of useless money to buy a bag of sweets did not adequately capture the extent of the crisis. In 2008, I traveled to Zimbabwe to participate in the elections. Families were eating baboon meat, and children were dying from eating poisonous leaves because there was no food. Most political parties would not have survived under such circumstances. The literature rightly points out that ZANU-PF used violence against citizens to suppress support for the opposition. Indeed, between 2000 and 2008, it was not uncommon to hear stories of massive brutality faced by citizens at the hands of local ZANU-PF militia members who routinely chopped off limbs of anyone they accused of supporting the opposition. In her groundbreaking work with activists, L. E. Young (2020) found that extreme violence had harmed the psychological well-being of activists, many of whom would end up withdrawing from political action. However, violence alone does not explain why the opposition could not get to the numbers it needed to oust the regime. Many opposition supporters continued to vote even in the face of extreme violence.

Zimbabwe is unusual in that it experienced large-scale outward migration without being in an active war. Before 2000, there had been other waves of migration. In the late 1970s, leading up to independence, many White Zimbabweans who were wary of living in a more democratic state left for South Africa or the United Kingdom, where they have ancestry citizenship. Still, their numbers were low; some returned in the early 1990s. The emigration in and after 2000 was unprecedented. A Harare hospital lost nearly all its nurses and doctors overnight after they emigrated to the United Kingdom (Chikanda, 2005). This was very detrimental, considering that the country was still in the throes of the HIV/AIDS pandemic. In the mid-2000s, South African President Thabo Mbeki claimed that at least a million Zimbabweans were illegally crossing the border into his country. While his claim was exaggerated, thousands of Zimbabweans were leaving the country daily. Many died from crocodile attacks as they attempted to swim across the Limpopo. The United Kingdom, in response to an influx of Zimbabwean migrants, implemented visa policies for the first time.

The arrival of AIDS, although it was not publicly identified until much later, coincided with the start of endless protests in the cities, sudden changes in the economy, and political unrest. A single dollar could no longer cover the cost of a loaf of bread or candy. Teachers who had worked at our schools for years started disappearing. We knew some had succumbed to the illness, but we learned that others had gone abroad. By the mid-2000s, it felt like everyone was leaving. Funerals had become fewer due to antiretroviral therapy medications, but we now spent our days shuffling between family meetings discussing who was going next, how to get passports, and what was needed for visas. I was in high school between 2000 and 2004. At school, it felt as though everyone's parents were leaving. If they had not died during the peak of HIV, they were going to the United Kingdom or South Africa.

At least two million Zimbabweans died from AIDS between 1990 and 2010. By 2010, an estimated four million people had emigrated outside the country. Most people who died from HIV or left the country in response to the declining conditions were young, urban, educated, and likely to have supported liberal democracy. The HIV/AIDS pandemic stalled democratic growth. Many pro-democracy civil society organizations abruptly shifted focus to matters related to the health crisis. The loss of active pro-democracy voices outside of political parties wrecked citizen engagement for years.

Given all this pressure, existing theories of regime survival would lead one to expect ZANU-PF would have lost power. Indeed, other regimes did – yet it remains because voter exit has helped sustain this electoral authoritarian regime. To provide context for the later chapters, the next section describes the political history of Zimbabwe and illustrates some of the tools ZANU-PF used to retain power. I compare ZANU-PF's actions to steps other regimes have taken, particularly in other parts of Southern Africa. I conclude that the existing theories fall short of explaining ZANU-PF's survival: Mugabe's party retained power while doing less in the face of conditions worse than those that brought similar regimes down.

EXPLANATIONS FOR THE PERSISTENCE OF ELECTORAL AUTHORITARIAN REGIMES

Scholars of democratization watched with bewilderment as former advocates for democracy turned into autocrats in Africa and much of the developing world. All the Southern African countries except Zambia and Malawi remain under the rule of the first independence party. Even in Zambia, the first independence party ruled for three decades before being kicked out in 1991, and the next party went on to rule for three more decades, until 2022. In Malawi, Kamuzu Banda also governed for three decades; after 1994, it has had more changes in leadership and parties.

Starting in 1999, the Zimbabwean economy contracted rapidly, a strong and popular opposition was founded, the international community rallied around the opposition, and voter turnout increased – yet ZANU-PF held on to power. Such conditions have toppled similar regimes that had more wealth and were more willing to use violence: Nicaragua in 1990, Kenya in 2007, Nigeria in 2014, and Gambia in 2016. A variety of explanations have been offered for the survival of ZANU-PF. Tendi (2013a, 2013b, 2020) argued that increasing militarization in Zimbabwe bolstered the ruling party. Closely tied to militarization was the increasing deployment of violence by the regime (Bratton, 2011; Masunungure, 2011; Raftopoulos, 2002; L. E. Young, 2019, 2020). ZANU-PF has used extreme violence to coerce voters in their rural base to vote for them and to suppress turnout in urban areas (Collier & Vicente, 2012). In 2008, the military intervened to thwart what could have been an electoral victory for the opposition (Mangongera, 2014; Masunungure, 2011; Tendi, 2017). Others have noted steps short of violence: blatant election manipulation and rigging of ballot boxes (Bratton et al., 2016; Chigora & Nciizah, 2007; Dorman, 2005; Magaisa, 2019; Moore, 2008; Mwonzora & Mandikwaza, 2019), as well as strategies the regime used to weaken civil society and the opposition (Chipato et al., 2020; Dorman, 2002, 2016; LeBas, 2006, 2013; Makumbe, 2002). The ruling party has also used patronage and state resources in elections (Arriola, 2009; Blessing-Miles et al., 2014; Maringira & Gukurume, 2022; Mpondi, 2015).

These explanations for ZANU-PF's survival deepen the puzzle rather than solve it. Certainly, the regime used these standard tools of authoritarianism to hold onto power. For the most part, however, it used them to a lesser degree than other regimes – yet it had more success. An accounting of the persistence of authoritarianism in Zimbabwe must consider how it benefited from events not of its own planning that gave it the breathing room it needed to survive many election cycles. ZANU-PF benefited from the death and diversion of so many of its citizens during the HIV pandemic and from the departure of many more of its citizens as they emigrated in search of better lives. That story comprises the bulk of this book. First, however, this chapter closes by describing standard but in this case insufficient explanations for regime survival: historical legacies, party performance, institutional manipulation, election fraud, patronage, weaponization of ethnic identity, and party organization.

Historical Legacies

ZANU-PF's party symbol, a clenched fist, sends a clear message to supporters and opponents alike that it is the party of the liberation struggle and the party to which Zimbabweans owe their independence. One of Mugabe's famous sayings, which has become a mantra for ZANU-PF elites, is that an X on the ballot cannot undo the work of the gun.

ZANU-PF claims full credit for freeing Zimbabwe from colonial rule and repeatedly tells voters it is the only party that can preserve the independence legacy. Mugabe, as one of the nation's founding fathers, is credited with masterminding the diplomatic missions that led to the end of the civil war and White minority rule. ZANU-PF has perfected the art of reframing history to suit its interests (Kenrick, 2016).

ZANU-PF's behavior fits into Samuel Huntington's theory of party survival, particularly in the immediate postindependence era. Huntington (1968) argued the "stability of a modernizing political system depends on the strength of the political parties. A party, in turn, is strong to the extent that it has institutionalized mass support" (p. 408). He also argued that one-party regimes that emerge out of social revolutions or independence movements have a distinct aura of legitimacy: "The stability of a one-party system derives more from its origins than its character. It is usually the product of a nationalist or revolutionary movement. The more intense and prolonged the revolution is, the deeper and stronger the ideological commitment of its followers and the greater its political stability."

Huntington's observation has proved to be accurate for most postcolonial states. Many long-ruling political parties – for example, the African National Congress (ANC) in South Africa, Botswana Democratic Party (BDP) in Botswana, and the Indian National Congress in India – were rooted in independence or liberation politics. Voters in countries that experienced transitions from decades of colonial rule or other types of authoritarian rule are likely to show loyalty to the parties that helped the country transition to democratic rule. A brief history of Zimbabwe helps explain the depth of ZANU-PF's claim to legitimacy.

From the beginning of settler colonialism in what was then called Rhodesia, Black people resisted White minority rule. In the early years, between 1896 and 1900, Blacks fought against Cecil Rhodes in the First Chimurenga (war of independence). They were underresourced, however, and the British had access to newer, more lethal weaponry. After their defeat, they continued to use methods like protests and boycotts to push back against White-minority authoritarianism. Rhodesian leaders responded with every brutal means of force available to them, legal and illegal. Black political parties and resistance movements could only exist underground. The first open opposition party, Zimbabwe African People's Union (ZAPU), was founded in 1961 by young Black political actors from unions and academic circles. Its founding leaders included Ndabaningi Sithole, Herbert Chitepo, and Joshua Nkomo. Many of them played an active role in the government after independence, and many used their experiences in the liberation struggle to continue ZANU-PF's hold on power.

In 1962, Ian Smith's Rhodesian government banned ZAPU, accusing it of militarism. Most of its members were forced into exile or jailed, and their operations went underground. Personality differences and the constant harassment from Rhodesian officials caused ZANU to split from ZAPU in 1963. Nkomo became the leader of ZAPU. Even though ZAPU had many leaders and members from Mashonaland, most people assumed it was a Ndebele faction because Nkomo was from Matebeleland and the party headquarters was located there. Sithole, Chitepo, Edgar Tekere, and Mugabe founded ZANU. Sithole was elected president, and Mugabe served as the secretary general. In the rewriting of national memory essential for elevating Mugabe, ZANU is considered the main liberation struggle party and Mugabe the most important founding member (Dombo, 2019). This historicization legitimated his stay in power for as long as he did. After Mugabe was ousted in 2017, his former comrades discounted his military role by claiming that he had been bookish and that it was, in fact, Emmerson Mnangagwa who was at the front lines. There is not much historical text placing Mnangagwa among the leaders of either ZAPU or ZANU at their founding.

Immediately following the formation of ZANU in 1963, Mugabe and many of ZANU's cofounders were arrested and sentenced to ten years in prison for political activism. Chitepo fled the country before Rhodesians could arrest him; he served as party leader from exile until his 1974 assassination in Zambia. After Chitepo's death, Mugabe was elected party leader. The arrests forced both ZANU and ZAPU to become more militant. Their efforts were bolstered by China, Russia, North Korea, and newly independent African states; they culminated in the Second Chimurenga between 1967 and 1979.

As the war raged in 1979, Smith struck a deal with Abel Muzorewa to try to sideline ZANU and ZAPU. Muzorewa led a small party that was more amenable to a transitional government with the White Rhodesians and was an opponent of military tactics. Their agreement in 1979 to form Zimbabwe-Rhodesia was rejected by ZANU and ZAPU leaders, who continued to fight for universal suffrage and Black majority rule.

After the Muzorewa agreement failed, the various factional leaders, including ZAPU's Nkomo, ZANU's Mugabe, and the Rhodesian Front's Smith, traveled to London to sign the Lancaster House Agreement. This brought the war to an end. Mugabe and the ZANU-PF have taken every opportunity to remind Zimbabweans that had they not made the trek to London, independence would not have been achieved.

In December 1979, Mugabe's delegation, which included Nkomo, signed a peace agreement at Lancaster House in London. The Lancaster Agreement voided the 1965 declaration of independence, so Zimbabwe was once again a colony of Britain until the first universal elections were held in 1980. Mugabe's ZANU won the majority of votes in the 1980 election, which was considered free and fair (BBC, 1980). In his inaugural speech as prime minister, Mugabe promised to work toward peace and democracy. Mugabe said he would create room for political actors from the opposition, including White Rhodesians. While Black Zimbabweans celebrated across ethnic and tribal lines, White Rhodesians were more apprehensive. About 60,000 White Zimbabweans left the country and moved to the United Kingdom (Brownell, 2008). This first wave of outward migration was critical to muffling the voices of White minorities in Zimbabwe's politics after independence. Most of those who left had been politically active and feared retribution from ZANU leadership. While this period is beyond the scope of this book, their departure supports my theory of how exit supports electoral authoritarian regimes.

To this day, ZANU-PF elites emphasize their liberation credentials. ZANU-PF referred to the farm takeover period in the early 2000s as the Third Chimurenga. ZANU-PF elites, army generals, and war veterans contrasted their leadership with that of the MDC opposition, many of whom were too young to have gone to war. By 2017, other elites within ZANU-PF considered Mugabe to have been compromised by his wife and by other actors who had no war credentials. Their ouster of Mugabe in the 2017 coup was justified as a necessary step to restoring the national legacy.

Weaponization of Identity for Political Gain

In the 1980 elections, only three political parties won any of the eighty parliamentary seats (out of 100) allocated to Black Zimbabweans. Mugabe's ZANU-PF emerged as the clear winner, with 63 percent of the votes and fifty-seven seats. Nkomo's PF-ZAPU came second with 24 percent of the vote and twenty seats, and Muzorewa's United National African Council (UANC) came third with only 8 percent of the vote and three scattered seats. The ZANU-PF won in its Shona strongholds of Mashonaland East, Central, and West; Victoria (now Masvingo); and Manicaland, where it won 71–87 percent of the vote in each constituency. PF-ZAPU's wins were in its base in Matebeleland, in Midlands, and in the southern parts of the country.

Although ZANU-PF came out of independence as the ruling party, opposition remained, especially in the Matebeleland region where Joshua Nkomo, the head of ZAPU, resided. A paramilitary created by Mnangagwa, then minister of state, targeted ethnic Ndebeles and accused them of disloyalty. This developed into a genocide known as Gukurahundi that killed over 20,000 ethnic Ndebele and some Shona allies (Catholic Commission for Justice and Peace & Legal Resources Foundation in Harare, 2008). As violence escalated, the state defended its position by arguing that the region was infiltrated by dissidents who wanted to destabilize independence. No evidence of dissidents in the region ever came to light. Nkomo, the leader of PF-ZAPU, faced many incidents of violence, including the infamous bombing of his house in Bulawayo (J. Alexander, 2021).

A common explanation for voting behavior and party survival in Africa is the ethnicization of African politics. Ethnic voting literature has roots in Horowitz's 1985 seminal *Ethnic Groups in Conflict*. Horowitz argued that voters in multiethnic countries seek affirmation of self-worth through their identities as members of ethnic groups. Ferree (2006) described elections in newly democratizing African states as nothing more than an ethnic census. This view of voting assumes people's ethnic allegiances are primordial and nonnegotiable. In this view, voters will sometimes vote against their individual interests to preserve group interests (Ferree, 2006).

More recent literature on the role of ethnicity in elections is moving away from this rigid explanation to a more constructivist understanding of voting behavior. This approach suggests that ethnicity is used by politicians and voters like any other political tool and, as such, is subject to change and manipulation (Basedau et al., 2007). Ethnic preferences interact with voter evaluations of the incumbent party's performance on the economy and policy (Ferree, 2006), delivery on promises (Kandeh, 2003), and other factors such as violence and intimidation (Bratton & Kimenyi, 2008). This view of ethnicity is more amenable to theories of voting behavior outside Africa.

Sociological approaches to voting argue "a person thinks politically as she is social" (Lazarsfeld et al., 1968, p. 27). This is consistent with ethnic voting because people tend to be socialized in communities of coethnics (Habyarimana et al., 2007). The same holds for the macro-sociological cleavage approach (Erdmann, 2007; Lipset & Rokkan, 1967) or for a sociopsychological approach that conceptualizes party identification and voting preferences as products of social ties (Dalton et al., 2000, pp. 20–21). Finally, ethnic voting fits neatly under the rational voter model (Aldrich, 1993; Downs, 1957; Fiorina, 1978), because voting for a coethnic candidate may serve a voter's interests. Lindberg and Morrison (2008) showed that in Ghana and elsewhere, ethnic voting is tied to expected benefits that a coethnic candidate might deliver once in office. In Zambia and Kenya, voters tend to choose coethnics if they fear other voters will do the same (Bogaards, 2007; Bratton & Kimenyi, 2008; D. J. Young, 2009). Bratton and Kimenyi (2008) found that voting in Kenyan elections remains highly ethnic even though, at an individual level, most voters do not identify in ethnic terms or see a candidate's ethnicity as a primary motivator for their vote. They also found that even though voters might want to vote in nonidentity terms, they tend not to do so because they fear other ethnic groups will not do the same. Although voters see themselves as not being biased against other ethnic groups, they see those groups as biased against them. Thus, voters fear that if they do not vote along ethnic lines, they will lose out due to ethnic favoritism (Posner, 2005, p. 104).

Zimbabwean ethnic politics is consistent with traditional views on the ethnicization of politics, though it is more subtle. Since independence, the status of racial minorities in Zimbabwe has been precarious. White Zimbabweans were slowly pushed out of politics unless they opted to join the ruling party. The land reform and various citizenship policies forced White minorities and others with migrant roots to leave the country. These measures for forced exit were violent in different ways. Whenever ZANU-PF is politically vulnerable, it unleashes violence on different subgroups. The four most dominant ethnic groups in Zimbabwe are the Shona and Ndebele, the two main Black ethnic groups (about 95 percent of the population), and Whites and Asians, who combine to make up 5 percent. Zimbabwe has never had a non-Shona president and is unlikely to do so.

After the 1983 genocide and the unification of ZAPU and ZANU, the government created a second vice president position. Unofficially, it is accepted that the position is reserved for a senior former ZAPU member who has become well entrenched within ZANU-PF. The forced unification of ZAPU and ZANU was supposed to address ethnic tensions, but this has not been entirely successful, as Mugabe rewarded coethnics with lucrative positions. The Matebeleland region remains one of the most underdeveloped areas in the country. Still, even the most repressive treatment of ethnic minorities has not sustained ZANU-PF rule. The opposition grew its strongest roots in Matebeleland, and it has received significant financial support from the White community.

Maintaining Elite Unity

The bombing of Nkomo's house in Bulawayo was a catalyst for the formation of ZANU (PF), a union of ZANU-PF and PF-ZAPU. While the Matebeleland genocide was occurring, Mugabe had pushed for a one-party state within the ZANU party structure (Shaw 1986). Mugabe was increasingly aware that ZANU could not afford to have a war raging on, yet he did not want to have an opposition party. In the second elections in 1985, ZANU-PF gained 77 percent of the vote and sixty-four seats and PF-ZAPU won only fifteen seats. UANC won less than 2 percent of the vote and no seats, but Sithole regained his hometown seat in Chiping with 1 percent of the national vote (Makumbe, 2006).

In 1986, Mugabe reached out to a weary Nkomo and convinced him they should unite to form ZANU (PF). The new party guaranteed political stability for both Nkomo and Mugabe, but Mugabe's promise of unity was short-lived for Nkomo's supporters in the South. Mugabe and ZANU were not content to have an active opposition, an attitude that continues to this day. Mugabe despised Nkomo, who remained popular and served as vice president until his death in 1999, and sought to destroy him and his followers. The seeds for antiopposition politics had been planted early, and ZANU utilized the tools it had inherited from White minority rule to suppress the voice of anyone who disagreed.

ZANU-PF followed Riker's (1976) model to ensure party dominance. As the incumbent party, it could divide and conquer by sticking to the center and splitting challengers to the left and the right. In the politics of developing nations, the ideological lines are not clear-cut, and parties tend to share many of the same values. However, ruling parties can divide the opposition by promising defectors benefits that newer and poorer parties cannot offer. Magaloni (2006) found this to be true for elite unity and mobilization within Mexico's Institutional Revolutionary Party (PRI). The PRI was able to coopt smaller parties and independent elites and create a supersize coalition.

This cooption is unusual in Africa, where parties tend to be wary of bringing opponents into their fold, likely because of a history of coups on the continent. For example, even when faced with growing opposition and defections, South Africa's ANC has not made any effort to reach out to opponents. If anything, the ANC seems committed to purging anyone who is not toeing the party line. Similarly, ZANU-PF functions in a very top-down process: older party loyalists and founders remain at the top of the food chain, and there is not much room for new people. Geddes (1999) argued that hegemonic parties survive because they are immune to elite splitting. Elites within the regime realize there are gains to be made from staying in a unified front. She argued:

> Factions form in single-party regimes around policy differences and competition for leadership positions, as in other regimes, but everyone is better off if all the factions remain united in office. This is why cooptation rather than exclusion is usually the rule in established single-party systems. Neither faction would be better off ruling alone, and neither would voluntarily withdraw from office unless exogenous events changed the costs and benefits of cooperating. (Geddes, 1999, p. 11)

The 1986 unification between Nkomo and Mugabe eliminated the largest opposition. Mugabe felt confident that he could push forward with his demands for a one-party state. The remaining opposition, led by former Mugabe ally Tekere, had substantial support in urban areas. Mugabe was wary of Tekere's growing popularity among urbanites. In the lead-up to the 1990 elections and before the multipartyism mandate's expiration, Mugabe renewed his demands for a one-party state. In the 1990 election, ZANU-PF won the majority of seats, 116 of 150, but turnout was low and there were rumors of discontent within the ruling party. Now that the mandate for multipartyism had expired and Mugabe had a two-thirds majority, he asserted ZANU-PF's electoral victory was "a mandate for all our policies, including one-party rule." It was not.

The call for a one-party state was not new. At the first national congress in 1984, Mugabe had said, "With such a mandate, we shall no doubt proceed toward the full attainment of our political goals and the establishment of a one-party state and the fulfillment of a socialist revolution" (Cowell, 1984, p. 1). However, unlike in neighboring Zambia and Malawi, Mugabe could not implement his plans because of a clause in the constitution drawn up at independence in 1980 that committed Zimbabwe to retain a multiparty system for ten years. That clause also reserved 20 percent of the parliamentary seats to the White minority, who had to give 100 percent support for any change in the constitution before 1987 and 70 percent support between 1987 and 1990 (Shaw, 1986). Essentially, Mugabe's hands were tied. Mugabe could not ignore the constitution because he was very committed to the public appearance of being democratic. The economy and his status with Western actors were also at stake. Shortly after independence, Mugabe had been given numerous honors, including a state visit with US President Jimmy Carter and a knighthood from Queen Elizabeth that was revoked in 2008 (New York Times, 2008). Mugabe was also given numerous honorary doctoral degrees, including one from the University of Edinburgh that was revoked in 2019 (Campsie, 2019). Mugabe was happy to use the rhetoric of a one-party state to keep his party cadre happy, but he had no real intention of following through within the first ten years of independence.

Leaders of other countries have manipulated constitutions and other democratic institutions to extend their rule, including shifting to presidentialism, creating a one-party state, and using emergency decrees. After independence, African leaders pushed to shift from a parliamentary to a presidential system, which is more amenable to centralizing power around a single leader (Van de Walle, 2003). A government centered on the presidency often finds it easier to distribute patronage. For example, during the Mwai Kibaki presidency, one in six Kenyan civil servants worked directly for the president's office. The president's office had the power to fire and hire new loyalists (Opalo, 2011).

In that postindependence era, most African states shifted to one-party states and eliminated opposition parties. Leaders pushing for one-party governments argued that newly independent states were too fragile to survive the tensions that come with multipartyism. The shift to a one-party state worked for three decades in a few countries, such as Zambia, Kenya, Tanzania, and Malawi (Bamfo, 2005; Venter, 2002). Their leaders were able to suppress opposition and keep their dominance. These ruling parties were forced to open political space for multiparty elections because of increased citizen demands and demands from the World Bank during the structural adjustment era. They all lost power when they did so. In West Africa, the strategy to shift to one-party governance never worked. In almost all cases, including Kwame Nkrumah's Ghana, one-party regimes were overthrown by a military junta.

As an alternative to setting up a one-party state, leaders seeking to extend their time in office have pushed for amendments to their countries' constitutions. Between 2000 and 2018, over forty-six attempts in twenty-eight countries were made to extend presidential term limits. A recent study by Reyntjens (2020) found four ways term limits have been manipulated. Leaders in Guinea (2001), Democratic Republic of Congo (DRC; 2002 and 2016), Rwanda (2003), Burundi (2015), and South Sudan (2018) delayed elections to extend their time in office. Other leaders changed the number of terms one could hold, as in DRC (2015). When a new constitution was introduced, such as in Zimbabwe (2013) and Rwanda (2015), incumbents reset the clock on their rule. Finally, several countries removed term limits altogether: Guinea (2001), Togo (2002), Tunisia (2002), Gabon (2003), Chad (2005), Uganda (2005), Algeria (2008), Cameroon (2008), Niger (2009), and Djibouti (2010).

Mugabe was unable to eliminate the opposition. Although suppressed and facing arrests and abuse, new activists emerged. Some ZANU-PF elites like Margaret Dongo defected, running as an independent and thus providing a small but critical opposition voice (Compagnon, 2000). The roots of opposition planted by Nkomo grew until the early 2000s. As years passed since independence and the economy continued to fail, even the most carefully crafted message about party unity did not insulate ZANU-PF from defections and small electoral losses. It was under the backdrop of these defections and citizen protests that the main opposition, the MDC, was founded by a group of young professionals and activists in 1999. Since then, ZANU-PF has been fighting for its survival against MDC.

Performance Legitimacy

Until the mid-1990s, however, ZANU-PF presided over economic growth. Steady growth in the middle class and widespread provision of affordable health care and education, especially in rural areas, certainly contributed to its survival. Perhaps the praise was inflated and not entirely deserved, but it was relative. South Africa was ruled by apartheid, Mozambique was caught up in a protracted civil war, and Zambia's economy had all but collapsed.

This approach to explaining regime survival is known as performance legitimacy: undemocratic regimes retain popular support by implementing good, sound policies that lead to economic growth (Hansen, 1994). Scholars and practitioners have used this approach to explain the survival of hegemonic parties in Asia's economic tigers – Taiwan, Malaysia, and Singapore – where the economy grew exceptionally well under one-party rule. Intuitively, the argument makes sense: parties should retain power when the economy improves and should collapse when the economy fails. There is empirical evidence of this from parties such as the United Malays National Organization in Malaysia, the People's Action Party in Singapore, the Liberal Democratic Party in Japan, and the BDP in Botswana. Each of these presided over sustained economic growth. When the economy is doing well, voters will often reward the incumbent party by voting for them again and again.

Lack of economic growth corresponds to losing political power. Before its demise at the hands of the MMD, the United National Independence Party (UNIP) governed Zambia from 1964 to 1991. Under Kaunda's leadership, Zambia had instituted one-party rule in the mid-1970s and banned all opposition political activities. A combination of bad economic policies, the 1980s global economic crisis, and Zambia's dependency on copper saw the country's economy decline at an alarming rate. Kaunda opposed capitalism, supporting a homegrown form of socialism that he called "humanism" (Maroleng, 2004). UNIP sponsored expensive spending commitments that ran the economy further into the ground. To make up for its overspending, UNIP borrowed heavily from international agencies. By 1990, Zambia owed over $7 billion, making it the most indebted country in the world (Chikalipah, 2021). UNIP faced increasing public discontent, riots, strikes, and demonstrations from labor and student groups. These all but paralyzed the already weakened economy. The Zambia Congress of Trade Unions quickly asserted itself in the political arena, challenging the one-party, one-state policy, and forcing UNIP to loosen its grip on power and open up political space (Posner, 2007). A combination of international and local demands and the joint opposition forces led to the ouster of UNIP in the 1990 elections.

Long-term hegemonic rule accompanied by economic failure is quite common. The puzzle is that ZANU-PF could withstand the international and domestic pressures that led to the failures of similar parties in Zambia and Malawi. By the mid-1990s, the Zimbabwean economy, which had been slowly declining, finally plummeted after the government issued unbudgeted compensation to the war veterans (Ndlela, 2011). In 1997, Harare was rife with civil servant strikes and riots headed by then-trade union leader Tsvangirai. That same year, ZANU-PF faced its first public outcry against their decision to send Zimbabwean troops to the Democratic Republic of Congo (DRC) to shore up Laurent Kabila's government against rebels. The two-year military intervention cost Zimbabwe an estimated $200 million at a time when its economy was already depressed (UN News Report, 2000). Zimbabweans argued that their government did not have the money and resources for the mission. There was also concern with the high number of Zimbabwean casualties in the war.

Since 2000, ZANU-PF has presided over the worst economic crisis since Germany's hyperinflation after the First World War. In 2005, I took a taxi into the city center and paid ZWD 5,000. On my return home about six hours later, the same ride was ZWD 15,000. I had to walk halfway home. This was not the worst of it. By 2008, inflation hit over 9.6 billion percent per month, with year-over-year inflation reaching an astounding 89.7 sextillion percent. In 2022, crippling inflation returned and was hovering at nearly 200 percent. In 2021, the fare for a taxi ride was ZWD 50 (the currency was devalued in 2016, 2018, and 2020). By June 2022, the cost had skyrocketed to ZWD 240 and continued to increase. In response to the high cost of living, citizens protested. Such protests and citizen anger would be enough to topple stronger regimes elsewhere, yet the ruling party in Zimbabwe survived.

Vote Buying and Patronage

In 1997, as the Zimbabwean economy began its decline, war veterans made public their demands for remuneration for war-related injuries and demanded compensation in the form of land and money. In November 1997, the government responded to their demands by initiating pension payouts of up to ZWD 50,000 ($4,500 at the time; Kanyenze et al., 2017). The estimated cost of the payout was about $4 billion, which was ten times Zimbabwe's 1997 budget. In addition, the war veterans were promised a ZWD 2,000 ($165) monthly income. Mugabe went on a national tour defending the release of the funds, even as critics, including members of parliament from his party, argued the money had not been budgeted. Mugabe said the cost would be covered by additional taxes (Reuters, 1997). The business and professional communities protested the payouts. The call for payouts provided common ground for White and Black urbanites who had until then largely stayed out of politics.

The payouts served as a final nail in the coffin for the Zimbabwean economy. The economy was struggling to recover from the negative effects of the World Bank's Economic Structural Adjustment Program and from corruption and banking scandals. On the day Mugabe announced the payouts, the Zimbabwean dollar fell from $11 to $21 and the country experienced its first national power blackout (A. Meldrum, 2006). By the end of the year, the Zimbabwean dollar had lost 75.5 percent of its value and the stock market had crashed by 46 percent. Civil society activism became more robust after the war veteran payouts debacle (Dorman, 2016).

Prior to the November payouts, the war veterans had laid out a series of demands, including hospital and school fees coverage for their families and government redistribution of land. The payouts did little to ameliorate tensions between war veterans and the ruling party. The ruling party leaders increasingly became agitated with the War Veterans Association, which was now openly hostile toward ZANU-PF. In 1999, the trial of Chenjerai Hunzvi, who was accused of fraud, dominated newspaper headlines and made public the tensions between party elites and the war veterans (Mail & Gurdian, 2000). The ruling party could not afford to fight two battles, one with the rising MDC and another with the war veterans, so it sided with the latter. Hunzvi was acquitted, which marked the beginning of the brutal land reform campaign that would become the center of ZANU-PF's messaging for a decade. Hunzvi led the initial farm grabs in 1999, and the government took over the process in 2000. The government tried but largely failed to formalize the equitable redistribution of farmland (Dorman, 2016).

The issue of land reform was not new. Land had played a critical role in the 1979 Lancaster House agreements. According to the agreements, the British government would give financial assistance to the new government to initiate land reform after a ten-year grace period. The Margaret Thatcher government had been primarily interested in protecting the property of the White minority. At Lancaster, British Foreign Minister Peter Carrington assured liberation struggle leaders that the British government would enlist the help of its allies to secure the money needed for land redistribution. Carrington assured the delegation that the "future government would be able to appeal to the international community for help in funding acquisition of land for agricultural settlement" (McGreal, 2002). This calmed the fears of the leaders, especially Mugabe, who argued that the "assurances (given in the Lancaster Agreement) go a long way in allaying the great concern we have over the whole land question arising from the great need our people have for land and our commitment to satisfy that need when in government" (McGreal, 2002).

During the first decade after independence, the new government was limited in what they could do to redistribute land because of the constitutional mandate that reform could not be initiated in the first ten years after independence. By the time the mandate expired, neither the government nor the White farmers took land reform seriously because the agriculture sector was bringing in a lot of revenue for the country. It seems there was an unwritten agreement between the new government and White farmers: the Blacks would run the government while the Whites would run the economy. This implicit compromise kept everyone happy until the late 1990s.

By then, time appeared to have slipped away from both the British and Zimbabwean leaders. The promise to give land to millions of poor Blacks hung in the air as the economy contracted. The demand for land caught the government by surprise. At independence in 1980, over 15 million hectares of land were devoted to commercial farming, and the White minority owned almost all of it. The first phase of land redistribution was a gradual process that started in the mid-1990s, when a little over three million hectares were redistributed. The amount of White-owned commercial land (about 12 million hectares) quickly declined after 2000, when the government allocated 4,500 hectares to new farmers, for a total of up to 7.6 million hectares (Scoones et al., 2010). The country experienced a dramatic shift from large-scale farming to smaller farms focused on mixed production that had very low levels of capitalization. The decline in agricultural production led to an increased need for imported foods and a decline in national exports, which negatively affected the nation's GDP. Between 2001 and 2010, GDP growth never made it above 10 percent. It was as low as −18 percent in 2003 and 2008 (World Bank Group, n.d.).

In 2001, the government had agreed to end land invasions in exchange for British funds to finance a more gradual and tempered land reform program, but the invasions continued. White farmers returned to politics by providing financial support that enabled the formation of the MDC. The return of White voters into active politics threatened to reduce ZANU-PF's dominance of the rural vote. After 2000, ZANU-PF invested in extensive tools to manipulate election outcomes.

African politicians are often accused of engaging in vote buying or patronage politics (Arriola, 2009; Bratton & Van de Walle, 1994; Lindberg, 2006; Omotola, 2011; Van de Walle, 2007; Vicente & Wantchekon, 2009; Wantchekon, 2003; D. J. Young, 2009). The two are often used interchangeably, but they mean different things. Sometimes African politicians blatantly offer money in exchange for votes (Bratton et al., 2012; Collier & Vicente, 2012); at other times, instead of cash, politicians promise to deliver gifts, goods, and services to voters who support them (Omotola, 2011; Wantchekon, 2003). Recent literature in the field shows that although patronage politics is vital, vote buying in terms of a vote for actual cash exchange is very rare. However, African voters do expect more personal gifts and attention from their representatives than do voters in more developed democracies (Arriola, 2009; Basedau et al., 2007; Carlson, 2010). Like most ruling parties in the region, ZANU-PF has benefited from having control over the state purse.

This has enabled them to deliver goods and services to voters, especially during election season. For example, ZANU-PF has consistently delivered fertilizers and other farming equipment to their rural voters.

By the mid-2000s, Zimbabwe could no longer afford to feed its people or import grain. Zimbabweans were depending on aid for every basic commodity. Once-booming industries were closed. Following the land reform initiative, the government banned foreign transactions in 2000. It became illegal for businesses to deal with foreign currency without prior approval from the government. This led to a further decline in business operations and industries as foreign companies fled. At the height of Zimbabwe's crisis between 2008 and 2010, Human Rights Watch reported that the food deficit in Zimbabwe had affected an estimated 4.1 million people. A drought worsened the food crisis, so most rural provinces did not have good harvests during that time, especially in the arid regions of Matebeleland. In May 2008, the government, via the Ministry of Social Welfare, issued a directive prohibiting international aid agencies from distributing food in a few rural provinces, including the ZANU-PF stronghold of Masvingo. The government argued that international agencies were using food to buy votes for the opposition, yet many rural Zimbabweans would have died without donor food. The government blamed food shortages on the drought, the MDC, and Western sanctions. Later, the government demanded that donor agencies give the food to their ministries, which then distributed the food.

Under the doctrine of a Third Chimurenga, Mugabe's regime introduced indigenization policies that came into effect in 2008 (Scoones et al., 2010). The Indigenization and Empowerment Act, officially signed into law on March 7, 2008, required all foreign-owned companies to offer at least 51 percent of their shares to indigenous Zimbabweans (Mugabe, 2001).[2] Foreign investors in Zimbabwe spoke out against the law, and a fair number withdrew their businesses. Market analysts worldwide expressed their outrage and concern over the policy, arguing the act would "effectively seal Zimbabwe's fate as a pariah to international capital" (Tupy, 2008). Marian Tupy, a Cato Institute policy analyst, condemned the law even more strongly as "yet another step on Zimbabwe's road to economic suicide" that would "expropriate non-Black owners, while providing the ZANU-PF elite with a new source of

---

[2] The full text of the Indigenization Act can be found at www.africayouthskills.org/images/pdf/lrg/National_Indigenization_and_Empowerment_Act.pdf

income. The biggest victims of the Orwellian measure ... will be the Black majority" (Zeldin, 2008).

At the start of the 2012 campaign season, ZANU-PF strategically delivered seed grain to rural voters in packaging engraved with ZANU-PF symbols. The strategy was met with outcries of injustice and accusations of vote buying from opposition leaders, who argued ZANU-PF was using state funds for campaign purposes (Mwonzora & Mandikwaza, 2019). The survival of ZANU-PF can be explained in part by the party's ability to consistently deliver patronage to its supporters. However, patronage delivery does not fully explain why voters remained loyal even when the party could not deliver such patronage.

Election Manipulation

The last resort for an authoritarian regime seeking to remain in power while maintaining a façade of democracy is to distort election outcomes. Well-documented evidence shows ZANU-PF routinely engaged in election fraud to maintain its electoral wins. In Zimbabwe, most electoral fraud happens before the election (Chigora & Nciizah, 2007). The ruling party manipulates the activities of the Zimbabwe Electoral Commission (ZEC), the only body with the constitutional mandate to manage Zimbabwean elections. ZANU-PF, via its control of ZEC, disenfranchises opposition voters via constant gerrymandering, unfair and unequal coverage of political parties on state media, unequal distribution of voting material materials, and legislation that criminalizes the opposition's political participation. While reports from local and international observers indicate that ballot counting has been relatively clean,[3] Dorman (2005) found there are often irregularities in vote counting that must not be ignored. Low levels of ballot fraud and the absence of actual ballot stuffing can be explained by the fact that all the Zimbabwean elections since 2000 have been high stakes and have drawn the attention of local political actors, civil society, and international observers. In such elections, ruling parties must seek other strategies to retain power (Laakso, 2002).

Around the world, the quality of elections appears to be in decline as authoritarian regimes continue to find creative ways to rig elections in their favor. Electoral fraud includes a myriad of clandestine and illegal efforts to change electoral outcomes, often done in favor of the

---

[3] See Zimbabwe Electoral Support Network (ZESN) 2000–2008 election reports and Electoral Institute of Sustainable Democracy (EISA) Zimbabwe election archive.

incumbent. Cheeseman and Klaas (2018) have categorized six ways that election manipulation can occur: gerrymandering, vote buying, repression, hacking, ballot stuffing, and international endorsements. In Zimbabwe, the government utilizes most of them clandestine ways. The main visible form of election manipulation is vote buying, as discussed in the next subsection.

All long-serving parties employ some of these tactics some of the time. A famous example of electoral hacking occurred in Mexico's 1988 election, when the long-ruling PRI was returned to office with a slim majority of 50.7 percent after computers malfunctioned (Magaloni, 2006). Similarly, it took over a month before the ZEC released the 2008 election results showing that although the incumbent ZANU-PF had finished second, the opposition had not garnered enough votes to prevent a runoff. The runoff was a bloody and violent affair that saw Mugabe win over 90 percent of the vote.

Preelection ballot staffing is now more common than postelection rigging methods. In Rwanda, like in Russia, the incumbent always wins with over 90 percent of the vote. Experts see this as evidence of ballot stuffing (Cheeseman & Klaas, 2018). Leaders who win with such large margins either have numbers prematched to the outcomes they want or add votes during the elections. In cases like Rwanda and Russia, there is a lot of fear of the incumbent and low trust in the judicial system, so opponents are unlikely to seek redress in the courts. Electoral manipulation has been a major fixture in Zimbabwean politics and yet even this alone is not enough to explain the survival of ZANU-PF.

STRUCTURE OF THE BOOK

The exit of millions via migration and death changed the political landscape in Zimbabwe. In this chapter, I introduced a novel way of thinking about exit: not only physical movement from one country to the next but also death as a permanent exit that has an impact on politics. Voter exit is a contributing factor to regime survival that complements the many other strategies that ruling parties can use to keep power. The remainder of the book is structured as follows.

In Chapter 2, "Theory of Exit and How to Study Exit," I detail the methodologies I used in the book as well as my adaptation and extension of Hirschman's theory of exit. My approach advances two types of exit: permanent exit, which comes about when voters die, and partial exit (whether forced or voluntary), which may or may not include physical exit. Partial exit through emigration often includes remittances to those who remain as expressions of loyalty. Partial exit may also occur through voter attrition related to pandemic fatigue. Exit, regardless of cause, impacts the electorate that remains and could participate. The government did not initiate the exit and initially had very little over these mechanisms, even though they have a great impact on political outcomes. However, over the years, they have found clandestine ways to benefit from exit. I also discuss the mixture of methodologies I used to study the link between exit and political survival.

In Chapter 3, "Death and Dearth of Democrats: HIV/AIDS and Voter Exit," I unpack the relationship between the HIV/AIDS pandemic and the political fortunes of the ruling and opposition parties. Governments can manipulate health pandemics to their advantage because of their power to determine access to care and move citizens from one location to another. Those who died had profiles and characteristics similar to those who voted for the opposition. I also show that due to its nature as a prolonged illness, HIV/AIDS impacted the functionality of the entire family unit. Caregiving for HIV patients led to fatigue and exhaustion. Caregivers had no time to focus on other things, least of all political participation, protests, or voting. HIV/AIDS led to the political exit of everyone impacted by the illness, whether as victims of the pandemic or as caregivers.

In Chapter 4, "Voting with Our Feet: When Voters Leave, the Regime Survives," I link the profiles of migrants to those who remained at home. Migrants tended to be young, educated, urban professionals – just like those who supported the ruling party. The moment they exited, most migrants gave up their right to vote. Asylees cannot return to their home country, Zimbabwe does not allow migrants to vote from abroad, and for many, the costs of returning home to vote are far too high. I also explore how migrants contributed to the politics of home by raising awareness of issues, writing in the media, and supporting activists, which are all important ways of participating. Although some migrants continued to use their voice by engaging in demonstrations abroad or participating in online engagement, their voice did not often translate to votes. Their physical absence, combined with barriers to voting, limited their ability to change the trajectory of politics in their home country. In this chapter, I draw from examples of countries where diaspora votes directly impacted the election outcome to illustrate the challenges in Zimbabwe.

In Chapter 5, "Remittances and ZANU-PF Survival," I show that remittances that migrants living abroad send to family members back home contributed to the political exit of those who remained in the home country. Most migrants remit with the noble goal of helping their family members. However, governments can also benefit from access to free money. Remittances sent as an expression of loyalty muffled the political voice of those remaining in Zimbabwe. Most receivers disengaged from political participation (use of voice) because they saw no need to engage with a state that could no longer deliver basic needs to them. Their basic needs were now met by remittances. In some cases, the diaspora also muffled the voice by discouraging political participation by their family members. I argue that authoritarian states place a premium on political participation that is too high for citizens whose primary needs are met elsewhere. Remittances also provided an important economic buffer for a regime that was very broke.

In Chapter 6, "Connecting the Dots: Voice, Exit, Loyalty, and Regime Survival," I conclude the book by showing the combined impact of exit on electoral participation and the practical and theoretical implications of my findings. I demonstrate how the theory of exit and party sustainability might work in other states, including Russia, Venezuela, and Syria – countries that have also experienced a mass exodus of citizens from authoritarian regimes. I also provide a brief comparison of the role of migrant voters in Ghana and Gambia's 2016 election where democracy struggled but ultimately thrived. I discuss the theory's policy implications in light of ongoing debates about the immigration crises around the world, especially the millions of Africans trying to make their way to Europe and ending up dead in the oceans.

2

Theory of Exit and How to Study Exit

The first time I went to Scotland for research, it was January and I was not prepared for winter storms. I ended up stuck for a couple of nights at the home of two lawyers who had emigrated from Zimbabwe in the early 2000s. They were my first interview. Inexperienced, I had rushed through my prepared questions and was now stuck in their home. I felt unsure how to spend my time until the wife asked me to explain again – slowly – what I was trying to do. I realized she had not understood my objectives during the interview, so we started over. This second attempt led to a much richer conversation that lasted over two days. I learned about their family dynamics and gained a deeper understanding of the political and economic costs felt by migrants. The wife, an established lawyer in Zimbabwe, had started over in Scotland. The asylum process had been difficult. Working multiple jobs to sustain themselves and the family back home took a toll on her health. One day, she fainted at the university campus where she was taking night law-school classes. When she woke up in the hospital, the doctor said her only ailment was fatigue. Later, I would realize AIDS caregivers had suffered the same deep fatigue, which made it impossible to care for themselves, let alone engage in political discourse. I would not have learned this from a survey, and my first attempt at an interview had failed. I took the lessons from this interview to the many cities I visited over the next two years. Studying the human condition is a slow, often unpredictable, and never linear process.

In this chapter, I have two main objectives. In the first section, I discuss Hirschman's exit–voice–loyalty (EVL) theory and how I adapt and extend it. I apply Hirschman's EVL theory to a type of regime, the illiberal democracy or electoral authoritarian regime, that has become more common. I extend exit to include the permanent exit of death, the effective exit of voter attrition, and the partial exit of those who return remittances. I also extend voice to include voting and allow it to be a factor even after exit. This continued engagement after exit extends the concept of loyalty to mean more than simply remaining in a country. I conclude this section by discussing how the predictions of my modified EVL construct differ from those of Hirschman.

In the second section, I describe how I gathered and analyzed data for this book. First, I used quantitative methods to link exit to the profile of Zimbabwean voters. To do this, I drew from Afrobarometer data gathered in Zimbabwe from 1999 to 2023 and from UNAIDS spectrum project data on HIV and migration from 1980 to 2023. I complement the large-scale data with smaller surveys and then turn to qualitative data. I discuss in detail my sampling method and my ethnographic interviews with 100 Zimbabweans living in four countries. I collected valuable insights by engaging with Zimbabweans and following their conversations in informal ways.

EXIT–VOICE–LOYALTY AND ELECTORAL AUTHORITARIAN REGIMES

Hirschman's Theoretical Framework

My argument stretches and modifies Hirschman's (1970) groundbreaking *Exit, Voice, and Loyalty*. Employing the analogy of a business firm, Hirschman discussed what happens "[i]f the performance of a firm or an organization (such as voluntary associations, trade unions, and political parties) is assumed to be subject to deterioration for unspecified, random causes which are neither so compelling nor so durable as to prevent the return to previous performance" (p. 3). In that case, customers can either stop buying the product (exit) or voice their displeasure. Hirschman's argument was directed at "firm(s) producing saleable products but [is] also applicable to organizations (such as voluntary associations, trade unions or political parties) that provide services to their members without monetary counterpart" (p. 3).

Hirschman defined *exit* as when people leave an organization such as a political party; recent studies have understood exit as including outward migration. Hirschman also defined exit as when people stop buying goods and services from a firm, which will result in a decline in profits. Hirschman assumed that in a normal or democratic situation, a firm or organization has competition but some latitude to determine prices or conditions to make members happy. He also assumed that customers or members have somewhere else to go. Under such circumstances, the choice to exit is a powerful tool that can destroy a firm or organization unless it makes changes or finds a way to attract new customers or members.

Hirschman defined *voice* as when members or customers express their dissatisfaction to leadership: "any attempt at all at changing the practices, policies and outputs of the firm from which one buys or the organization to which one belongs" (1970, p. 3). Hirschman's exit was clear-cut – people either leave or stay – but voice could range from "faint grumbling all the way to protest" (p. 16). Voice does, however, have to be publicly expressed – it is "articulation of one's critical opinions rather than a private 'secret'" (p. 16) – so it does not include the private act of voting. Voice is only an option for those who have not exited, and it is most effective when there is a credible threat of exit. Hirschman assumed that the person to whom voice is directed – a company or government – is responsive and cares about the views of customers or citizens. The leadership will then work to resolve people's concerns. Hirschman did not consider the cases of authoritarian regimes and business monopolies that do not much care what their citizens or customers think because they control the means for entry and exit. In this, Hirschman did not appreciate that individuals might exit even under authoritarian conditions when the cost of doing so is very high.

Hirschman defined *loyalty* simply as not exiting despite voice being ineffective. A person who despises a company's ethics and products but continues to use them is loyal. For example, a person who finds it abhorrent that Apple's products are made under conditions that might be abusive but continues to buy the latest iPhone or MacBook is loyal. American citizens who opposed the Biden government's position on Gaza but continue to vote for the Democratic Party would be defined as loyal. A customer or member may opt to put up with dissatisfaction and forgo exit and choose to remain loyal when the costs of exit are too high or they are uncertain about the options available elsewhere.

Hirschman's concept of loyalty and the role of choice in exit are complicated and have elicited debate (Dowding et al., 2000; Huefner & Hunt, 1994; Leck & Saunders, 1992). As Huefner and Hunt (1994) pointed out, many readers misread Hirschman by assuming that he defined loyalty in the standard way, as synonymous with devotion, dedication, support, or commitment. It is easy to make this error because

Hirschman's use of the term loyalty is anything but standard. A person in North Korea or Zimbabwe who opposes those regimes and even tries to expose government atrocities but stays in the country would be considered loyal. For Hirschman, any form of nonexit is loyalty. Hirschman also did not clearly define the different circumstances in which choice and loyalty apply. Loyal members will voice their concerns if they think there is a credible chance they will be heard, but the threat of exit must be credible before the firm or leaders will respond to the demands of voice. This narrow view of loyalty does not explain consumer or voter behavior in a world that is more complicated and less monolithic than the one Hirschman was writing about.

Hirschman also wrote about the relationship between exit, voice, and the state. Applying his theory to the politics of nineteenth- and twentieth-century European states, Hirschman (1978) argued that the enormous outmigration at that time was not resisted by governments because "the outflow of [migrants] did not provoke any visible political problems or dangers" (p. 101). Hirschman argued that European governments that had prohibited emigration in earlier centuries were willing to allow it because it "alleviated several economic as well as political problems" (p. 101). The governments viewed many of those who left as troublemakers. They saw outward migration as more beneficial to the government because those who emigrated were dissatisfied with the regime. The governments would rather those people exited than used their voice while being loyal and remaining: "The ships carrying the migrants contained many actual or potential anarchists and socialists, reformers and revolutionaries" (p. 102). In other words, the exit of outward migration reduced the voice of social protest in European states.

Hirschman argued that this exit had a democratizing effect in these countries because once the most vocal opposition actors exited, regimes felt it was safe to extend democratization to the quieter or silent loyalists who remained. While Hirschman found it evident that "the emigration of dissenters [from repressive eighteenth-century regimes] will strengthen an authoritarian regime in the short run," it would lead to liberalization as the governments catered to the needs of those who chose to remain loyal.

Much of the literature that engages with Hirschman has done so in democracies, where exit, voice, and loyalty have very different implications than they do in authoritarian regimes. The expansion of the European Union (EU) created new opportunities for exit from poorer democracies like Poland and Romania to wealthier countries like France and the United Kingdom. Instead of pushing for polices that made their lives better, Polish citizens found it easier to exit to wealthier democracies that could provide them the democracy and welfare that were not abundant at home (Meardi, 2007; Szent-Ivanyi & Kugiel, 2020).

Even though much of the application of Hirschman has been to Western democracies, some literature has applied EVL to situations more akin to the absolute monarchies he wrote about. Boyle (2022) studied refugees from North Korea under conditions in which voice and exit were illegal and could lead to one's death if exercised. Those who remain there have not done so by choice; loyalty is forced upon citizens. Boyle (2022) found that people are willing to take extreme risks to exit a society; once they do, they also take the risk of using their voice to expose the state. In a similar way, Denaro (2020) noted that Syrian refugees found voice once they emigrated to Europe, where their voices could be heard and they could exercise agency in ways that they had not been able to do at home. Heins (2020) noted, "Hirschman could not foresee the emerging global possibilities of cultivating 'the art of voice'" (p. 1) that allows exiled people to express themselves and sometimes challenge the governments they have left behind. In these countries, as I discuss later with Zimbabwe, exit allowed authoritarian regimes to consolidate power.

Between these two extremes, illiberal democracies like Zimbabwe have very little interest in encouraging the disgruntled to remain loyal by staying, lest they become angry and voice their demands for change. The only way electoral authoritarian regimes can appease disgruntled voters is to become more democratic. The next subsection adopts EVL to this relatively new type of regime.

My Theory of Voter Exit and Party Survival

I stretch and modify Hirschman (1970) to explain the impact of the mass exodus of millions of people from a country that has an electoral authoritarian regime (also known as an illiberal democracy). How are such political systems impacted by exit, whether through emigration, disengagement, or death? How can those who exit still exercise voice and show loyalty? My theory is that exit bolsters the survival of electoral authoritarian regimes because those people are not available to participate in the voting process. Paradoxically, however, their exit does not encourage democratization because they continue to use voice in a way that threatens the regime and because the loyalty they show by sending remittances dampens resistance and funds the government in power.

In this section, I expand Hirschman (1970) in four ways. First, I discuss a different type of regime. Hirschman wrote about exit from institutions, democratic societies, and absolute monarchies; I study the impact of exit from illiberal democracies. Second, I expand exit to include death and the diversion of caregivers. Third, I show that voice can be available after people exit, but that voice has limited influence on elections. Fourth, I show that emigrants can express loyalty after they leave through remittances and other support to family members. All these factors combine to help electoral authoritarian regimes retain their hold on power.

Before addressing my innovations, another area where I differ with Hirschman is the matter of choice. Hirschman (1970) emphasized the role of choice: voters can choose to exit without using voice, choose to use their voice to try to change the behavior of institutions, or choose to be silent and loyal. After they use voice, they again have a choice to exit or remain loyal. Hirschman treated these as simple economic decisions; in reality, the situation is very complicated. There is a lot of anxiety for those deciding whether to stay or leave when the cost associated with either decision feels very high. Hirschman thought individuals could choose to stay or leave as easily as changing brands when providers and products are plentiful in a market. But even in consumer conditions, sometimes choice is impossible. Individuals might continue to patronize a business they dislike because it is the only provider. People continue to pay taxes to a government they do not support, and they consume government propaganda when there are no independent media options.

The extent to which any of these choices are free is complicated even in a context where basic human and economic rights are respected, but this is even more questionable for individuals in authoritarian regimes. Those who exit such regimes do so in response to circumstances that leave them no real choice. If one leaves home because staying would result in death, is that a free choice? If a mother leaves her children behind because she can no longer feed them, is that comparable to choosing to move within the United States or from one part of Europe to another? In regimes where the government responds to any expression of dissent or displeasure with violence, is it a choice whether or not to use one's voice? The answer to all these questions and many others is "No." In the end, exit, voice, and loyalty matter regardless of how freely individuals choose them. Thus, I place less emphasis on choice than Hirschman (1970) did, which he backed away from himself upon reflecting on his own experience as a Jewish exile:

Most of the young emigrated, like myself, in the years after Hitler's seizure of power and left a severely weakened [Jewish] community behind. There was certainly no longer any practical possibility of effective voice, regardless of whether one left or stayed. Still, the true origin of the book may be a carefully repressed sense of guilt, which is simply there, even if it seems intellectually absurd. (p. vii)

Electoral Authoritarian Regimes and Illiberal Democracies

My arguments speak to what Levitsky and Way (2002) defined as competitive authoritarian states. These are also known as illiberal democracies (Zakaria, 1997) or electoral autocracies (Bogaards, 2009). Illiberal democracies or electoral authoritarian regimes did not exist when Hirschman proposed his theory: a regime was either a liberal democracy or fully authoritarian. I use these terms interchangeably in this book.

A defining feature of illiberal democracies is that even though they may operate as de facto single-party states, they are not formalized as such because they do not criminalize political opposition per se. Electoral authoritarian regimes behave differently than pure dictatorships because they want to gain legitimacy from elections. But they are not willing to lose power in those elections, so they expend a lot of effort manipulating the electoral system in their favor. They deny civil liberties, influence if not control the media, and devise election rules that make it difficult for the opposition to convert support into victories at the polls. Some of them use brutal methods to suppress dissent while formally allowing opposition activism and protest. Journalists and activists are often jailed, and in more extreme cases, they are disappeared or killed for their activism. States in this category vary in their level of openness and brutality toward opposition elites and citizens. Some of them, like Hungary and Turkey, are fairly open to opposition parties. On another extreme are states like Egypt, Zimbabwe, Uganda, and Russia. In these countries, it is possible to be in opposition and speak out against the regime, but the costs can be very high and the chance of success is very low.

Anything that reduces turnout for the opposition bolsters the survival of an authoritarian regime by reducing how much it needs to manipulate election outcomes – such regimes prefer not to go so far as to ban elections altogether. The massive exodus of those who would have supported the opposition strengthens their position. A common feature among these states is that they tend to have one leader in power for a long time. Examples of contemporary states with a single leader include Russia, Uganda, Rwanda, and Zimbabwe.

Russia's Vladimir Putin has been in power for over twenty years, with support from first the United Russia Party and then the All-Russia

People's Front (ONF), which he formed in 2011. Prior to the formation of the ONF, Putin had enjoyed the support of the United Russia Front, but he chose to govern as an independent rather than as a formal member (Reuter, 2010). In most dominant party systems, leaders benefit from party membership; in Russia, the situation is reversed. Putin is stronger than the party. The party is a vehicle for loyalists to serve in the government, but they only do so if they remain in Putin's favor. The party is also a vehicle to reward loyalists by distributing patronage. Russia's massive oil reserves have given him enormous leverage among oligarchs who are mainly interested in lining their pockets. However, patronage is not enough to keep him in power. Putin also relies on the repression of opposition activists and manipulation of democratic institutions to his benefit. Putin's survival and by extension that of his party is heavily dependent on his ability to distribute state resources to loyalists.

In Uganda, President Yoweri Museveni and his National Resistance Movement have been in power since 1986. When Museveni came into power after the ouster of his mentor Idi Amin by the military, he said the problem with African leaders is that they overstay their welcome. I was born the year he came into office, and he does not show any signs of letting go. Elections under Museveni have not been free or fair. Opposition leaders are routinely brutalized. In 2020, the opposition, led by thirty-eight-year old popular musician Bobi Wine, suspended its campaign after thirty-seven of its members were killed. In a previous election, Wine had been assaulted beyond recognition. Museveni maintains popularity because of his control over the war in the northern regions, and his government continues to receive support from Western nations that support his homophobic agenda. Museveni has used his majorities in parliament to change rules to stay in power. In 2004, the parliament scrapped a constitutional age limit that would have forced him to retire in 2005. When he reached the new age limit of seventy-five in 2017, the constitution was again changed to accommodate him. Museveni has also done a good job of distributing patronage to loyal supporters. There is very little incentive for those within the government to go against the president.

In Rwanda, President Paul Kagame, leader of the Patriotic Front, has been in power since 2000. In 2015, at Kagame's request, parliament voted to extend his rule by a third term and possibly two more five-year terms after that. Kagame is set to govern until at least 2035 and may very well request more changes to the constitution. Kagame has a lot of support because he is credited with ending the 1994 genocide against the Tutsi.

In recent years, his country has seen impressive economic growth, although the numbers may not be as good as his government reports. However, even with all the goodwill he supposedly enjoys, Kagame is opposed to being challenged. Opposition leaders are routinely jailed on bogus accusations or forced into exile. Anyone who opposes the narrative that Kagame has pushed forward can find themselves imprisoned or dead.

The nature of ZANU-PF's authoritarian rule has changed over the years, but like most long-ruling parties, it governs from the center as the party that first brought democracy. After a short period of democratization, ZANU-PF built strong oversize coalitions through the unification of the two largest rival parties in the 1980s. In more recent years, the regime has employed various methods of electoral fraud, intimidation, and violence.

Exit Includes Death, Disease, and Disengagement

Hirschman considered exit a binary choice: someone is either present in or absent from the firm, organization, or state; if they are present, they are considered loyal. Exit is not a free choice for those who may face death or deprivation if they use their voice – sometimes, even if they do not – but it may not be easy to get travel papers and find a destination. Exit has the same effect on a regime whether the exit was freely chosen or compelled by the government. Exit also has the same effect if people die from disease or famine, rather than move to another country. The premature death of millions of voters in a short period of time affects electoral outcomes: they have no voice and cannot vote.

Hirschman does not consider another form of exit: disengagement from politics while remaining in the country. HIV/AIDS, like other terminal illnesses, demands a lot of attention from caregivers for an extended time. This is another situation in which people have no real choice. Caring for one individual is more than a full-time job and so requires at least two others dedicated to the task. In Zimbabwe, most of these were young women who sometimes quit work or school to become full-time caregivers. Most such caregivers are left with little energy for themselves, let alone for politics. They, and of course the patients they are caring for, become disconnected from the state and remove themselves from participation. Their voices become silent, but not because of loyalty or state action.

Voice after Exit

Hirschman argued that once people exit, they cannot use their voice. Unlike Hirschman (1970) and Warren (2011), I argue those who exit (except through death) can retain their voice by participating in conversations via the internet, radio, or television. Contemporary exiles are more like Hannah Arendt than Karl Marx, in Heins's (2020) formulation, and technology has increased the number of ways that people can express their opinions and contribute to political discourse and the politics of home. Their use of voice is easier through the internet than it was in the era of shortwave radio. Regime opponents may even have more voice after exit. Authoritarian regimes work very hard to suppress people's voice by criminalizing protest and independent journalism. Even in these days of broad access to social media, a government can choose to switch off the internet or police people's social media to deny them choice about what media to consume.

In Zimbabwe, both radio and television are dominated by the state. Independent journalists are routinely harassed, and their offices are heavily policed. At extreme times, the government has banned independent media and even the consumption of international music. A regime that can jail radio personalities for playing a Michael Jackson song can do worse to those who use their voices to publicize atrocities committed by that regime. Those who do not exit are limited by how they use their voice because the regime punishes them.

On the other hand, citizens who exit through emigration can renew their use of voice by sharing their thoughts via the internet from places where such actions are not criminalized. The activities of exiled activists are well documented (Kuhlmann, 2010). The use of voice encourages opposition supporters in the home country and might even translate to financial support from friendly regimes. Indeed, Zimbabweans in exile have used their voices to bring global awareness to the plight of their country and have been active supporters of the opposition.

Hirschman required voice to be active and visible, so he did not include voting as voice. Here again, I stretch this concept by including voting as a form of voice. For citizens who are limited in their ability to protest, to write to the editor, or to use voice in other ways, the only way they can voice their displeasure with a regime might be through the ballot, even in flawed elections. While the individual ballot may be secret and silent, the election results can be heard as a public voice. Those who exit may lose their ability to use their voice by participating in elections.

While exit may not silence voice, the voice can be lost in authoritarian regimes even without physical exit. The state can criminalize the expression of opinion. People can also decide that using their voice is not worth the risk, so they self-silence. Living under authoritarian conditions is exhausting because of the multiple ways people experience violence, criminalization, and lack of basic services. Fatigue can also silence people. A regime can even influence what exiles say by inducing fear for the safety of their family members who have not exited.

Loyalty after Exit
My fourth modification to Hirschman is that I do not equate exit with the end of loyalty to a country. Hirschman saw exit as a "symptom and a consequence of the disappearance of 'loyalty' to a state that betrays its own citizens" (Heins, 2020), but this is not always so for those leaving authoritarian countries. A decline in loyalty to the ruling elites does not always translate to a decline in loyalty to one's country. Loyalty can even lead people to exit. Wong et al. (2023) argued that citizens loyal to Hong Kong as it had been became more likely to exit because they were sensitive to the performance of its new authoritarian regime.

I use loyalty in more conventional ways than Hirschman did. Loyalty is an attachment to a space that leads one to continue participating even after exit. It is attachment to the imagined community of a diaspora, to a place one may have never lived. This attachment leads one to use voice and advocate for change or improvement in that community. I argue that individuals may express their loyalty to their home country by using technology to voice views on politics from abroad and sending remittances to families. However, as noted in the previous subsection, their voices will be less effective than the voices of those who remain within the country.

Remittances are more effective expressions of loyalty to country, but they can bolster the regime by inadvertently funding it and reducing the intensity of opposition. The regime can profit by taxing remittances and by setting itself up as the channel for remittance payments. While most remittances do not lead to large-scale development, they reduce the number of aggrieved citizens who might otherwise raise their voices against the government because their basic needs have not been met. Remittances allow receivers to afford food, shelter, healthcare, and education, which are the issues that lead people to take to the streets. Furthermore, senders may remit fear. This is especially true of mothers – and most Zimbabwean emigrants are women. They might encourage their children and other family members to stay out of politics now that their primary needs have been met. This reduces the use of voice by those who remain in the country but disagree with the regime, which is something Hirschman (1970) did not address.

Impact of EVL on Electoral Authoritarian Regimes

My theory is that large-scale voter exit provides a lifeline to authoritarian parties that would lose power if free elections were allowed. When voters are not physically present to vote for their preferred party, either because they have moved abroad or have died, their party will receive fewer votes. Authoritarian regimes benefit when the profile of those who exit matches the profile of those who support the opposition. When voters in certain areas exit en masse, it is easier for ruling parties to suppress opposition. Voters who exit can use their voice, but without the right to vote from exile, they are disenfranchised, which benefits the regime. Other forms of exit come without voter choice – death, of course, but people who are sick for a long time or engaged in caregiving responsibilities are also less likely to participate in politics. They have effectively exited the system. The support of those who have exited but express loyalty to their families through remittances can also lead to political exit of those families and offer economic benefits to the regime.

While regime opponents in exile may use their voices, doing so is not always an effective tool for change in illiberal democracies. The regime has no way to stop them from using their voices, but it can make it impossible for migrants to vote from outside the country. If electoral authoritarian regimes disallow voting from abroad, exit favors the party in power. The regime can also introduce laws that would lead to the arrest of those who speak against the government if they return. This might not suppress voice, but it keeps migrants away from political participation. Because the voice of those who exited does not translate to actual votes, it does not hurt the electoral chances of the regime.

Electoral authoritarian regimes can also directly benefit from those who have left. The regime might manipulate the channels of money transfer by increasing the cost of getting remittances or by becoming the money transfer agency. This gives the government direct access to foreign currency, which is often difficult for them to come by. Regimes might also find ways to receive direct payment for the labor of citizens working abroad. For example, the Egyptian government of Anwar Sadat (a full authoritarian regime), faced with mass exodus of its human capital to oil-rich Arab countries, required emigrants to remit a fixed portion of their income directly to it (Hadley, 1977). Egypt had tried to curb migration, but growing unemployment and other problems faced by the population led the regime to change its policies (Tsourapas, 2022). The Philippines, an illiberal democracy, also gets money from receiving countries when its citizens go abroad to work.

MULTIMETHOD APPROACH

The aim of my research was to learn how the exit of millions from an illiberal democracy affects the politics of that country. In this section, I discuss the multimethod approach I used for data collection and the analytical models I used to make inferences about how exit via death and migration sustained this competitive authoritarian regime. This research question is difficult to study because one must make inferences about people who can no longer speak for themselves because they are dead and about what people would have done if they had not emigrated. In the empirical chapters, I show that the profile of those who died and the profiles of those who emigrated are both skewed toward the profile of opposition voters, which reduced support for the ruling party. My multimethod approach included case study and other qualitative methodologies alongside quantitative ones. A multimethod approach "offers scholars the opportunity to test more of their assumptions and therefore to produce better and more empirically grounded causal inferences" (Seawright, 2016, p. 49). I adopted a multimethod approach to use the strength of each methodology to compensate for the weaknesses inherent in the others. I begin this section by discussing how I measured regime survival.

Authoritarian Survival

I started by establishing ZANU-PF's durability in elections from 1980 to 2023. I included years outside my main period of interest to establish that the regime at any point did not lose power. As shown in Figure 2.1, ZANU-PF has won every election. While the legitimacy of the wins is up for debate because the regime used illegal methods to retain power, these victories have maintained the regime's control of parliament and the presidency. The ZANU-PF government has been recognized within Zimbabwe and internationally as a legitimate government since 1980.

Between 1980 and 2023, ZANU-PF won a majority in every presidential election, although in 2008 it had to win a runoff. In 2008, opposition parties combined to win 56 percent of the vote, but the leader among them (the MDC) garnered only a plurality of 47 percent. In the ensuing runoff, ZANU-PF won a hard-to-believe 90 percent of the vote. The authenticity of the initial 2008 results is highly debatable, as it took a month for the election commission to release them. To effectively defeat ZANU-PF, the MDC would have needed to win with a larger, rig-proof

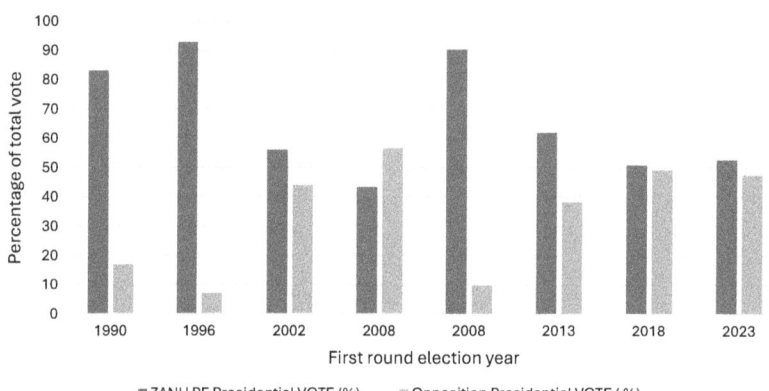

FIGURE 2.1 ZANU-PF durability showing combined opposition votes.
Source: Data compiled from Kubatana.net, Zimbabwe Electoral Commission (ZEC), and Electoral Institute for Sustainable Democracy in Africa.

margin. Cheeseman and Klaas (2018) argued that the opposition must win with at least 5 percent above the required threshold to protect against rigging by authoritarian regimes. In Zimbabwe, I argue that the opposition would need an even larger margin – at least 20 percent – to be safe. In the next section, I will discuss the partisan profiles of Zimbabweans and how they vote, which is a prerequisite for understanding how exit impacts regime durability.

Partisan Profile

To examine the preferences of the Zimbabwean electorate from 1999 to 2023, I used the nationally representative surveys conducted by Afrobarometer. These longitudinal surveys provide individual Africans' views of governance and society in eighteen countries, including Zimbabwe. Zimbabwe has had nine full surveys and a handful of smaller ones: 1999, 2004, 2005, 2009, 2010, 2012, 2014, 2017, 2018, and 2021. Over the years, Afrobarometer has interviewed a nationally representative sample of over 7,000 Zimbabweans. Data from Afrobarometer provide crucial information on citizen participation in elections and organizations, intent to emigrate, relationship with migrants (remittances), and citizen evaluation of government officials. Afrobarometer manages to get people to answer questions that a single researcher would have difficulty in extracting responses to, especially in rural areas. Using Afrobarometer, I can tell a longer story about the ebbs and flows of citizen participation.

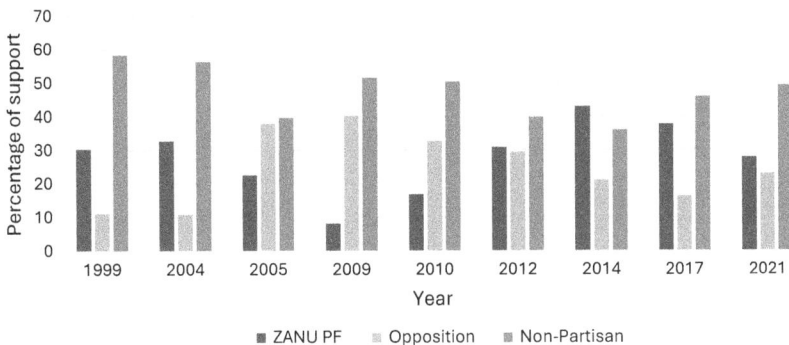

FIGURE 2.2 Support for ZANU-PF and opposition.
Note: The percentage of Zimbabweans who support ZANU-PF, opposition and non-partisans.
Source: Data compiled from Afrobarometer from 1999 to 2021.

Afrobarometer shows that the support ZANU-PF had enjoyed since 1980 declined, especially after 1999. In 1999, 30 percent of respondents said that they felt very close to ZANU-PF and only 11 percent said that they felt close to the MDC. By 2009, only 8 percent of respondents said that they felt close to the ZANU-PF but 40 percent of respondents said that they felt close to the MDC. Over time, support for other opposition parties declined as support for the MDC rose. In both of those years, a majority of Zimbabweans said they were close to neither party. See Figure 2.2.

A troubling pattern in Zimbabwean surveys is the high number of respondents who refuse to identify a political party preference. More than a third of respondents are likely to say they do not feel close to any party. This supports a general theory of voter exit or withdrawal from politics. I was able to get a deeper understanding of Zimbabwean apprehension about political conversation during in-depth unstructured interviews with the respondents.

While it is common practice to recode "Refuse" and "I don't know" responses as missing data, doing so in the Zimbabwean case would not only reduce the number of observations available for analysis by as much as 30–39 percent (see Table 2.1) but also ignore the meaning in those responses. Bratton and Masungure (2012) argued that most such responses reflect fear, especially during election years. I followed the Bratton and Masunugure (2012) strategy and modeled a large proportion of these individuals, especially those in rural areas and places prone to

TABLE 2.1 *Zimbabwean responses to sensitive questions*

Response	2005 (R3) (%)	2009 (R4) (%)	2012 (R5) (%)	2015 (R6) (%)	2017 (R7) (%)	2022 (R8) (%)	2023 (R9) (%)
Would not vote	7.8	3.9	10.0	6.5	10.5	10.3	5.8
Refused to answer	29.1	24.5	23.8	24.3	22.4	19.9	27.2
Don't know	2.1	3.9	2.3	3.8	3.5	8.9	3.1
Total	38.0	32.3	36.1	34.6	36.4	39.1	36.10

Note: Data from Afrobarometer. Questions were: Do you usually think of yourself as close to any particular political party? If yes, which party is that?

political violence, as opposition supporters because ruling party supporters would be unlikely to fear sharing their preferences.

Another problem is that voters might lie about preferring the ruling party to keep themselves safe. I account for this by considering the proportion of respondents who report fearing to speak up about politics. Zimbabweans, like most people living in authoritarian countries, are wary of surveys because most people believe the state spies on them. There are no repercussions for supporting the ruling party, but many voters believe that if information on party preferences lands in the wrong hands, retaliation might lead even to death. Rural voter preferences were made much clearer in intimate conversations I had with people during my semistructured interviews. In these interviews, I was mindful that Zimbabweans are more sensitive to political violence than voters in most other African countries.

There are differences between people who support ZANU-PF and those who support the opposition. I used these numbers as a guide for estimating opposition supporters among those who exited via death or emigration. I used regression analysis and cross-tabs to draw partisanship patterns from the Afrobarometer data. Regression analyses are important for measuring the strength of relationships between variables, but they are not always helpful when there are very few observations. This happens a lot with Zimbabwean data because people refuse to commit to responses. Opposition voters are younger than their ruling party counterparts, most are aged 18–45 years.

Opposition voters also tend to be urbanites compared to their rural, ruling party supporting counterparts. Urban voters became increasingly more comfortable with declaring support for the opposition party.

In 1999, 58 percent of urban voters refused to say which party they felt close to. If one only looks at the binary responses of ruling party and opposition supporters, one would not be faulted in concluding that ZANU-PF won over the opposition, but this is not the full story.

Overall, as shown in Table 2.2, opposition voters were young, with an average age in their thirties across all rounds of Afrobarometer. They had at least a high school diploma, which is quite significant, as most people in the country had only a primary school education. In 1999, at least 56 percent of opposition supporters were formally employed, but that number declined as unemployment skyrocketed. Still, even in 2009, when the economy was at its worst and inflation was the highest in the world, at least a third of opposition voters were employed and expressed dissatisfaction with the state of democracy.

Profile of AIDS Pandemic Victims

To calculate the population of the electorate that exited because of HIV, I used data from the Joint United Nations Program on HIV/AIDS (UNAIDS) spectrum model.[1] The spectrum model is not perfect, but it is the only expansive source of data on AIDS. Makota et al. (2023) found no substantive differences between the most widely used AIDS data models. Given the fluctuation in HIV numbers and the difficulty of getting accurate data, especially in the early years, the models are more likely to underestimate the impact than overestimate it. Thus, more complete data would reinforce my findings.

As of 2022, the spectrum model has data from 160 countries. The spectrum model is used by national programs and UNAIDS to prepare annual estimates of the status of the HIV epidemic in those countries. The model and assumptions are updated regularly. The model is the brainchild of researchers from UNAIDS. They pull together demographic data and other measures of the impact of HIV, including migration, and estimate adult and childhood prevalence. The prevalence is transferred to the model to estimate the consequences of the HIV/AIDS epidemic,

---

[1] I give a lot of credit to Nicoli Nattress of the University of Cape Town. During an early presentation of this work, she pointed out that the data I had been using was inadequate to give a full picture of the relationship between AIDS and political outcome. She suggested I use the spectrum data, which are often used by economists but rarely by political scientists. Our collaboration on building the model I would use for this project fit into my multimethod research approach. It is not often that economists and political scientists agree on matters related to predictive analyses.

TABLE 2.2 *Profile of opposition supporters*

Opposition support	R1 1999	R2 2004	R3 2005	R4 2009	R4.5 2010	R5 2012	R6 2014	R7 2017	R8 2021
Age	32.30	33.81	34.67	36.58	37.31	37.43	37.28	36.01	38.94
Urban (%)	70.63	57.27	32.77	34.14	36.21	39.25	44.44	35.19	52.16
Education level	3.51	3.93	4.00	3.97	4.15	4.65	4.28	4.58	4.90
Employment (%)	56.59	40.00	23.44	24.61	39.19	40.81	35.51	31.84	44.70

Note: Afrobarometer. Age = average age in years; Urban = percentage of supporters in urban district; Education level coded on a 0–9 scale: 0 = no formal schooling, 1 = informal schooling, 2 = some primary schooling, 3 = primary school completed, 4 = some secondary or high school, 5 = secondary or high school completed, 6 = postsecondary qualifications short of university, 7 = some university or college, 8 = university or college completed, 9 = postgraduate degree; Employment = percentage with jobs (respondents with part-time jobs are counted as employed).

including the number of people living with HIV by age and sex, new infections, AIDS deaths, AIDS orphans, treatment needs, and the impact of treatment on survival (Stover et al., 2006).

The Zimbabwe data are drawn from the UNAIDS-funded Zimbabwe Population-Based HIV Impact Assessment cross-sectional surveys (Gonese et al., 2020). The model was particularly helpful for this study because it accounts for non-AIDS mortality, migration, and HIV infection as the population ages. The data on migration have been criticized because they do not reflect real-world observations. This is not a problem of the model; rather, migration data are generally inadequate. I complement spectrum migration data with data from the Southern Migration Project, which provides data on migration in the region, and original ethnographic data.

I used the model's default assumptions because I was most interested in the population effects of AIDS over time. From the model, I used default data on those in the electorate living with HIV, those taking antiretroviral drugs, those not taking them, and HIV-related deaths from 1990 to 2002. The electorate includes people aged eighteen and over who would be eligible to vote in Zimbabwe. For each year, I calculated the number who died (exited) from HIV. The available data show that although the first case of HIV was reported in 1980, data were not yet available. HIV deaths peaked in 2004. The data allowed me to estimate the population that had access to antiretroviral drugs when they first became available in Zimbabwe in 2004. I used that data to estimate the population that was very ill from HIV over time. I used the profiles of those impacted by HIV to estimate the population that might have exited politics due to fatigue from the pandemic.

Afrobarometer asked about families impacted by the HIV crisis. Among those surveyed, 67.7 percent of Zimbabweans reported in 1999 that they had lost someone close due to HIV; that number jumped to 79 percent in 2005. The Afrobarometer data is consistent with data from UNAIDS that I used to calculate the impact of the exit of the electorate via death. At the height of HIV, one in four Zimbabweans was dying from HIV. I complemented these data sources with interviews of family members and with funeral homeowners, who had a lot of insight into the proportion of HIV deaths. In Chapter 3, I will discuss in more detail how I used the HIV data to calculate the impact of lost votes on opposition returns and ZANU-PF durability.

Profile of Migrants

Data on African migrants is not regularly collected, and the methods used are not uniform. As such, it is very difficult to get an accurate account of

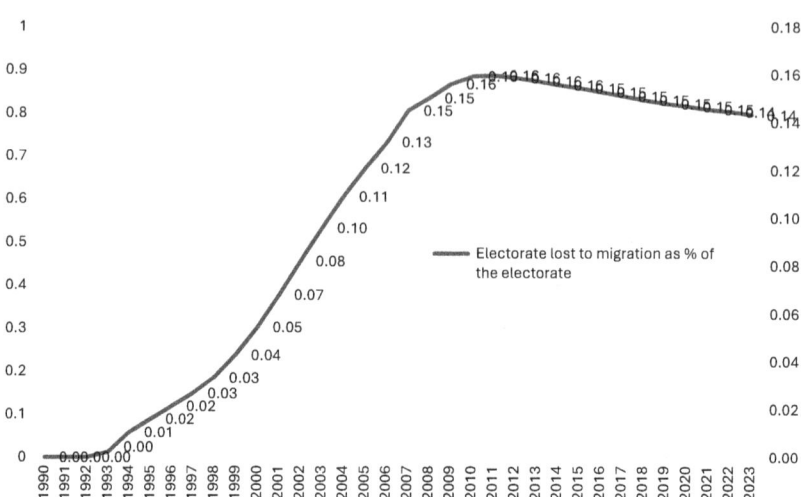

FIGURE 2.3 Electorate lost to migration, 1990–2023. *Source*: Data from UNAIDS Spectrum model.

who has left the country. To calculate the population that exited because of emigration, I used data from multiple sources. Data from the UN AIDS spectrum model are shown in Figure 2.3. I also drew on data from the International Organization for Migration and the Southern Migration Project.

In addition to these large-scale data sources, I relied on published regional studies of Zimbabwean migrants. Pasura (2008, 2012) created a profile of migrants in the United Kingdom, as did Makina (2008) on Zimbabwean migrants. Pasura (2008) divided the waves of Zimbabwean migration into five, dating back to 1960 when an estimated 300,000 migrated for labor. He argued that Phase 5 started in 1999, and he estimated that 3–4 million have emigrated since then. This is the figure most cited as the estimate of how many Zimbabweans have left the country (Ndoma, 2017; Vanyoro, 2023). I complemented this data with official reports of Zimbabwean asylum seekers.

Both Makina (2008) and Pasura (2008) showed that the profile of most Zimbabwean migrants was young, urban, educated, and professional – the same profile as those who supported the opposition back home. This was also the profile of those who showed intent to emigrate in Round 7 of Afrobarometer. Although that data is outside my period of study, the fact that the profiles are similar is important for future research. Because 80 percent of those who intended to emigrate supported the opposition, I estimate that 80 percent of those in the diaspora would have voted for the opposition. I also draw heavily on my in-depth interviews to analyze the relationship between exit via migration and regime survival. In my interviews, I asked migrants about their political support.

Another proxy I used to estimate opposition support for migrants was asylum applicant data from the UN Refugee Agency. The Refugee Agency reported that political asylees from Zimbabwe were largely opposition supporters who left the country out of fear. Asylum applications went from close to zero in 1999 to a peak of 158,000 in 2010. From this data, I estimate that the opposition lost close to 1 million votes. In Chapter 4, I will discuss in more detail how I used the emigration data to calculate the impact of lost votes on opposition returns and ZANU-PF durability.

Remittances

The biggest challenge with remittance data is that it is scarce and unreliable, especially in weak states (Bracking & Sachikonye, 2010). While remittance flows in Zimbabwe have overtaken foreign direct investment, data on remittances are scant – even the World Bank has yet to include Zimbabwe. Remittance flow into developing countries is complicated by the fact that most remittances come via informal methods that are difficult to track. Furthermore, formal remitting institutions have no duty to share the data publicly. I tried and failed to get data from those institutions. To analyze the political behavior of individuals who receive remittances, I drew data from Rounds 4 and 6 of Afrobarometer. The profile of receivers cuts across urban and rural constituencies. Most of those who receive remittances say they are unlikely to vote. Data from studies, including Maphosa (2005), Muzondidya (2007) on South Africa, Mbiba (2004) and Bracking and Sachikonye (2010), helped me understand the demographic profiles of receivers, but none of them asked about the voting and protest behavior of receivers. In Chapter 5, I will discuss in more detail how I used remittance data to calculate the impact of lost votes on opposition returns and ZANU-PF durability. To study the political behavior of receivers, I conducted in-depth interviews with people in Zimbabwe. I now discuss those methods in greater detail.

Concerns with Surveying At-Risk Populations

The secondary sources described so far in this section allowed me to understand the demographics of those who exited through emigration or death and the voting preferences of Zimbabweans who remained in the country and shared those demographics. Missing from this data were the preferences of the actual migrants. The secondary data also did not describe the voting intentions of people affected by HIV/AIDS. Based on my political science training, my initial instinct was to collect primary data using an online survey. Surveys produce numeric data that can easily be analyzed and allow one to make claims about causality and generalizability. They also can be replicated by other scholars interested in the same question. I planned to survey 2,000 Zimbabwean migrants in a manner that would complement the Afrobarometer surveys. An online survey would have allowed me to reach Zimbabweans worldwide, including in places that are difficult for political researchers to enter like Qatar, where small but significant populations of Africans have been moving to. The men residing in and around the Middle East tend to work in the oil industry, while women tend to be domestic workers. Russia is another top destination where it would be challenging to conduct research: doing so attracts government attention, and migrants living there fear surveillance.

After I sent out pilot surveys, it became apparent that this methodology would not work. Online surveys are accessible for respondents who are comfortable with technology and have unlimited internet access. Most migrants, especially older and working-class people, do not have the resources to access such surveys. My responses were biased toward a younger and more privileged group.

Furthermore, when I sent out my pilot survey, respondents answered demographic questions, including their location, but not the political participation questions. I asked questions like those in the Afrobarometer surveys, for example:

- Have you ever voted?
- Please tell me the year you last voted.
- Do you feel close to any political party in your home country?
- Are you a member of any political group in the host country?

Although most respondents did not complete the surveys, some shared their email address or phone number and permitted me to contact them. I also reached out to leaders in the migrant communities to find out why the response rate was so poor. They said Zimbabweans are afraid to take surveys because they fear government surveillance. Often, researchers struggle to survey migrants because they lack a sampling frame (Agadjanian & Zotova, 2012; Chung et al., 2020). Fear is not a common challenge for researchers studying migrants, especially those from less authoritarian states, though it is more common for researchers who have a different identity than the surveyed population. I thought sharing my name on the survey might signal my in-group status.

The issue I faced was fear of government surveillance via electronic sources. Conversations with migrant community leaders and in-person interviews revealed that people feared that even fellow Zimbabweans might report them to the government. I had not realized there had been severe issues in the United Kingdom with the Home Office using in-group informants to target migrants for deportation. Although there is no documented evidence that this happened in the United States or South Africa, fear of deportation was also present there.

Most of my target population was unfamiliar with email and online surveys, which likely heightened their fears. Zimbabweans are a low-trust community, even compared to other Africans. In 2013, economist Elisabet Rustrom and I conducted field experiments in Zambia and Zimbabwe that measured trust. Zimbabwean participants were the most risk-averse and least trusting. I attribute this to years of living under a ruthless regime. Even migrants who had legal status to reside in the host country retained fear about discussing politics anonymously with someone on the internet.

I could understand the concerns raised by the respondents and community leaders. During my undergraduate studies at a small school in Oregon, I was invited to an interview with a local TV station in a town of 34,000 people. I was terrified even though they only wanted to know about my life and to ask me to comment on inflation. I was confident the government would not be interested in the views of a nineteen-year-old. However, like the migrants I sought to interview, I grew up being told the government was to be feared.

I have a Russian friend who is afraid to travel back home with their American-born son because they believe Putin has a database of all foreign-born children. Those fears have intensified because of the Russian war in Ukraine, just as each act of aggression against civilians by the Zimbabwean government increases fear. Like other authoritarian regimes, Zimbabwe is notorious for surveilling citizens. As a result, most people not linked to the government fear being accused of not supporting the regime enough or plotting to oust government officials. Zimbabweans are often loud and joyful in public settings, but their voices will drop to a whisper at the mention of the government. Author Chimamanda Ngozi described the same experience growing up in postwar Biafra. Her parents, who were loud and joyful, would become quiet, almost inaudible, at the mention of the government. Those fears remain even when Nigerians or

Zimbabweans have left home and are safely relocated to democracies. People never stop being afraid that the government will find them out and punish them or their loved ones back home.

When discussing politics, most Zimbabweans say the walls have ears. An interviewee in Scotland, Mary, fifty-one, kept checking the door even though we were as far as one can get from the Zimbabwean government and a blizzard was keeping me at their house for three days. Mary, like most Zimbabweans I spoke to, believed the government could gain access to electronic communication. Government policies that punish citizens with jail time for tweets or other social media engagements bolster these beliefs. Researchers must take these fears seriously, regardless of how real the threat seems to them.

Surveys pose other challenges as well. Without follow-up, it is hard to know what respondents mean when they choose one of five options on a survey. When respondents are asked to evaluate the performance of a sitting president, for example, and a majority report dissatisfaction, what does that mean? For those who voted for the president, dissatisfaction might mean they wish they were doing more on issues they care about; for opponents, it might imply they do not like them and will not vote for them. Because researchers have no way of knowing what voters mean by their survey answers, predictions of election outcomes have been off the mark lately, at least in the United States. People lie in both interviews and surveys, but the challenge is greater in surveys because researchers do not always have the ability to ask follow-up questions.

In 2017, for example, there was an uproar across Zimbabwean social media spaces when Afrobarometer results showed that most Zimbabweans trusted the government. The results were inconsistent with people's lived experiences. Zimbabweans wanted to know what the survey meant by trust. How can most Zimbabweans say they trust the president and yet report the country is going in the wrong direction and they are worse off than in the previous year? Afrobarometer held a town hall meeting to explain the results. It explained its survey procedures and then issued several reports suggesting presidential trust was about fear of the president and not about trust per se. The opposition MDC attributed the high levels of reported trust in ZANU-PF leadership to fear among respondents; they also questioned the structure of the questions and how they may have been misinterpreted (News24, 2017). Moyo-Nyede (2020) found that fear shaped respondent responses and that 82 percent of respondents who believed Afrobarometer had been sent by the government were likely to say that they trusted the government.

If I had only asked people to respond in an anonymous survey whether they intended to return to Zimbabwe, their yes or no responses would not have told me anything about the reasoning behind that response. Even if they all had the same response, I would not be able to tell if they had the same reasons. Contrast this with my interview experience with Maeve and Sarudzai, who both said they did not intend to return to Zimbabwe.

Sarudzai, fifty-five, an NGO executive interviewed in Washington, DC, said she would not return simply because she did not think her single vote mattered. Maeve had a more complex reason for saying, "I don't think I will ever return to Zimbabwe." There was a finality in how Maeve said those words. I had asked her whether she would return home to vote. After a long pause, she repeated, "I will never go back to Zimbabwe." She seemed even more confident in her response, but soon she started crying. I was worried that perhaps I had misread her file and that she was one of the victims of political violence I had been advised to approach with delicacy. I was sure she was not. My informant said she had come to the UK at the invitation of her sister, also an accountant. They now lived in Edinburgh after having worked in London. It turned out that Maeve was a victim of a different kind of abuse. Maeve had left the year before from Zimbabwe, leaving behind her husband and their six-year-old. Shortly after she relocated, her husband took a second wife. Her young son had died in a hit-and-run accident while in the care of the father's second wife – the partner she had been sending thousands of pounds to. He later moved to the UK with his new wife using sponsorship papers Maeve had prepared for him. Maeve blamed her ex-husband, the new wife, and the Zimbabwean government's failed medical system for her son's death; hence, she would never return to vote.

Maeve and Sarudzai responded similarly when asked if they would return home, but different circumstances shaped their responses. A survey asking for a yes or no answer would have given only part of the story: two women living in the diaspora will not return home to vote. This information provides a count, but it does not explain why Zimbabweans feel alienated from their politics. Interviews may provide additional context. Five years after the interview, Sarudzai returned to Zimbabwe on a business visit; while there, her husband convinced her to register to vote. In 2018, they reluctantly voted. Meanwhile, Maeve has kept her promise never to return to Zimbabwe. The two responses had very different implications for political participation.

Using Ethnographic Strategies in Political Science

Given these conditions, I decided to pivot my methodology toward a modified ethnographic study. This approach is more commonly used in anthropology than in politics, but a number of key political science works on ethnography have shaped my thinking on methodology (Fujii, 2015; Schatz, 2013). Political science generally tends to be more concerned about institutional behaviors than about individuals. Yet institutions are designed by individuals, and individuals work to strengthen or weaken institutions. Therefore, I committed to getting additional training in ethnography. I took a class on ethnography from anthropologists at Stanford. Taking the course was accidental; one might even say my decision to take the course and live among anthropologists was real-life training for my fieldwork. I had gone to Stanford to visit a friend in graduate school. After discussing my project, she suggested I attend her ethnography class.

The American Anthropology Association defines ethnography as the study of human behavior in a natural setting, in which investigators must immerse themselves in the community. There is no set requirement for how long one must live in a community or the number of interviews to conduct. I used semistructured interviews with ten questions and lived in communities for three to six months. While ethnography is a well-established field, I had some concerns about my positionality and the generalizability of my findings.

Positionality is a very important concern in ethnography. In some ways, I was a group insider; in others, I was a group outsider. I was aware that my being a Black Shona, specifically a Karanga woman from a middle-class background who was highly educated and grew up in the capital city of Harare, might impact the responses I would get and influence the pool I interviewed. I never interviewed my friends or family and avoided pooling too many people from adjacent circles.

No matter how similar I might be to my interviewees, our individual experiences were different. I took measures to the best of my ability to ensure I never projected my thoughts on respondents because of our perceived similarities. One strategy I used was avoiding a conversational style that might result in my inserting my own opinion. It was not always easy to do this, especially when respondents shared opinions that were similar or very different from mine. For example, I interviewed someone who supported the ruling party. Like me, they were young, urban, and educated. It was tempting to interrogate their beliefs and even challenge what I felt were mischaracterizations of politics back home. I have stayed in touch with this respondent even as they have returned home and risen in the ranks of government service. As another example, in Khayalitsha, Cape Town, I interviewed a young woman in her small shanty cottage. At the start of the interview, her husband kept interrupting her (she was the interviewee; the husband had refused to participate). It was tempting to jump in and ask him to let her speak. As a self-identified feminist, I was very upset by the entire setup. I was glad I did not interject. After I left, the woman called me and asked if I wanted to meet up. She said her husband was sizing me up, and she also found it interesting to hear his views. She was glad I had not tried to interject on her behalf because her husband would have likely become violent. It took many failed attempts to develop a strong ability to separate myself from the interview process.

My academic and public profile changed greatly during my research years. I started as an unknown graduate student. Anonymity allowed me to enter many important spaces without much suspicion. People find young, unknown women less intimidating, so they are more comfortable sharing their views. By 2017, I was a public intellectual with a bigger profile. At this point, it became especially important to let my respondents speak. I was also aware that although I am not an active member of the opposition, I have testified before the US Congress on issues related to Zimbabwe, and my comments were viewed as pro-opposition. Since the 2017 coup, I have regularly provided political commentary on CNN, BBC, and Al Jazeera. I also have a significant Twitter/X following. With all this in mind, I began each interview by emphasizing my academic credentials and downplaying the activist side of my identity. Thankfully, by then, I had known most of my respondents for years, and the changes in my professional life did not affect our relationship. The biggest change was that most people wanted me to talk to their children about college application processes. I was always glad to do this after the interviews. It felt like a small way to say thank you to people who had given me so much.

Generalizability is another important consideration in ethnography. Suppose I spoke to twenty or thirty Zimbabweans, as is standard in ethnographic work. Would their stories say enough about why millions of Zimbabweans were leaving the country and how their exit contributed to the survival of ZANU-PF? How many stories would be enough? I needed to develop a strategy to ensure that my results would represent Zimbabwean migrants as a whole.

Sampling Strategy

I devised a three-stage snowball strategy to reach a stratified sample of 100 interviewees. In the snowball method, research participants help the researcher reach additional participants. Snowballing increases trust between the researcher and participants because people tend to be more open to someone known within their community. The initial contact would reach out to a potential participant on my behalf and ask whether they would contact me for a conversation.

A colleague reading over an earlier draft of my work asked whether I had considered just interviewing members of my family living in the diaspora. This strategy has been used by other Zimbabwean scholars who fear retaliation. I briefly considered this, especially since autoethnography is growing in popularity and would get me past my fear of an intense recruitment system. But I wanted to get further from my immediate social network. In my strategy, the first person often had strong ties to someone I knew or were themselves very active in political conversations. I wanted more diversity in the pool so I could learn about the views of Zimbabweans outside my circles. As I will show later, I had reason to be concerned about speaking primarily to individuals with close ties to the political communities.

To achieve my goal, I created a list of Zimbabwean community and church leaders in different countries, with the help of people I already knew. The existing connections helped me test my interview questions and map out immigrant locations, but I excluded them from the final respondent group. I would contact Person A, ask them five basic questions about their knowledge of the Zimbabwean community, and ask them to introduce me to Person B. I would ask Person B an additional five questions about political participation and networks, then Person B would introduce me to Person C. My final list of respondents was comprised of Person Cs; but where someone had died or I had an underrepresented community (e.g., White Zimbabweans and those above age sixty), I interviewed some Bs. I added another layer of Person Cs to the interview if I had an overrepresented community. In South Africa, I added Person B.1 because the neighborhood was quite densely populated, and I wanted more distance between Person A and Person C. In places with fewer immigrants (e.g., Stirling, Scotland), I sometimes ended up with multiple recommendations to the same Person C. In such cases, I added Person C.2.

My sampling strategy was intertwined with my interview process. The first interviews occurred in three countries in 2013 and 2014, with subsequent rounds in 2017, 2020, and 2022. If I could not reach some respondents because they had moved or died, I recruited a new respondent from their family or community network or pulled someone from my list of Person Bs for an extended semistructured interview. I tried to find someone with characteristics similar to the original interviewee. In the years since the COVID-19 pandemic, I have sometimes replaced face-to-face interviews with phone calls. Face-to-face interviews are richer in detail because people often communicate more with their facial expressions and are more open than on the phone. I had conversations with over 300 Zimbabweans about transnational politics. I also attended many community meetings, church meetings, and community functions in the United States, United Kingdom, and South Africa. These meetings and events provided additional information about communities. In the next section, I detail my sampling process.

Recruiting Participants

I began planning for ethnographic fieldwork by looking at diaspora mapping work created by Pasura (2008) in the United Kingdom, Makina (2008) in South Africa, and Crush and Tevera (2010) in Canada. While migrants tend to move frequently from the places they first land, I knew they follow network patterns. I used similar methodologies to recruit interviewees in each location, with minor modifications to accommodate community differences.

I wanted my sample to improve on previous studies of Zimbabwean migrants, which had been less representative of host countries, racial groups, and ethnolinguistic communities. A lot was known about the experiences of Zimbabweans in London (Bloch, 2005; Kuhlmann, 2010; Pasura, 2010), but there was very little on the experiences and opinions of migrants in the United States and South Africa other than in Johannesburg. I wanted my study to cover multiple countries and cities. I believed posing similar questions in a similar time frame to people in different host countries would add richness to the study. I could also learn whether there were fundamental differences in how the diasporas viewed the ruling party back home. Indeed, when I began my work, I found the diaspora to be more active in transnational politics in the United Kingdom than in the United States and South Africa. After the 2017 coup, the American diaspora became more vocal and anti-ZANU-PF than those in the United Kingdom. At the same time, support for the regime back home grew and became more open. The rest of this subsection discusses the recruitment, and interview processes I used in each country, as well as how I handled returnees and AIDS-specific interviews.

UNITED STATES Because I am based in the United States, I began my fieldwork there. At the time, there had been no study of Zimbabwean migrants because their population was not as large or well known as in the United Kingdom or South Africa. I had an advantage because of my experiences as an immigrant in the United States since 2005. I also had access to US census data on the immigrant population. In 2012, about 20,000 Zimbabwean-born immigrants were living in the United States. These numbers do not capture the entire population. My sources at the US embassy in Harare told me that over 100,000 Zimbabweans had been issued visas during the same period (2008–2018). Most migrants came on visitor or student visas, and those on visitor visas are not counted in the census. Both census data and community knowledge informed me that most Zimbabwean migrants first arrived in Texas (US Census Bureau, 2012), except for people who came to the United States primarily to attend college (like myself). Zimbabweans make up almost 5 percent of the African-born population in Dallas, Texas. My US-based sample was drawn from people residing in Atlanta, Georgia, Texas, Oregon, Indiana, and Washington, DC.

Students are more spread out geographically, so I used different methods to reach the student population. In the early 2000s, active political groups existed in most diaspora cities. After 2010, as more people gained legal status in the host country and became more settled, groups with political affiliations dwindled and most people connected via church groups. The decline in political groups in the United States coincided with the rise of Zimbabwean churches. One of the largest Pentecostal churches in Zimbabwe, Forward in Faith Ministries International (FIFMI, often known as ZAOGA), which had created strong roots in the United Kingdom, was becoming rooted in the United States. In 2007, during a summer undergraduate internship at the Carter Center in Atlanta, I was invited to visit the first ZAOGA church, which had been launched just outside the suburbs. At that time, it was a small outfit of fewer than twenty people; today, the church has thousands of members all over the United States. In 2013, I reconnected with a pastor I had met in Atlanta. She was now based in Texas.

The move made sense for her because Texas remains the biggest hub for Zimbabweans and African migrants in general. From the perspective of Zimbabweans accustomed to warm temperatures, the weather in Texas is excellent. Although the politics of migration is changing, it is still easier for new arrivals to get jobs and settle in Texas than in other parts of the United States. My first contact in Texas invited me to their home, where they were hosting a birthday party for a Nigerian friend. It was not the environment I expected for a serious academic interview. My graduate school jeans and sweatshirt were not adequate for an African party in Texas. The host and their guests were unforgiving of my attire. I was offered a designer black dress and heels much higher than I was used to. Still, they indulged my questions, and I gained valuable insight into migrant experiences. In Texas, I learned that many Zimbabweans had moved to the Midwest, to Indiana specifically. Indiana! I did not expect that. It is freezing. While I was in Texas, I was introduced to a community leader from Indiana; she was not a politician or religious leader but was someone many respected. She was Ndebele, which helped me because, being Shona, my Ndebele networks in the United States were quite slim. In the United Kingdom, I would also benefit from having Ndebele migrants introduce me to their church networks.

Despite having done much work to build community trust, only some people were comfortable talking to me. During a meeting in Atlanta, where I was meeting respondents and establishing community ties, one guest spent more than thirty minutes berating me. I understood her frustration with the Shona people, whom she blamed for the genocide against her Ndebele community. Although she and I shared a Shona first name, Chipo, she did not identify with that heritage. Her single Ndebele mother raised her after her Shona father abandoned them. Unfortunately, what her father did was common, especially in the 1980s, shortly after independence. It is also common for anger and frustration to be expressed in diasporas. Studies of Somali migrants living in Minneapolis have shown that conflicts from back home can sometimes carry over into the host country (Brinkerhoff, 2006; Darboe, 2003; Lindley, 2022). I held no grudge, but the incident led me to cancel the interviews I had planned. It took me months to rebuild trust with the Ndebele community in Atlanta. I was lucky to have graduate school friends from South Africa and Lesotho who worked hard to facilitate conversations with the community, including with Chipo. Later, Chipo and I learned we had friends in common – she had even gone to high school with some of my Ndebele cousins, one of whom was her school's head boy. This connection was and continues to be beneficial.

Oregon is an unlikely place to seek out Black interview subjects, let alone Zimbabweans, but I went to college there and knew the community well. In the mid-1990s, the University of Zimbabwe built relationships with several schools in the United States, including Portland State, known for its strong chemistry program, and the University of Michigan. I had no direct connections in Michigan, so I returned to Oregon. During my undergraduate years, I attended many meetings of Zimbabweans in the USA (ZUSA), a short-lived organization that brought Zimbabweans together monthly. In fact, I attended one of the very first ZUSA meetings in Portland in 2005. The organization had been focused on transnational politics. Members raised funds to support the opposition party back home. I think the earliest seeds of my interest in transnational politics were planted at that first meeting in a two-bedroom apartment packed with Zimbabweans eating Zimbabwean foods and trying to figure out how to support the victims of Murambatsvina, a 2005 program initiated by the Zimbabwean government that displaced 700,000 and caused the deaths of hundreds who could no longer access HIV medication. ZUSA groups were also instrumental in helping victims of political violence relocate. Portland, like Atlanta, is an amiable city for political refugees. In Portland, I interviewed a lot of political activists who fled Zimbabwe between 2000 and 2008.

I also spent much time in Washington, DC, where I interviewed Zimbabweans in the area. I lived there after my undergraduate studies in 2008–2009, which made it easier to connect with community leaders. During my year in DC, I had volunteered as a translator for Zimbabwean asylum seekers, a position that kept me in touch with political party wings in the city. I connected with people who self-identified as members of the opposition party. The very active opposition party group in DC had hundreds of members. At the time, no one admitted to supporting ZANU-PF, although after 2017, more admitted to supporting the ruling party. Like in other states, family networks shaped how people ended up in the area. Many people in the DC area settled there because that was where the relative who sponsored their move was living. I sometimes traveled to New York City, where I met a lot more affluent Zimbabweans than I did in other cities. I found Zimbabwean New Yorkers to be less connected to migrant communities.

My sampling experiences validated my choice to take a wide-ranging approach. If a researcher only focused on Texas, they might conclude the Zimbabwean community was very close-knit and religious. If they only spent time around Washington, DC, where opposition party members routinely organized protests, they might conclude Zimbabweans are heavily engaged in transnational politics. If they only interviewed those living in New York, they would conclude connections to home have become weak. Extensive interviews allow one to differentiate the mechanisms through which voter exit sustains regimes in the home country.

UNITED KINGDOM The United Kingdom is the largest hub of Zimbabwean migrants after South Africa. The first large wave of migrants from Zimbabwe moved to the United Kingdom after independence. This wave was mostly White Zimbabweans worried about destabilization. The second wave started in 2000 because of failing economic conditions in Zimbabwe. A growing need for teachers and nurses in the United Kingdom created the perfect conditions for exit. My mother was among those who left during that wave. In my diary, I wrote that it felt as if everyone's parents were going away. In the months after my mom emigrated, our home became a sort of migrant processing center, a farewell hub for family and friends leaving for the United Kingdom. Unlike the United States, the United Kingdom did not require visas for Zimbabwean migrants until 2004. People only needed to raise money for airfare. Many of those seeking to relocate sold furniture and, in extreme cases, houses to fund their relocation. They expected to recoup their wealth once they settled in the United Kingdom.

Early arrivals in the 2000s would land in Greater London, Leeds, or Birmingham. I relied on Pasura's mapping projects as a starting point for my research. I also contacted people I knew in a few cities frequented by Zimbabwean immigrants to understand the diaspora movement and settlement better. As was the case in the United States, most migrants followed family networks for settlement.

For example, Blessing arrived in the United Kingdom in 2000 at age forty-three. She moved to Herefordshire, where she joined a family member, Jane, 73 years old, who was working on a potato farm. About twelve other Zimbabweans were working there, all with some connection to Jane. After six months on the potato farm, which is how long it often takes to repay the primary contact for financial expenses related to hosting new arrivals, Blessing moved to Slough, part of Greater London, where she knew a cousin, Mary, age 40. London provided more work opportunities. Mary was working in the care industry with at least thirty other Zimbabweans.

Within a year of arriving in the United Kingdom, Blessing had facilitated the arrival of six family members, all younger women in their thirties. They joined her at the hotel where she was working after leaving the care industry. The younger women soon moved into the care industry, where they would earn more money in a sector that welcomed those without professional credentials. Within two years, many began to move north to Scotland, where it was much easier to secure immigration paperwork.

Recruitment was easier and faster in the United Kingdom, perhaps because my skills were more refined after a year of traveling and doing interviews in the United States or because the UK population was more accustomed to interviews. My double in-group status burdened me less because, as a nonresident, I had little knowledge of UK subcultures and it was easier to not impose my beliefs on respondents. The United Kingdom had a more active political and politicized community. I quickly learned that certain parts of the community, especially those with links to political groups, had much experience with academic interviews. Indeed, most researchers working on Zimbabwean migrants reached out to the same political and professional communities. This was not good, because I sensed that people were telling me what they thought I wanted to hear rather than their truth. I increased the number and length of interviews for people from political groups so I could cross-check their previous comments. I also asked that we meet in new locations, hoping the change of venue would help them lower their guard. It also became clear that I needed to find respondents who were not closely tied to the political community. Thus, I once again modified my recruitment methodology. In addition to community groups and churches, I began recruiting from hair salons and joined the care work industry.

I mapped out the hair salons most frequented by Zimbabweans. Most women would visit a hair salon regardless of their level of political engagement. I could also meet more younger people and those who did not have formal professional credentials. I spent a lot of money on getting my hair done, though perhaps not as much as I did in the United States. Better hairstyles earned me approval from older interviewees, who only sometimes approved of my academic fashion choices. One of the first people I met at a hair salon was Betty, age 26. She had worked as a domestic worker in Zimbabwe. A wealthier cousin sponsored her ticket to the United Kingdom. Without this help, her family would not have been able to fund the trip. Through Betty, I met more people from similar backgrounds. She also introduced me to barbers, including Z, who worked at an exclusive barbershop in London. I am still trying to figure out Z's line of work in Zimbabwe. I am grateful for his wide network, which included bankers and other high earners in London who work very hard to avoid the rest of the Zimbabwean community. Fortunately for me, everyone needs a barber, and Z was one of the best.

Although I did not interview my family members for my work (not even my mother, who has many opinions), I benefited from their connections. A cousin who emigrated when she was eighteen, the same age I was when I came to study in the United States, was working in a care home. Most very young migrants ended up working long hours in care work. My cousin Seth spoke to her boss, who allowed me to volunteer at various care homes. Most care workers did not like to be interviewed. Although care work was well paid, those working in this industry often felt a lot of shame. Zimbabweans pride themselves on being highly educated professionals. However, care workers were the highest remitters and kept the economy back home afloat. Once I started working in the care home, the barrier that had existed between me and the subjects melted. It is very easy to find friendship when working together to clean adult bodily excrement.

In each city, I recruited from political groups, churches, and salons, and I continued with my care work. I could not get paid work due to my immigration status, but I could volunteer anywhere once I made connections in the care industry. The employers were quite willing to have free labor. I was able to build a very long contact list in the United Kingdom. I decided not to spend a lot of time at universities even though that would have made recruitment much easier. I wanted to meet people outside the academic community in spaces where they lived and engaged with politics of home more naturally. It took me a few years and multiple visits to speak to most of the people I had been connected with.

SOUTH AFRICA Nearly 85 percent of Zimbabwean migrants are in South Africa, mostly in Johannesburg and Pretoria. As such, most research is based on data drawn from the experiences of migrants living in those places. I decided to go to Cape Town because I had not read much about migrant experiences in the Western Cape. It was a lot further from Harare and would require more resources. I also wanted to oversample White Zimbabweans. In the United States and United Kingdom, I had only managed to speak to a handful of White Zimbabweans. While most Zimbabweans had been forced to leave the country because of economic and political conditions, the majority of White Zimbabweans had been expelled.

Making connections with people from ethnolinguistic communities different from my own was always challenging, but it was especially hard with White Zimbabweans. I grew up in a predominantly Black neighborhood and could count on my hands the number of times I had interacted with White people before going abroad. I decided to start my recruitment efforts at the University of Cape Town, where most White Zimbabweans attended university and Zimbabwean faculty were a majority.

I was very anxious about the reception I would get as a Black Zimbabwean, given that most White Zimbabweans had been violently kicked out of their homes and country of birth by Blacks. While the government had orchestrated and planned the violent land reform program, it was their Black domestic workers and neighbors who had delivered the physical blows. I was very excited to have been connected to a White Zimbabwean whose family had owned one of the largest farms in the country. In most reporting about victims of land reform, the perspectives came from men. Women were rarely interviewed.

My excitement for our interview was not matched. I have a vague memory of how everything transpired. One moment, I was getting up to greet her, and the next I was wiping spit from my face. She had spat on me in a restaurant full of people. I was mortified, afraid, embarrassed, and angry, but I also wanted to continue with the interview. Ultimately, this was one of the best interviews I conducted. I am not sure why I did not leave the restaurant. Perhaps it was because I did not react that she sat down. I informed her I was going to wash my face. I expected she would have left when I returned, but she was there. She had ordered two pots of tea. For a while, we both just drank our tea quietly. Without prompting, she began telling me about the night the war veterans invaded their homes. Although she had no right to abuse me, she was right to be angry. Her once flawless skin had a huge scar that cut across her nose from being stabbed by a dagger. She recounted a harrowing story of being forced to watch her horses burn to death. I might never be able to appreciate her wealth, but I can empathize with death, especially of loved ones. I only read about the invasions, first in Zimbabwe, where state media never mentioned violence, and later in the United States, where the media focused on violence but never the nuances of land inequality. Through this interview, I was connected to a community of White Zimbabweans who remained in the country. As luck would have it, some of them became vendors for my wedding. After the land reform pushed most farmers out of business, they pivoted to a different kind of entrepreneurship.

I had a much easier time recruiting within the Black community. Nearly every other cab driver was Zimbabwean. In addition to recruiting from the university, churches, and the few political groups in Cape Town, I started getting contacts via cab drivers. I spent a lot of time and money on taxis. Talking to cab drivers took me out of the leafy southern suburbs of Cape Town, where I felt safe, to the more diverse communities in the North. I had valid reasons to be anxious.

I interviewed several people who showed me frightening scars from being robbed in Khayelitsha by fellow Zimbabweans, South Africans, and other migrants. Poverty has a way of bringing out the worst in people.

Jabu, who was now a professor at one of the universities, told me he was homeless when he first arrived. He had been a university lecturer back home. Every day, he would pack his cardboard box covers and hide them in a city tunnel. One day, he was robbed and physically assaulted by a group also seeking shelter. The assault left a large scar on his back. Somehow, he made it out of those circumstances to find a lectureship position.

The young Zimbabweans in Cape Town were living in harsher conditions than their American and English counterparts. I interviewed people living under bridges. Some were caught up in the drug crisis, and others were just seeking shelter until they could find a break. I also met very wealthy Zimbabweans. A lot of the wealthy class, both Black and White, worked extra hard to blend into the South African community. One might leave Cape Town thinking no wealthy black Zimbabweans lived there. They did not want to be found. However, with the help of high school friends who had gone to university in Cape Town, I entered those communities. I am glad I did, because their politics and views on transnational politics were very different from their wealthy counterparts in New York.

OTHER LOCATIONS Over the years, I have met in other parts of the world with people I had interviewed in one of my three main locations. A young woman I interviewed in Washington, DC, moved to Tanzania. We reconnected while I was traveling in East Africa for other projects. She introduced me to other communities of migrants there. I eventually made my way to the Middle East. Someone I interviewed in South Africa started a business buying hair supplies in Dubai. They asked me to tag along to visit a community of more recent migrants, most of whom were domestic workers. A friend from graduate school was doing a short teaching stint there; she split airfare with me and offered me housing. I am grateful to the many friends and family who subsidized my research with their generosity. In these communities, I did not follow a strict methodology, but I did take note of transnational and remittance activities.

RETURNEES Among the diaspora, I was asking Zimbabweans about their feelings and engagement with politics back home. I also wanted to know whether they return home to vote. I was fortunate that there were two elections – in 2013 and 2018 – while I was doing my research. In 2013, I reached out to my diaspora contacts to see if any of them would be returning home to vote. I was also interested in the impact of remittances on the political participation of recipients, so I asked my contacts whether I could speak to their receivers. In 2009, the Zimbabwean government had signed an agreement with the opposition to govern together. This resulted in a small wave of migrants returning home. Some people I interviewed had also returned home. This was a good opportunity to inquire about their political participation in their home country and check whether they had voted.

In Zimbabwe, I spent time at the Zimbabwe Electoral Commission (ZEC), where I checked registration numbers and locations. I also had unexpected luck. I had gone to the ZEC offices to interview one of the commissioners about voter registration processes. While I was there, their computers crashed, and there was a power outage. They asked whether they could load the voter roll on my computer. I agreed. With this access, I could search whether my respondents had been registered to vote later that evening. This helped me verify the information I was given during interviews. Almost everyone had told the truth. I was also struck by the number of registered voters aged over 100 – but that is a conversation for later chapters!

In 2017, the Zimbabwean government announced it was creating a new voter roll ahead of the 2018 election. Anyone who intended to vote in that critical election, the first since the coup that ousted Mugabe, would need to reregister. Those in the diaspora would need to return home before February 2018 to register to vote and then again in July to vote. This provided a natural experiment, an opportunity to assess the impact of voter exit on political engagement. How many would come back home? I traveled to Zimbabwe to register and interview my respondents who had returned home and those who had made promises to do so. I was also able to purchase the 2018 voter roll. I could now compare data from 2017 and 2018 to see how many of my respondents had managed to register to vote. While in Zimbabwe, I dug through historical and current records at the national archives on migration, elections, and HIV.

In the early years of my research, I was able to spend time in ZANU-PF and MDC headquarters. Being young and female was very beneficial. The first month I was at ZANU-PF headquarters, I found myself in a high-profile meeting after being asked to make tea for the teams. Once, I was sent to buy a light bulb after I told one of the security guards that the library did not have working lights. ZANU-PF has been very meticulous at documenting party manifestos, campaign regalia, and other materials. They gave me insight into their political activities.

During election years, I attended political rallies. It is a lot easier to gain access to politicians during election cycles. During the 2013 election, I attended at least ten rallies. The ruling party often provided buses to their rallies, which made them a lot more accessible than opposition rallies. Opposition parties did not always have the resources to provide free transportation to their members.

HIV-SPECIFIC WORK How does one study the impact of exit because of HIV on political outcomes? In the interviews I conducted with the diaspora and returnees, I asked about the impact of HIV on family life. I asked people to describe their relatives impacted by HIV: their education levels, economic class, children, and their political participation. I was interested in the predicted voting behavior of the deceased and how the pandemic changed life. To supplement the interviews with members of the diaspora, I interviewed business owners who had lost employees. I spoke to insurance company owners who had data on death rates and could speak to how this impacted their businesses. I spent time at orphanages getting information on the inflows of children since the start of the pandemic. Where possible, I interviewed adult orphans on how they thought the pandemic impacted their trajectories. Because most of the publicly discussed impact of HIV was on musicians, I also interviewed musicians, including high-profile people like the late Oliver Mtukudzi, who had served as an HIV ambassador, Thomas Mapfumo, and Tsitsi Dangarebga.

Avoiding Bias in Analysis

How does one make effective use of 100 interviews to tell a truthful story and not just select comments that support one's argument or theory? Each time I concluded a set of interviews, I gave myself a few days or months away from the data. When I first thought of my project, I never imagined I would end up talking to people about their most vulnerable moments. How would I use a story told to me by a young man in Scotland named Chris, who was introduced to credit card fraud and ended up spending nearly five years in jail? Back home, he had been an upstanding member of society working what he called a boring bank job. I interviewed him in his freezing council flat. I could not bring myself to sit on his couch, which had a gaping hole and what I thought were rat droppings. Many years later, I still feel guilty about being afraid of him. My methodology had worked so well that I found myself in an unlikely part of Glasgow, afraid for my life, judging a stranger but still intrigued to ask about his political views. How would I make any sense of his responses – or those of Ashely, the high-end lawyer I had spoken to in Edinburgh a few hours before my interview with Chris? This work was more emotionally taxing than I had anticipated. There were so many sad stories, anger, and pain among the diaspora. There was joy, too, but the sadness weighed heavily on me. The literature had no suggestions about what to do with my feelings, so I allowed myself time off.

Afterward, I hired a native Ndebele speaker who was fluent in English to do the transcriptions for me. I almost always asked questions in English during interviews, but most respondents would switch between their native languages and English, especially when narrating difficult times. For example, I interviewed Vusa in the United Kingdom. He had been a teacher in Zimbabwe before he left in a hurry after being hunted down for his political beliefs. Vusa knew I was not a fluent Ndebele speaker; however, as he got into the more complicated details, he switched to Ndebele. The interview was over an hour long. The same happened with Maria in Washington, DC, who switched to Shona.

After completing the transcriptions, I tapped into my training and created a codebook for each respondent with much commentary. When respondents told me they engaged in political activity, I did not just code them as active, but I also coded the type of activity and length. I saved interesting commentary about each question to draw on for direct quotes to include in the book only if they explained a broader pattern of behavior. I also categorized the responses by the year in which events were reported to have happened, not just by the year of the interview.

To avoid selection bias for data that supported my argument, I divided responses into five categories: strong and medium opposition supporters, strong and medium ruling supporters, and those who said they did not support any political party. This allowed me to carefully analyze responses from each group and compare them to people who were politically similar. Responses from the seventeen ZANU-PF supporters were very important in this analysis because they challenged my assumptions about young, educated urbanites and their support for the opposition. To preview findings that I will discuss in greater detail in Chapter 4, ZANU-PF supporters tended to be nostalgic about better life at home and believed Zimbabwe was superior to their adopted home. Even more curious is that over half of strong ZANU-PF supporters were self-reported victims of political violence back home and were now living as refugees.

A lot of good groundbreaking work is drawn from a few case studies, such as Skocpol's work on revolutions (Skocpol, 1979). Findings from extensive semistructured interviews can say a lot about the role of exit on politics, but I cannot and do not make claims about the entirety of the Zimbabwean diaspora or other diasporas.

CONCLUSION

In this chapter, I discussed the theoretical and methodological approaches I used to study the impact of exit on the political survival of ZANU-PF's authoritarian regime. In the first section, I discussed Hirschman's EVL theory and how I adapt and extend it. I apply Hirschman to a different type of regime, the illiberal democracy or electoral authoritarianism that has become more common in the world. I extend exit to add the permanent exit of death, the effective exit of voter attrition, and the partial exit of those who return remittances. I also extend voice to include voting and allow it to be a factor after exit. This continued engagement after exit extends the concept of loyalty to mean more than simply remaining in a country. I concluded that section by discussing how the predictions of my modified EVL construct differ from those of Hirschman.

Questions should drive methodology. The choice of using surveys or experiments should not be determined by the most popular method at the time but instead by what strategies provide the best chance of learning new information. No single methodology would be enough to study how an authoritarian regime was bolstered by large-scale migration, death from HIV, and the related negative consequences on communities. This chapter discussed my multimethod strategies, including quantitative and qualitative methodologies. I used two decades of quantitative data on citizen opinions, HIV, and migration from nationally representative Afrobarometer and UNAIDS spectrum samples. I also collected extensive ethnographic data through semistructured interviews with 100 Zimbabweans living abroad and those who have returned home.

3

Death and Dearth of Democrats

HIV/AIDS and Voter Exit

> I thought both Angelo and Michael were friends that I would grow old with. As it turned out, I didn't even have a chance to say goodbye.
> —Michael Shnyaerson (2013)

In the 1990s, when I was enrolled in primary school in Harare, Zimbabwe, something shifted in our family, allowing my cousins and me to spend more time together than was usual. We were together during school days, day and night, something our middle-class parents, typically very strict about education, would not have previously allowed. We were spending time away from school because we were always at funerals. This was happening in my family and among my friends and teachers. Our parents were missing days of work because they were also at funerals or caregiving for sick relatives. Friends were losing their parents and having to move from our middle-class suburb to their ancestral village if there was no one to take care of them in their home. Many families converted bedrooms into in-home clinics. At the time, the disease killing so many of our people did not have a name. When someone died, people would whisper that they "died from the new illness." Doctors were not allowed to name HIV as the cause of illness until after 2005.

A fifty-three-year-old woman I interviewed in the United Kingdom lost five of her eight siblings to the illness, all within three years. The eight siblings reflected a typical 1990s Black middle-class family in Zimbabwe. Everyone had a university degree, owned their home, sent their children to good schools, was employed in a high-earning job, and paid taxes. Together, they left eight orphans. None of their children made it to university. Another woman in her mid-thirties lost both her parents within months, orphaning her and her three siblings. These are some of the stories I gathered from over 300 interviews. Each of my respondents had a personal story related to HIV/AIDS loss, and most of them lost relatives who were young, urban, educated professionals at the time of their death.

Like most others, it is hard to account for the number in my family who died from HIV/AIDS. In only one year, we lost fifteen people, all under the age of thirty-five, all with at least a high school education or higher, all living in the city when they got sick, and all active workforce members. They either left a child who died soon after they did, or their young children preceded them in death. The high death rate would continue well into the early 2000s. A groundbreaking study by Chigwedere et al. (2008) estimated that over 22 million years of human life were lost prematurely in the years South Africans could not access HIV medication. It is reasonable to assume that millions of years of life were also prematurely lost in neighboring Zimbabwe, which was experiencing a similar purge. Unofficial statistics from a doctor working at the largest public hospital in 2002 estimated that about 2,500 deaths per week were from HIV. By 2003, there were about 1.8 million cases of HIV. Unofficially, doctors told me that over 80 percent of those people died. Many of these people died before reaching the age of thirty.

When I first thought about the explanations for ZANU-PF's survival, I had no idea the work would lead me to HIV. I did not make the connection between HIV/AIDS deaths and fatigue to politics until much later. During a talk at Stanford University in 2018, I came across a *Vanity Fair* article about the impact of HIV on the arts community in San Francisco. Until then, I had no idea about the extent of the HIV pandemic in America, as I had assumed it was only an African issue. The article featured photos of several artists who had died young, and the authors speculated on the kind of work these artists could have produced if they had lived longer. The report highlighted how the HIV pandemic had a significant impact on the cultural scene in most metropolitan cities, as it caused the loss of several decades' worth of great work.

The HIV cases affecting the LGBTQI (lesbian, gay, bisexual, transgender, queer, and intersex) communities were discovered after the Stonewall uprisings. These uprisings had expanded significant rights and increased political activism among minorities. The pandemic erased many of those gains and suppressed the voices of activists. LGBTQI persons were once again forced to live in hiding during the early years of the HIV pandemic (Miachel, 2013). HIV scholars, including Halkitis (2019), have pushed back against assertions that the sexual liberation that came after Stonewall increased HIV infections. In fact, health systems were not well equipped or ready to deal with the health challenges facing LGBTQI communities.

Learning more about the impact HIV had on the LGBTQI community in America, especially their art, got me thinking about how different political life in Zimbabwe, South Africa, Zambia, Malawi, Kenya, and Tanzania would have been had it not been for HIV. Millions of people who were the most fit, young, and educated had died. How did the pandemic affect not only social structures and economy but also the political trajectories of the communities it impacted the most? Would Zimbabwe's politics have been different if the pandemic had not occurred, if the voices of hundreds of artists, activists, professionals, and urban working-class people had been heard? What was the impact on the political activism of those who had to step away from participation due to becoming caregivers, and what about the millions of orphans who grew up without stable family structures where they could learn about political engagement?

In this chapter, I argue that the exit of voters from the political system because of the HIV/AIDS pandemic bolstered the survival of ZANU-PF. While most explanations and data used in this chapter are drawn from the Zimbabwean case, I also show patterns in other parts of the world, particularly the other six Southern African countries that have experienced high rates of HIV infection and deaths. Adding to Hirschman's EVL, I show that the involuntary exit of millions of voters from the political system created opportunities for ZANU-PF's survival. Most of those who died or stopped their political participation because of being ill themselves or being caregivers would have been opposition voters or activists. Their exit thus weakened opposition support and helped the regime sustain itself. Had Zimbabwean voters not died or been too incapacitated to participate in politics due to HIV/AIDS, the opposition would have won more votes in elections. Using multiple sources of data, I show that ZANU-PF benefited from an AIDS premium of at least two percentage points in the elections between 2000 and 2013.[1]

FORTY YEARS OF THE HIV PANDEMIC

Over the last forty years, AIDS has wreaked havoc on African societies, economies, and social structures. Nevertheless, political science has been

---

[1] ZANU-PF had a 1–3 percent gain in the 2000, 2002, and 2008 elections but no HIV premium in 2005 or 2013.

slow to study its impact on democracy. In the late 1990s, at the height of the pandemic, Boone and Batsell (2001) lamented the lack of political science analysis of the impact of AIDS on politics. Nearly two decades later, the literature remains scant. Still, with the benefit of time, one can now engage in a more robust analysis of the negative consequences of HIV on politics in Southern Africa, where the disease killed the most people. And indeed, critical works by Alex de Waal (2006), Amy Patterson (2005, 2011, 2018), also engaged on the political aspects of the HIV pandemics on the African continent. My work also benefits from a rich Zimbabwe-specific literature on the myriad of ways ZANU-PF officials engaged with the HIV crisis (Gregson et al., 2006; Halperin et al., 2011; O'Brien & Bloom, 2010; Price-Smith, 2004).

On June 5, 1981, the US Centers for Disease Control and Prevention (1990) published about five cases of *Pneumocystis carinii* pneumonia among previously healthy young men in Los Angeles. There was no name for the illness now known as AIDS. The 1981 case marks the official start of the AIDS crisis in the United States, but the spread of the disease likely began decades earlier. Scientists say AIDS originated in Central Africa, in what is now called the Democratic Republic of Congo (DRC). Although the origins of the illness are linked to Africa, the first cases of HIV/AIDS in several countries on the continent were not reported until the mid-1980s. The first reported incidence of the HIV in Zimbabwe was in 1985 (Dzimiri et al., 2019), following reports in South Africa and Uganda in 1982 and in Zambia in 1984.

It would be a few more years after these cases before the term human immunodeficiency syndrome (HIV) or AIDS would be widely used or even linked to the illness. For years, in most African cases, the official diagnosis was that someone was suffering from or had died from either the short or long illness. This was derived from how long it took someone to die after acquiring the virus. Progression to active AIDS after HIV invades the body can be quite long, often six to twelve years, but human deterioration after that point can be quite quick. HIV targets and weakens the body's white blood cells, which fight infection and diseases. The virus also mutates quickly, manifesting in different illnesses, which is why it was very difficult to properly diagnose it in the early days and find treatment. Rose, forty-five, a nurse in Zimbabwe from 1990 until she emigrated to the United Kingdom in 2000, described HIV as a cruelly opportunistic illness: "Each time we thought we had a handle on one problem, say a cough, then the mouth sores would come or bed sores or headaches – we never could get ahead of it."

My most vivid memories of watching relatives suffering from HIV are of my aunt, who died at just twenty-three in 1995. Before she was ill, she had always been very beautiful and plump. People said we looked alike because of our similar round cheeks. She moved to Harare in 1992 to care for me while my mother traveled for work. It was an exciting time to be a young woman in Harare. Born in 1972, she had been too young to remember the war, but she was coming of age at independence. Her youth had been full of euphoria, joy, and hope. Harare was only too happy to welcome a naïve young woman. Her deterioration was quick. By the time she died, she weighed less than 30 kg, just a third of her previous weight. She was just bones. Her baby preceded her in death at just three months old. In the same way that it destroyed bodies, leaving young women like my aunt former shells of themselves, it was decimating the political capital that young people could have provided to a young country still trying to figure out its politics.

By the late 1990s, the World Bank had identified AIDS as the largest threat to development in Africa since independence. In the view of many, AIDS would reverse the gains made in health, education, and life expectancy (Boone & Batsell, 2001). Although much progress has been made in HIV treatment and health outcomes, it remains among the top twenty causes of morbidity and mortality in the top ten high-prevalence countries, mostly in Southern and East Africa. In the 2000s, at its peak, HIV was among the top five global causes of death. It was also during this period that many countries in Africa experienced democratic regression.

Of those who died from HIV globally, nearly half were from Southern Africa. UNAIDS data show that at its peak in 1999, nearly 25 percent of the hardest-hit Southern African population lived with the illness, and most of them succumbed to their illness. When I was in high school in the mid-2000s, children would play catch using the one in four statistics as a scare tactic in games: "Every fourth person has it," meaning AIDS, although we never actually used the term. By 2020, an estimated 79 million people were infected with HIV/AIDS, and more than 42 million people had died since the start of the HIV pandemic. Today, fewer people are dying from HIV because of advances in medication and increased knowledge about the disease. There are still no vaccines or cures for AIDS, but the infected now have access to antiretroviral medicines that work by preventing the virus from mutating within the body. According to a 2017 UN report, more than half of people living with HIV worldwide have some access to medicine, and nearly 20 million were on treatment, including the life-saving antiretroviral therapy (ART).[2]

There is no doubt that widespread access to ART is a good thing. However, the cost of providing ART falls on governments and donor organizations. In Southern Africa, this has placed a heavy financial burden on young countries. While high-prevalence countries have made strong inroads toward self-funding HIV treatment, most still depend on donor funding. Nearly 60 percent of HIV funding in the region comes from donor governments and agencies. In East and Southern Africa, the region worst affected by HIV, eight of the fifteen countries reporting data to UNAIDS in 2017 were dependent on donors for more than 80 percent of their HIV response. For example, while the Zimbabwean government instituted a 5 percent income tax levy for AIDS, over 80 percent of the HIV budget still comes from donor agencies. As donor governments continue to reduce foreign aid, this raises concerns about the future of treatment for the millions who depend on ART and other therapies.

To combat HIV, Western embassies all over Africa added an AIDS agenda to their work, and there was an initial significant global increase in the number of HIV-focused organizations. However, available funding is not meeting the targets. A twenty-year study on health funding found that nearly $9 trillion was spent on global health spending between 1995 and 2019 (Global Burden of Disease Health Financing Collaborator Network, 2018). Between 2000 and 2015, $562.6 billion was spent globally on HIV/AIDS. In-region governments funded 61 percent ($29.8 billion) of total HIV/AIDS spending in 2015. Sub-Saharan Africa and other developing regions, where the HIV disease burden remains high, are very dependent on donor development assistance for health, which accounts for about 63.9 percent of HIV/AIDS spending in the region. Of the $48.9 billion spent on HIV/AIDS in 2015, 55.8 percent ($27.3 billion) was spent on care and treatment, and one-fifth ($9.3 billion) was spent on prevention (Global Burden of Disease Health Financing Collaborator Network, 2018).

Celebrities raised millions of dollars for HIV. The most popular fundraising efforts by musician Bono's nonprofit RED claim to have raised over $650 million for AIDS, although the actual numbers might be higher. Despite all this effort and focus on the disease, very few efforts have been

---

[2] The COVID-19 pandemic has reduced these numbers. In 2020, WHO estimated that more than half of those who depend on ART could not access their medication during the pandemic.

made to understand how a pandemic with such a broad sweeping impact on millions of lives has shaped the political landscape.

During the transition from colonialism to independence, the HIV pandemic had a significant impact on most countries in Southern Africa. The countries that gained independence late – such as Zimbabwe, South Africa, and Namibia – were severely affected. Meanwhile, in the countries that had gained independence early – such as Zambia, Kenya, and Malawi – the pandemic coincided with the end of the postindependence authoritarian era, marked by authoritarianism moving toward more democratic governance (Kerr et al., 2024). In these countries, leaders who came into power after independence had prohibited opposition participation in politics.

Thus, at a time when the newly independent governments still recovering from years of civil war, as was the case in Zimbabwe, or economic sanctions, as was the case in South Africa, and working to restructure society and expand rights and opportunities that had been restricted under colonialism, they also faced an unprecedented crisis that demanded more resources than anyone could have imagined. HIV was financially and physically draining on the entire system. The state's control of life-saving medication is at the heart of how politicians manipulated the pandemic to suit their goals. The initial response from most countries was to deny the existence of HIV and its impact on society. Piot et al. (2009) suggested that politicians denied the existence of HIV because of shame about how the disease is transmitted. In the next section, I provide more detail about the politics of HIV/AIDS.

THE POLITICS OF HIV

Everywhere in the world, governments were slow to act on HIV; for a period, the global community was unsure how to handle the pandemic. The slow reaction was partly because little was known about the illness and partly because, in the Western countries where the first cases were reported, the illness mainly impacted marginalized communities. However, by the mid-1980s, HIV/AIDs had become a hot political issue in Western countries. LGBTQI activist groups organized protests around the United States and in the United Kingdom, demanding government action on research and provision of care (Morley, 2016). In the 1990s, AIDS was a top agenda item for both the United Nations and the World Bank. However, AIDS was never a major election issue in most African countries. In Africa, the response to HIV was extremely slow and mostly government-led. Africans who just a decade earlier had been fighting for independence did not take to the streets to demand that governments act on HIV.

Although Zimbabwe, like most countries, was slow to respond to HIV, its government made big strides in the early 1990s, far ahead of its peers. Robert Mugabe was among the first to admit his country had an HIV crisis and encourage access to condoms and ART, unlike Thabo Mbeki next door in South Africa, who denied the existence of the crisis, which led to the premature deaths of millions of people (Hawker, 2002; Weinel, 2009). Still, thousands of Zimbabweans were dying each year. By the 2000s, when the government began engaging in rogue political behavior, the impact of their actions, especially Operation Murambatsvina which saw the destruction of hundreds of HIV care centers and the displacement of gravely ill people, worsened the HIV crisis (Harris, 2008; Potts, 2006).

African governments were often quick to punish HIV activists. Why did they do this when earlier intervention could have saved millions of lives? Why did African urbanites who were most impacted by the pandemic not unite in protest for faster research and access to care, which might have saved more lives? Often, the protests were led by the same handful of activists, making them easy targets for government crackdown (Human Rights Watch, 2003; Patterson & Cole, 2006; Robins, 2006). In 2018, I interviewed Zimbabwean activist Frank Guni in Washington, DC. He had fled the country after the government made multiple attempts to harm him. Guni suggested that a lack of information contributed to the shame associated with HIV/AIDS, resulting in poor citizen buy-in and government support. African governments were displeased with the protests; in Zimbabwe, HIV activism was entwined with calls for political reform, which the government saw as an endorsement of the opposition. Healthcare workers in Zimbabwe said that the system was also under strain due to the high prevalence of HIV. Cecelia, a doctor who had worked in Zimbabwe and then South Africa in the 1980s and 1990s, said:

Part of the problem with AIDS is that we did not know what we were dealing with. Once people in Europe said it was killing homosexuals, people here got scared even as our fellow doctors were dying. Even in Uganda, where research was more advanced, it was hard to unify around something we did not fully understand. After I got sick, I was ostracized. My workmates wanted nothing to do with me even though everyone was getting it from patients, so I went into hiding. I was there, but I was dying.

African governments held the same attitude.

Another reason for the lack of citizen action is that in the United States and other Western nations, the responsibility for addressing the pandemic was on the government, whereas it quickly became a donated aid issue in much of Africa. There were no policy debates about the impact of HIV on the economy or society, even as hundreds were dying each month from the illness. It was certainly an ever-present reality, but it was not considered a political issue, at least not until the late 1990s – and by then, millions were already suffering and dying. HIV activism would come in the mid-2000s, but it was too late. The damage to the political fabric had already been done.

After gaining independence, Zimbabwe made progress in many areas of welfare. In the early 1980s, demographers anticipated even more improvement in infant mortality, fertility, and life expectancy. The government made efforts to improve rural healthcare accessibility and built more schools, resulting in increased enrollment of children in primary schools. However, progress made during the early years after independence in reducing child mortality and improving life expectancy was lost between 1994 and 2008. In 2003, the average life expectancy of a female was thirty six years. However, by 2007, this had declined to just 34 years (McClure, 2020). In Southern Africa, life expectancy was predicted to reach seventy years by 2020; unfortunately, it remained well below this number in countries like Zimbabwe (thirty three), Botswana (twenty nine), Namibia (thirty three), and Swaziland (thirty three; Stanecki, 2000).

Between 1994 and 2008, Zimbabwe experienced a decline in its population growth. During this period, the country's infant mortality rate remained persistently high. At the peak of the HIV epidemic, sixty of every 1,000 children born to Zimbabwean mothers died in infancy. Without HIV, this number would have been just 30 of 1,000 (Stanecki, 2000). In 1994, the earliest year for which data are available, the maternal mortality rate in Zimbabwe was only 2.83 deaths per 1,000 mothers. By 2004, the maternal mortality rate had tripled to 6.80 deaths per 1,000 mothers. Analysis by Bicego et al. (2002) showed that the majority of maternal deaths were directly related to HIV infections. They also found that in the early 2000s, the number of women dying due to HIV was significantly higher. The HIV epidemic had a detrimental impact on Zimbabwe's population growth. Between 2000 and 2005, the peak of HIV prevalence in Zimbabwe, the country experienced negative population growth. HIV/AIDS was raging a silent war around the country. The escalating pandemic reversed the gains from early government policies that improved infant and maternal mortality rates.

It took too long for the government and even citizens to realize the broad impact of the pandemic. By 1995, life expectancy was down to

52.95 years. The 1990s were a bloodbath, but things would worsen between 2000 and 2008: life expectancy never exceeded forty-six years old. In 2005, UNICEF estimated that every fifteen minutes, a child was dying of AIDS in Zimbabwe. The infant mortality rate had been 50 percent lower in 1990. Although there has been some improvement, the situation is still dire. In 2019, 38 babies out of every 1,000 were dying after birth. Each year since 2009, when we buried my young cousin who died from complications related to HIV at just twenty-two years old, I have taken note of the number of graves of small children. Today, it is impossible to count because tiny graves cover the entire cemetery. The Zimbabwean population was staying young because most people were dying young from HIV and AIDS. Economic research shows that stagnant population growth harms economic development because it directly impacts the labor force. Missing from this discussion is the fact that premature deaths are also bad for politics and democratic growth.

In 2014, when I began collecting data on political participation in Victoria Falls, people would casually point to neighbors who were living with HIV or children who had lost family members to the illness. The pandemic hit tourist destinations and border towns like Victoria Falls hardest because they are high-traffic areas with higher ratios of truckers and sex workers (UNAIDS, 2017). Additionally, Victoria Falls is in the Matebeleland region, which never recovered from the genocide that occurred in the 1980s shortly after independence. In the early 1980s, Mugabe targeted the Ndebele minority ethnic group, accusing them of being dissidents. The genocide killed over 20,000 people (Catholic Commission for Justice and Peace & Legal Resources Foundation in Harare, 2008). As a result, upheavals in the economy or health sectors have a worse impact there than in any other part of the country.

People were dying young. Young democrats were dying. France Lovemore, an activist medical practitioner who dedicated her career to victims of political prosecution, said the 1990s were a paradox: "On one hand, there was so much good happening. We were taking a breath from student activism against racism and apartheid and just starting our lives as our friends were starting to die." When I asked why they did not protest earlier, she said, "I do not know why. I do think we were trying to live for a moment." Her reaction was shared by many who turned the question back at me: "What would we have protested?" Zimbabwe's democracy activists exited the political conversation because of the demands and fear of HIV/AIDS's impact on their lives.

HIV came to Zimbabwe at a time (the 1980s to mid-1990s) when people were mostly satisfied with the government and there was a lot of hope and trust that the new government would do well. People trusted that individuals could change their circumstances, and in many ways this was true. Most families moved young members like my aunt from rural areas into urban areas where job and education opportunities were abundant. Regis moved from rural Matebeleland to join his six older siblings in Bulawayo to finish his education and later moved to Harare for university and a job as an executive. His trajectory was much brighter; he was born in 1975, and he came of age when Zimbabwe was at its best. In university, they protested for better living conditions:

> Not because things were very bad, but because that is what we did in university. But when my friends and siblings started dying, it never occurred to me that protest was an option for ending the HIV crisis. It felt personal. Before age thirty, I had adopted my four orphaned nephews. In my thirties, I was taking care of more than people. I came from a family of eight, but only two of us remain. How do you protest that?

What if Regis and his friends had been able to raise the alarm and organize against HIV? What if citizens had been quick to place responsibility for ensuring their health and well-being on the government? Would that have changed the trajectory of Zimbabwean politics? Any of these actions would have likely led to better outcomes. In South Africa, which is more democratic, citizens took the government to court and forced them to acquire ART (New Humanitarian, 2011).

Evidence from other places shows that when citizens protested for better healthcare, it modeled a culture of citizens as stakeholders. This happened in Poland. Owczarzak (2009) found that democracy in post-communist Poland was closely tied to citizen activism against HIV in the early 1990s. HIV protests and demand for care in Poland also occurred during a period of political transition and joined unlikely allies – LGBTQI activists and the Catholic church – in demands for more space and voice, setting a standard that democracy meant more engagement and not less. The chaos and cruelty of AIDS broke political structures that could have otherwise channeled more citizen voices toward a more stable democracy and thus created opportunities for authoritarian survival.

HIV impacted people in the prime of their lives. Prior to wide access to HIV treatment, the debilitating impact of HIV greatly reduced quality of life, forcing people to lose their jobs, income, homes, and life. Those affected by HIV were less likely to engage in politics during the course of the illness, and young democracies lost nearly 25 percent of eligible voters. In 2000, the UN estimated that half the teenagers in Africa would die from HIV, with the small population in southern countries being the most impacted (Gottlieb, 2000). In 2018, more than 32 million had died from the disease, making HIV the greatest threat to human life – more than civil conflict and even the COVID-19 virus that arrested the world in 2020. The remainder of this chapter details how exit induced by HIV/AIDS helped the ZANU-PF regime stay in power. Authoritarian regimes are masterminds at manipulating crises for their own benefit. It is not surprising that the ruling party politicized the HIV crisis for its own benefit.

ZANU-PF BENEFITED FROM AN EXIT PREMIUM

In this section, I present a detailed analysis of how the political landscape of Zimbabwe would have been different if not for the impact of HIV/AIDS. I use extensive quantitative data to model the additional electorate that would have existed if not for deaths and incapacitation due to HIV. Then, I project how the elections would have turned out if that additional electorate had been present. My findings suggest that ZANU-PF benefited from an exit premium created by the death of about a quarter of the electorate between 2000 and 2013. Furthermore, the worst impact of HIV was in opposition strongholds in urban areas, particularly among the urban poor. ZANU-PF benefited from a combined premium of at least two percentage points because people died or were too sick to engage in politics. My calculations are very conservative. I make predictions based on the lowest possible turnout for the electorate. Using these calculations, had the people severely impacted by HIV been able to vote, the opposition would have made small gains in the 2000 and 2002 elections, but they would have gained an additional 3 percent in the 2008 elections, increasing Morgan Tsvangirai's vote from 49 percent to 52 percent and fending off a runoff.

To estimate the size of the electorate that exited because of HIV, I used data from the Joint United Nations Program on HIV/AIDS (UNAIDS) spectrum model. Spectrum is not perfect, but it is one of the major sources of data on AIDS. Makota et al. (2023) found no substantive differences between the most widely used AIDS data models. Given the fluctuation in HIV numbers and the difficulty of getting accurate data, especially in the early years, models are more likely to underestimate the impact than overestimate it. More complete data would reinforce my findings.

As of 2022, the spectrum model had data from 160 countries. Spectrum is used by national programs and UNAIDS to prepare annual estimates of the status of the HIV epidemic in those countries. The model and assumptions are updated regularly by researchers at UNAIDS, who pull together demographic data and other measures of the impact of HIV, including migration, and estimate adult and childhood prevalence. Prevalence is transferred to the model to estimate the consequences of the HIV/AIDS epidemic, including the number of people living with HIV by age and sex, new infections, AIDS deaths, AIDS orphans, treatment needs, and the impact of treatment on survival (Stover et al., 2021). The model was particularly helpful for this study because it accounts for non-AIDS mortality, migration, and HIV infection as the population ages. The Zimbabwe data are drawn from the UNAIDS-funded Zimbabwe Population-Based HIV Impact Assessment cross-sectional surveys (Gonese et al., 2020).

I used the model's default assumptions because I was most interested in the effects of AIDS over time. I used its data on those in the electorate living with HIV, those receiving ART, those not receiving ART despite needing it, and HIV-related deaths from 1990 to 2022. The electorate includes people aged eighteen and over who would be eligible to vote in Zimbabwe. For each year, I calculated the number who died (exited) from HIV as well as the number who were in need of ART and thus incapacitated by the disease. The HIV pandemic also took away an unknown number of people from the electorate who had to leave their jobs and other activities to take care of their sick family members. This expectation is supported by data from interviews with caregivers and studies by other scholars on caregiver experiences in high-prevalence countries. These studies found that caregiving responsibilities had a paralyzing effect on caregivers' social and economic lives (Amoateng et al., 2015; Chitura & Chitura, 2014; Hlabyago & Ogunbanjo, 2009; Ogunmefun et al., 2011). While some among the very sick group may not have fully exited from politics, the spectrum model is unable to capture the people who have exited because of their caregiver responsibilities. The latter group is probably larger than the former, so my figures are likely to underestimate the number who exited to the benefit of ZANU-PF.

The prevalence of HIV among Zimbabweans of voting age, those aged; 18 and above, rose sharply from 1990 to 2013. Figure 3.1 divides Zimbabweans into effective and alternative electorates. There are four groups of potential voters. Group A comprises those who are not affected by HIV. Group B is made up of those who are living with HIV but are not incapacitated because they are receiving ART. Group B only grew after 2004, when Zimbabwe received its first doses of HIV treatment. Groups

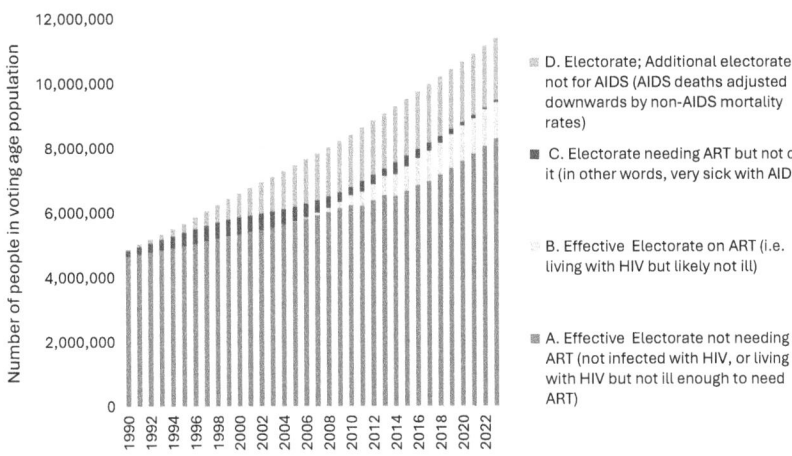

FIGURE 3.1 Impact of HIV/AIDS on the effective electorate.
Source: Data from UNAIDS Spectrum model.

A and B comprise the effective electorate – those Zimbabweans who were alive and healthy enough to participate in elections. Group C consists of those who are very ill and dying from the virus. Group D includes those who have died due to complications related to HIV. These two groups are the most important for understanding the political implications of HIV on national politics. The population in the electorate critically ill from HIV rose from 163,195 in 1990 to 504,766 in 1999. The exited electorate of Groups C and D, when added to the effective electorate, comprise the alternative electorate – those Zimbabweans who would have been alive and able to participate in elections if not for HIV/AIDS.

Access to care was not widespread until much later, and, as I will show in subsequent sections, anti-HIV programs were halted and negatively impacted by government policies, especially Operation Murambatsvina, which targeted and destroyed HIV care access points in peri-urban areas. From 1999 to 2004, nearly all HIV patients died. The actual deaths and numbers of those who had the illness are likely underestimated because, in the early years, it was difficult to get an accurate measure of how many people were suffering from HIV.

As shown in Figure 3.2, starting in 2006, more people began living healthier lives with HIV. Access to ART had increased, and much of the damage done to healthcare access points by Operation Murambatsvina was being addressed. Getting an HIV diagnosis was no longer the death sentence it had been just a decade earlier. The decades from when HIV was first discovered to 2013, when there was a decline, are what matter

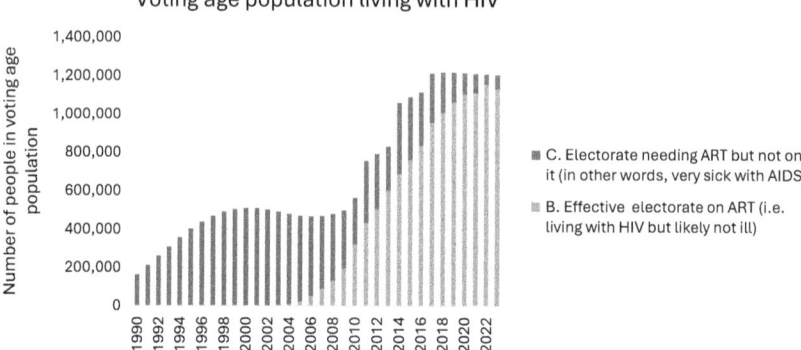

FIGURE 3.2 Impact of HIV and the population of voters.
Source: Data from UNAIDS Spectrum model.

the most for understanding how ZANU-PF manipulated and benefited from a healthcare crisis.

The opposition would lose out on crucial votes because of the HIV crisis. The formation of the MDC coincided with the exit via migration and the death of many of its potential supporters. The reasons that propelled the formation of the MDC were the failing economy, a growing middle class, frustration with corruption, failed policies, and increased exit. The failing economy worsened the HIV crisis, and the HIV crisis deepened the crisis. In the next chapter, I will discuss the impact of migration.

Before 1990, less than 1 percent of the electorate was living with or dying from HIV. By 1999, when MDC was formed, presenting the largest and most formidable opposition to ZANU-PF, a cumulative 8 percent of the population had died from HIV (see Figure 3.3). In 2002, the first election in which the MDC ran a candidate for president, 14 percent had died from HIV, and the other 10 percent were critically ill from HIV with no chance of getting medication or surviving. Almost 25 percent of the population had exited either because of death or critical illness. By the elections of 2008, the cumulative HIV death rate was 24 percent, and more than a quarter of a million people were critically ill. Thus, close to 28 percent of the voters had exited either because of death or critical illness. The prime years of the opposition movement, when citizen activity was likely to have the most impact on ousting the ruling party, was also when the time when almost everyone in the electorate who was living with HIV was very sick.

The question I address in this chapter is: How would Zimbabwean politics have changed if so much of the electorate had not exited through

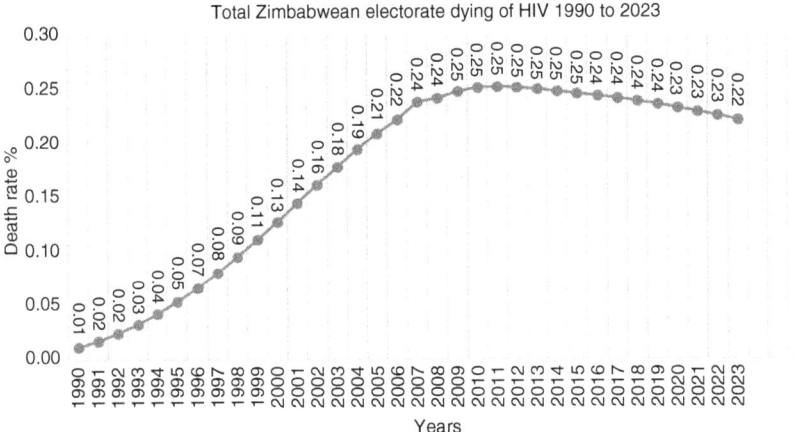

FIGURE 3.3 Cumulative HIV deaths. *Source*: Data from UNAIDS Spectrum model.

death or illness? While Zimbabweans had a fairly equal chance of being impacted by HIV, rates of infection were higher in urban areas where nonregular partnerships and sex work were more prominent (Lopman & Gregson, 2008). To discern the impact, I broke down the national numbers into provincial effects and then estimated the effect on the national vote if HIV/AIDS were assumed to have had a proportionate effect within each province.

To do this, I first calculate the additional people who would have been part of the electorate – Groups C and D, those who are alive but incapacitated by HIV/AIDS, and those who have died from it. I multiply this alternative electorate by the turnout in the election to calculate the number of additional voters. Note that this method omits those who did not vote because of their caretaking responsibilities; in the absence of HIV/AIDS, turnout would have been higher among both the actual electorate and the alternative electorate. I then assume that the distribution of votes within each province or electoral district would have remained the same. In formal terms, the calculation is:

$$\text{Additional votes for Party X} = (\text{sick} + \text{dead}) * \text{turnout} \\ * (\text{Party X's vote share}).$$

To illustrate this in round numbers, say that by a particular election, 90,000 citizens in a province had died of HIV/AIDS who otherwise would not have, and another 10,000 citizens were alive but in need of ART. This would add 100,000 to the alternative electorate. Suppose turnout in the actual electorate was 80 percent. In that case, I assume an additional 80,000 Zimbabweans would have voted in that election in that province. If the actual election results were 60 percent opposition and 40 percent regime in that province, that translates to an additional 48,000 votes for the opposition and 32,000 votes for the regime – a net margin of 16,000 for the opposition. By repeating this across provinces (I do not have data by electoral district), I calculate each election's net gain (or loss) for the opposition. If this had happened, perhaps the regime would still have stolen the election through violence or fraud, but the exit premium allowed ZANU-PF to survive without being more ruthless.

The reason ZANU-PF reaped a grim premium from HIV is that the pandemic tended to take a greater toll in provinces where there were more opposition supporters. As shown in Figure 3.4, HIV/AIDS death rates were consistently highest in Harare (by far), where the opposition received 68 percent of the vote in 2005, in Mashonaland Central (17 percent for the opposition), Matebeleland North (62 percent), and Bulawayo (79 percent). In the rest of this section, I use the differential vote shares and voter exits to demonstrate how the opposition party

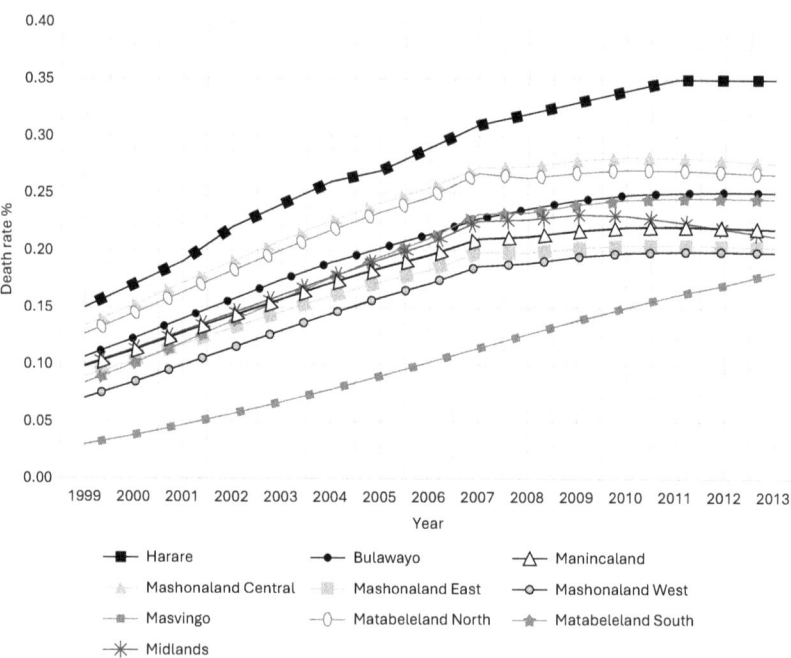

FIGURE 3.4 HIV death rates by province, 1999–2013. *Source*: Data from UNAIDS Spectrum model.

would have performed in the elections. I refer to official numbers released by the Zimbabwe Electoral Commission (ZEC) and the Zimbabwe Election Support Network (ZESN) for accurate election results and voter registration figures. ZESN is known for maintaining more reliable records of election data than other election agencies or the government. To ensure consistency in my analysis, I rely on ZESN reports, except for 2005, when the ZESN report was incomplete and the available numbers are inconsistent. Unless otherwise noted, I also use Spectrum data instead of data from government records.

HIV/AIDS had already begun to affect Zimbabwe by the 1996 elections, the last conducted before the emergence of an effective national opposition. At that time, 5,062,748 people were eligible to vote. But the effective electorate was much smaller: 438,279 people (8.7 percent) of them were too sick with AIDS to be able to vote. Another 365,579 had already died of AIDS. With HIV, the effective Zimbabwean electorate in 1996 was 4,624,469; in the absence of HIV, the Zimbabwean electorate would have been 5,428,327 (17 percent larger). Without competitive opposition, this did not make a difference in the election outcome.

As summarized in Table 3.1, HIV affected the voter population from 2000–2013. In 2000, the newly formed MDC participated in its first set of elections, the parliamentary election. Before 2008, when the government introduced harmonized elections, the parliamentary and presidential elections were held in separate years. In 2000, the total number of registered voters was 5,288,804. The total voting-eligible population was 5,861,408, but an additional 1,255,621 potential voters were excluded from elections because they were either too sick to vote or had died.[3] To calculate the exit premium received by ZANU-PF in these elections, I distributed the potential votes of exited voters proportionally to the votes received by ZANU-PF and the opposition in each province.

In the 2000 parliamentary election, across all nine provinces, ZANU-PF received 2,397,177 votes against the opposition's 2,953,976 (see Table 3.2). In the previous election, ZANU-PF had won all 118 elected seats. In 2000, the new opposition won fifty-seven seats to ZANU-PF's sixty-two. The opposition received five fewer seats, but had more votes because of higher turnout in provinces with more urban districts. ZANU-PF received over 50 percent of the vote in predominantly rural Mashonaland Central (78.6 percent), Mashonaland East (72.6),

---

[3] Other voters excluded because Zimbabwe voter's roll has many missing voters, especially young urbanites.

TABLE 3.1 *Summary of impact*

Election year	Registered voters	Votes cast	Living voters	Healthy electorate	Exited electorate	Additional voters	Net opposition gain
2000*	5,288,804	2,556,261	5,861,408	5,351,154	1,255,621	582,079	49,493 (2%)
2002**	5,607,795	3,032,577	5,980,845	5,480,571	1,323,880	689,135	34,261 (1%)
2005*	5,658,624	2,520,850	5,724,627	6,502,947	1,720,488	740,236	-117,605 (-2%)
2008***	5,611,304	2,572,245	6,024,000	6,502,947	1,916,692	788,541	116,300 (3%)
2013***	5,695,706	3,378,320	7,364,202	6,533,443	1,933,866	2,061,989	-223,877 (-5%)

Note: Data from UN Spectrum, ZEC, ZESN; *Only parliamentary election; **Only presidential election, ***Harmonized election, Healthy electorate = Not sick or healthy enough to vote because on ART, per Spectrum; Exited electorate = Dead or too sick to vote (not on ART), per Spectrum; Additional voters = Alternative electorate multiplied by turnout.

TABLE 3.2 *2000 elections*

Province	Votes cast	Healthy electorate	Exited electorate	Additional voters	ZANU gain	Opposition gain	Exit premium
Midlands	350,505	588,677	174,022	193,612	40,949	31,018	(9,931)
Matebeleland South	159,579	247,926	88,435	102,975	12,736	22,350	9,614
Matebeleland North	147,828	242,281	98,382	110,899	8,342	31,381	23,039
Masvingo	286,741	498,134	134,296	146,233	30,642	21,382	(9,260)
Mashonaland West	246,783	578,596	164,327	184,581	23,221	20,758	(2,463)
Mashonaland East	278,221	538,731	159,938	178,523	38,713	14,611	(24,103)
Mashonaland Central	247,953	413,540	164,696	183,155	53,511	14,569	(38,942)
Manicaland	272,909	601,686	186,256	212,002	26,248	30,444	4,195
Harare	394,073	1,280,166	554,442	629,619	26,910	95,966	69,056
Bulawayo	171,669	361,416	112,212	120,388	5,021	33,308	28,287
Total	2,556,261	5,351,154	1,837,006	2,061,989	582,079	266,293	49,493

Note: Data from UN Spectrum, ZEC, ZESN; Only parliamentary election. Healthy electorate = Not sick or healthy enough to vote because on ART, per Spectrum; Exited electorate = Dead or too sick to vote (not on ART), per Spectrum; Additional voters = Alternative electorate multiplied by turnout.

Mashonaland West (63.7 percent), and Masvingo (58.9 percent) but had low vote percentages in urban and other marginalized provinces like Harare (21 percent), Manicaland (46 percent), Bulawayo (13 percent), and Matebeleland North and South (21 percent, 36.3 percent).

If all eligible voters had been able to cast their votes, both parties would have received more votes, but the opposition would have received 49,493 more additional votes than ZANU-PF. The highest gains would have been in Harare (69,056) and Bulawayo (28,287). This could have led to significant gains in urban and marginalized communities, resulting in the opposition winning more seats. However, it is hard to say for sure, as my data does not allow me to analyze voting patterns at the precinct level. Provinces with large urban populations, such as Midlands, Mashonaland East, Mashonaland West, and Manicaland, would have been most affected by the additional votes. Manicaland has historically been a challenging region for ZANU-PF, as it was home to some of Mugabe's earliest opponents. The opposition may have also done better in Matebeleland South. Although I cannot provide exact numbers without precinct-level data, the additional votes would have changed perceptions of the election and made it harder to rig the results.

In 2002, Zimbabwe headed for its first presidential election in which Mugabe faced a viable opponent. In that election, Mugabe received 56 percent of the vote to Tsvangirai's 47 percent. In 2002, the total living electorate was 5,980,845, but the effective electorate, those alive and well enough to vote, was only 5,480,571. The missing electorate, those unable to vote because they were very sick from HIV or had died, was 1,323,880. Assuming the turnout for the missing electorate would have been proportional to that of the effective electorate, then there would have been 693,297 additional voters. If the additional voters had been able to participate, Mugabe would have received 329,518 more votes and the opposition 340,649, as shown in Table 3.3. The net gain for the opposition would have been 34,261, giving them an additional 1 percent. Using these conservative estimates, HIV illness and death alone would not have changed the election outcomes in 2002, as MDC would have received only 42 percent, but voters missing from HIV fatigue would have also likely increased turnout in pro-opposition areas. While Harare had the largest electorate, its voter turnout was the lowest, likely due to many factors that forced voter exit.

The next election was the 2005 parliamentary election. In 2005, the total eligible electorate had increased to 6,194,847. The effective electorate of those with a reasonable chance of voting was 5,750,161, as

TABLE 3.3 *2002 presidential elections*

Province	Votes cast	Healthy electorate	Exited electorate	Additional voters	ZANU gain	Opposition gain	Exit premium
Midlands	418,024	45,183	71,686	69,724	42,532	27,192	(15,339)
Matebeleland South	162,179	26,853	27,658	25,700	11,308	14,392	3,084
Matebeleland North	175,935	26,661	38,443	33,869	11,515	22,354	10,838
Masvingo	372,095	36,608	53,769	51,332	28,233	23,100	(5,133)
Mashonaland West	322,641	50,378	52,732	58,091	40,664	17,427	(23,237)
Mashonaland East	349,565	43,951	59,302	61,261	45,946	15,315	(30,630)
Mashonaland Central	300,613	43,950	69,594	71,100	58,302	12,798	(45,504)
Manicaland	355,954	51,632	73,358	67,544	32,421	35,123	2,702
Harare	412,935	139,567	314,630	212,604	51,025	161,579	110,554
Bulawayo	162,616	31,490	62,434	42,072	7,573	34,499	26,926
Total	3,032,557	500,273	823,607	693,297	329,518	363,779	34,261

Note. Data from UN Spectrum, ZEC, ZESN: Healthy electorate = Not sick or healthy enough to vote because on ART, per Spectrum; Exited electorate = Dead or too sick to vote (not on ART), per Spectrum; Additional voters = Alternative electorate multiplied by turnout.

1,720,488 were unable to vote because they were too sick from complications related to HIV or had died. If not for AIDS, the total eligible population would have been 7,470,649.

In 2005's parliamentary elections, ZANU-PF experienced another decline in the number of seats they had in parliament. Their biggest losses were in provinces with large urban populations, Harare and Bulawayo, and in regions that historically preferred non-ZANU-PF candidates. Voter turnout increased at a time when the prevalence rate of HIV and associated death rates was also peaking.

As shown in Table 3.4, in 2005, across all nine provinces, ZANU-PF received 1,569,867 votes and seventy-eight seats and the opposition 1,041,292 votes and forty-one seats. The period leading up to this election had been extremely violent, contributing to the decline in opposition votes. The impact of violence on turnout has been extensively studied (J. Alexander & McGregor, 2013; Blair, 2002; LeBas, 2006; L. E. Young, 2019). Daxecker and Rauschenbach (2023) argued that in the Zimbabwean case, the regime used violence in opposition strongholds to suppress turnout and threats of violence in their own strongholds to encourage turnout. In addition to violence, land reform, and voter intimidation, HIV/AIDS was also wrecking voter turnout. By 2005, half a million voting-age people were critically ill from HIV; two million had died. The impact of HIV was the biggest in Harare. Nearly half of all the critically ill (115,009) and dead (402,771) were from Harare.

The HIV pandemic further disrupted democracy. After the 2005 elections, seven members of parliament, six from ZANU-PF and one from MDC, would die during their terms in office. Their deaths were attributed to long or short illnesses, which were used then as the stand-in for HIV diagnosis. In this set of by-elections, the opposition was able to retain their seats, but they would not have the same luck in subsequent by-elections, almost all of which were due to the premature deaths of members of parliament.

In 2008, Zimbabwe held its first harmonized elections, combining the vote for president and legislature. I begin with an analysis of the presidential vote. The 2008 election was also very contentious. The government refused to release the election results for over thirty days. The results showed a win for the opposition, but the officials claimed the opposition had failed to win with the required 50 percent + 1 to fend off a runoff. My analysis is based on the first round of elections, which, while contentious and violent, gave the opposition the best chance to win.

As shown in Table 3.5, across all nine provinces, ZANU-PF received 1,079,730 votes, and Tsvangirai's opposition faction received 1,195,562.

TABLE 3.4 *2005 parliamentary elections*

Province	Votes cast	Healthy electorate	Exited electorate	Additional voters	ZANU gain	Opposition gain	Exit premium
Midlands	311,003	608,454	125,495	167,545	54,589	31,049	(23,539)
Matebeleland South	107,667	263,924	56,792	84,702	17,304	17,250	(54)
Matebeleland North	144,444	265,880	68,056	92,884	19,312	31,149	11,837
Masvingo	319,178	555,704	95,413	130,478	50,691	24,251	(26,441)
Mashonaland West	286,576	628,391	107,872	156,964	51,560	20,023	(31,537)
Mashonaland East	285,844	587,653	109,101	150,119	55,942	17,078	(38,864)
Mashonaland Central	272,217	448,567	117,404	154,003	78,576	14,882	(63,694)
Manicaland	338,813	654,716	129,888	176,918	51,403	40,152	(11,251)
Harare	347,043	1,338,761	401,166	516,175	43,055	90,752	47,697
Bulawayo	108,065	372,576	81,548	107,634	6,489	24,730	18,242
Total	2,520,850	5,724,627	1,292,735	1,737,421	428,920	311,316	(117,605)

Note. Data from UN Spectrum, ZEC, ZESN. Healthy electorate = Not sick or healthy enough to vote because on ART, per Spectrum; Exited electorate = Dead or too sick to vote (not on ART), per Spectrum; Additional voters = Alternative electorate multiplied by turnout.

TABLE 3.5 *2008 presidential election results in harmonized election*

Province	Votes cast	Healthy electorate	Exited electorate	Additional voters	ZANU gain	Opposition gain	Exit premium
Midlands	341,787	617,914	150,804	99,989	48,795	51,194	2,400
Matebeleland South	119,183	280,012	72,575	39,942	15,458	24,485	9,027
Matebeleland North	151,112	287,065	83,230	53,935	15,264	38,671	23,408
Masvingo	316,245	596,258	115,661	75,266	37,257	38,009	753
Mashonaland West	255,161	671,097	136,903	66,386	35,052	31,334	(3,718)
Mashonaland East	292,734	631,294	134,736	78,105	42,958	35,147	(7,811)
Mashonaland Central	316,245	479,115	141,450	111,622	72,889	38,733	(34,156)
Manicaland	369,098	697,057	158,746	103,337	39,681	63,656	23,974
Harare	313,995	1,381,670	477,832	129,652	25,282	104,370	79,088
Bulawayo	96,685	382,518	98,062	30,306	3,485	26,821	23,336
Total	2,572,245	6,024,000	1,570,000	788,541	336,120	452,421	116,300

Note. Data from UN Spectrum, ZEC, ZESN; Healthy electorate = Not sick or healthy enough to vote because on ART, per Spectrum; Exited electorate = Dead or too sick to vote (not on ART), per Spectrum; Additional voters = Alternative electorate multiplied by turnout.

Although the election was very violent and the opposition was reeling from divisions, the turnout rate was higher than in other elections. That said, the turnout rate was still low: only 2,497,265 voted. By 2008, over half a million voting-age people were critically ill from HIV, and over 1.5 million had died. Assuming proportional numbers of the exited electorate would have participated and cast their votes by province in the same way the actual voters did, the opposition as a whole would have received an additional 491,050 votes and Tsvangirai's vote share would have been 451,766[4] more votes against Mugabe's 294,793. Tsvangirai would have garnered an additional 3 percent votes, giving him 52 percent, enough to avoid a runoff. In the next chapter, I will show that the exit premium from HIV and migrant votes would have earned them an additional 493,840 votes (13 percent), putting him well over the 50 percent + 1 mark, notwithstanding votes lost to violence and other forms of electoral fraud in the 2008 election.

The parliamentary election results are not very different from the presidential, as shown in Table 3.6. ZANU-PF and MDC received more votes because only one of the other six third-party candidates won any seats. In 2008, ZANU-PF lost thirty-four seats between the House and Senate. Meanwhile, MDC gained an additional twenty-four seats in the Senate and seventy-eight in the House. A smaller MDC faction won ten seats from the main MDC faction. Without HIV exit, the larger Tsvangirai faction would have gained 471,103 votes to ZANU-PF's 314,740. Adding the exit premium from migration would have put the opposition past the 50 percent + 1 mark. Zimbabwe would have avoided the bloodiest runoff in the country's modern history, one that resulted in hundreds of deaths. The political turmoil from the 2008 elections also worsened the economic and health crisis, resulting in a cholera pandemic that caused many deaths in urban areas.

Following the disputed 2008 election, Zimbabwe entered a negotiated government with Mugabe as president and Tsvangirai as prime minister. This government of national unity stabilized an economy that was in free fall, and the country started to experience a steady decline in HIV-related deaths. Therefore, I would not expect much of an exit premium for that election. As shown in Table 3.7, there was no HIV exit premium for the 2013 election. By then, ART was once more readily available, resulting in better outcomes for those living with HIV.

---

[4] This is assuming that opposition vote distributed the same way among the third-party candidates Simba Makoni and Aurthur Mutambara.

TABLE 3.6 *2008 parliamentary election results in harmonized election*

Province	Votes cast	Healthy electorate	Exited electorate	Additional voters	ZANU gain	Opposition gain	Exit premium
Midlands	323,704	617,914	150,804	94,699	43,882	50,817	6,935
Matebeleland South	109,629	280,012	72,575	36,740	15,324	21,416	6,093
Matebeleland North	148,902	287,065	83,230	53,146	15,844	37,302	21,459
Masvingo	314,752	596,258	115,661	74,911	40,422	34,489	(5,934)
Mashonaland West	245,512	671,097	136,903	63,875	36,030	27,845	(8,185)
Mashonaland East	288,791	631,294	134,736	77,053	44,492	32,561	(11,93)
Mashonaland Central	228,581	479,115	141,450	80,680	52,412	28,268	(24,145)
Manicaland	348,953	697,057	158,746	97,697	41,304	56,393	15,088
Harare	311,386	1,381,670	477,832	128,575	30,071	98,504	68,434
Bulawayo	84,917	382,518	98,062	26,617	3,572	23,045	19,473
Total	7,549,617	6,024,000	1,570,000	733,994	323,354	410,640	87,286

Note. Data from UN Spectrum, ZEC, ZESN; Healthy electorate = Not sick or healthy enough to vote because on ART, per Spectrum; Exited electorate = Dead or too sick to vote (not on ART), per Spectrum; Additional voters = Alternative electorate multiplied by turnout.

TABLE 3.7 *2013 elections**

Province	Votes cast	Healthy electorate	Exited electorate	Additional voters	ZANU gain	Opposition gain	Exit premium
Midlands	420,924	725,770	174,022	112,289	73,420	38,869	(34,551)
Matebeleland South	156,129	300,551	88,435	53,493	27,952	25,541	(2,410)
Matebeleland North	195,273	313,089	98,382	69,168	29,084	40,084	10,999
Masvingo	406,352	646,471	134,296	91,918	67,730	24,188	(43,542)
Mashonaland West	388,851	734,734	164,327	97,688	70,434	27,254	(43,180)
Mashonaland East	419,308	699,301	159,938	107,044	80,739	26,306	(54,433)
Mashonaland Central	380,880	532,170	164,696	131,086	115,604	15,482	(100,122)
Manicaland	455,795	762,041	186,256	126,803	71,068	55,735	(15,333)
Harare	423,854	1,426,859	554,442	187,031	74,506	112,525	38,020
Bulawayo	130,954	392,457	112,212	40,171	9,748	30,423	20,675
Total	3,378,320	6,533,443	1,837,006	1,016,692	620,284	396,407	(223,877)

Note. Data from UN Spectrum, ZEC, ZESN; *Harmonized election, Healthy electorate = Not sick or healthy enough to vote because on ART, per Spectrum; Exited electorate = Dead or too sick to vote (not on ART), per Spectrum; Additional voters = Alternative electorate multiplied by turnout.

HIV AND FORCED EXIT: DEATH, CAREGIVING, AND GENERATIONAL LOSS

In the previous section, I presented quantitative data that provide only a partial view of the impact of HIV/AIDS on the survival of the Mugabe regime. In this section, I supplement the numbers with stories that reveal more about the issue. First, the deaths of musicians and activists due to HIV made it much easier for ZANU-PF to censor their voices. If these individuals had been alive, it would have been much harder for the regime to silence their messages. Due to the absence of a strong community of musicians, the government was able to bribe some artists and force others out of the country. Additionally, although HIV did not differentiate between ZANU-PF and opposition MPs, when opposition-affiliated MP deaths resulted in runoffs, ZANU-PF gained more seats in parliament. Long-serving regimes with access to state funds find it much easier to manipulate smaller elections. Between the 2000 and 2005 parliamentary elections, ZANU-PF won eight seats in by-elections that arose from the deaths of MPs.

Additionally, citizens started to disengage from politics as they became burdened with caregiving responsibilities. The cost of voting in countries such as Zimbabwe is already high, and the HIV crisis only increased the cost. Finally, the HIV pandemic had far-reaching consequences that affected different aspects of Zimbabwean society. One of the consequences was that a whole generation of younger voters lost their parents and guardians to the crisis. These young people did not have the opportunity to witness political engagement from their elders. The pandemic caused more children to fall into poverty and limited their access to education, further compounding the issue. These effects of the pandemic ultimately strengthened ZANU-PF's position at a time when conditions were favorable for the party's ouster.

Exit of Music Activists

In Zimbabwe, as in most countries, music and the arts are an integral part of life. During my travels for this book, I often found my interviewees humming along to the latest track in Zimbabwe even as they sat thousands of miles away from home in conditions far different from the family members they left behind. Music carried Black Zimbabweans through the liberation struggle. Famed musician Thomas Mapfumo told me in 2018, "We were at the frontlines of the battle. We were fighting just as hard as those holding the guns, and sometimes our friends held the gun while singing." The struggle for independence would not have been won without musicians who kept the spirits of the fighters alive. Their lyrics motivated young men and women to leave their homes and join the battle. Music was the only weapon the colonial regime could not ban or control. Black people were allowed to have their radio stations and concerts. It was through music that people at home learned about activities at the front line and the status of war. They learned about the deaths and losses. Musicians were the teachers of war. They were the historians reminding people what life was like before colonialism. They were the narrators of contemporary hardships and the prophets of a better and brighter future. Wartime music provided communities with details on signing up for war and told parents how they could send their children to war and other ways they could help the fighters. The voices of musicians kept the struggle and hope alive. Their voices were also an active tool against an oppressive regime. The Rhodesian government would harass musicians and arrest them. They accused them of treason against the state and argued their lyrics were encouraging violence.

At independence, Mugabe's government brought in Bob Marley, the most famous musician in the world at the time. Marley's hit "Zimbabwe," written for the occasion, not only became the unofficial anthem but stayed at the top of music charts in many countries across the continent for a very long time. At the end of his set, Marley stood quietly crying as the cluttered green and white Rhodesian flag came down and was replaced by the colorful red, yellow, green, black, and white banner of Zimbabwe's freedom. Mapfumo closed the show with an inspiring track of revolutionary music.

Through music and drama, the new government shaped the rhetoric of the type of country they wanted to have. Music was used as a tool for educating the young nation, what Singhal et al. (2003) called education–entertainment, defined as "The process of purposely designing and implementing a media message to both entertain and educate, in order to increase knowledge about an issue, create favorable attitudes and change overt behavior" (p. 9). Early 1980s music prophesied that the future would be bright and resources abundant. The same tool used to build hope was politicized in the Southern region during the genocide. Those who failed to sing Shona voluntary songs were marked as sellouts and killed. When government officials were accused of corruption in 1989, Mapfumo's music cautioning them to stay true to the liberation promises hit the airwaves, igniting discussion across the country about corruption and calling on citizens to hold politicians accountable. Artists have the power to shape the politics and ideologies of an entire nation.

It was no surprise that the earliest education about the HIV/AIDS crisis came via music. In 1986, legendary musician Oliver Mtukudzi released the cautionary song "Stick to One Woman," warning people about the dangers of promiscuity. Mtukudzi would spend much of his career singing about HIV and other social ills. Mtukudzi was personally impacted by the death of almost half of his band from HIV.

Worldwide, artists, especially musicians, were the first public faces of AIDS. The shocking deaths of high-profile individuals like Freddie Mercury at age forty-five in 1991, Eric Lynn Wright (Eazy-E) at age thirty in 1995, and Fela Kuti at age fifty-nine in 1997 forever changed the music world. The HIV pandemic silenced the voices of critical social activists whose work did more than most in shaping views on inclusion and the importance of democracy. Bhundu Boys was one of the first Black Zimbabwean bands to perform in Europe, and that it did so with Madonna was an incredible achievement. Bhundu Boys is also credited with popularizing African music in Europe. The death of Bhundu Boys' lead guitarist Mankaba in 1991 was the first time AIDS was listed as the official cause of death of a prominent person and would remain unique for a very long time (M. Meldrum, 1991). Mankaba was diagnosed during their European tour and asked that his status be made public after his death to help spread awareness of the HIV crisis. Three more members of their band would die and eventually the band collapsed. Those who remained have been recluses, living in poverty and hiding away from the limelight. Bhundu Boys had its origins in *chimurenga* music. The name Bhundu Boys, which translates to bush boys, was a nod to the young men who aided liberation struggle fighters in the bush. Lead singer Biggie Tembo had been one of the bush boys. At the top of their career, they were called the African Beatles. Their *jiti* music influenced new generations of musicians, not just Zimbabweans but also other Africans who sought to become global influencers. Rise Kagona, the founder, former band leader, and only surviving member of Bhundu Boys, described their genre of *jiti* saying, "sometimes we play rhumba and sometimes we play whatever, we actually gave it one name, and we thought of putting 'jiti' because to us it's like [saying] 'pop music' – 'African pop'" (Kagona, cited in Brusila, 2002, p. 42).

The deaths of artists impact communities that are tight-knit and highly influential. As talk of AIDS became more common, Zimbabwean artists answered the call to educate the nation. They sang warnings that taught about an illness that could not be treated: *chirwere chisingarapike*. In a 2022 interview, one of the artists who had been involved in the production of "*Nechirwere*," a famous collaboration on HIV, said, "Even as they were working, I was not big enough to be on the song, but I was helping, there was a sense of fear that they were singing about their own deaths. It was surreal."

Indeed, within a few years of the song's release, many of the lead contributors on the album were dead or dying. They more than anyone else knew how dangerous this disease was. There was a lot of shame too. In Zimbabwe and much of Africa, it would take a long time before individuals with HIV were not shunned and ostracized for being sexually promiscuous. The HIV music of the 1990s was highly moralized, so it would have been very difficult for the artists to publicly advocate for themselves and their community without appearing to admit they had participated in shameful acts.

The loss of thousands of artists dramatically changed Zimbabwe, but more importantly, it changed the role of activist music. Much of the music in the 1990s emerged out of the liberation struggle. As holders of the national memory, they knew the true narrative of independence and could challenge ZANU-PF's attempts to reshape national memory. Music continues to be an important tool for ZANU-PF propaganda. One of the reasons this works for them is that there are not enough musicians with liberation struggle credentials to challenge their narrative. Mapfumo, who remained an important critic of regimes with hit songs like "*Nyika Yaita Mamvemve*/You Have Torn the Nation to Pieces," was forced into exile in the early 2000s. When I asked him why he did not stay, he said:

> It got harder to stay when I was now the only voice singing critical things. Oliver [Mtukudzi] was too polite and singing HIV jingles, so the regime rarely went after him. But most of our bandmates were gone. My friends from the liberation struggle were gone. The long illness had taken them, and if I had stayed ZANU-PF would have taken me.

The devastating impact of HIV on the previously politically active artist community created an opportunity for the increasingly paranoid ZANU-PF to censor musicians. ZANU-PF took more and more control of broadcasting, using state media as their mouthpiece more openly. Just like the Rhodesian government had done decades earlier, ZANU-PF sidelined musicians who spoke against the regime and instead elevated hand-picked, younger artists. In 2001, Minister of Information and Publicity Jonathan Moyo announced a series of repressive laws under the

Broadcasting Services Act. There was no constitutional basis for the act other than to infringe on the rights of citizens and silence vocal artists, replacing them with artists who only sang praises of the government. Moyo directed financial resources to musicians he favored, including his own band.

Artists rely on conducive environments to produce their work, and financial support and broadcasting access are also important. Without this, their voices are silenced. In the mid-2000s, it became common to hear that songs critical of the government had been banned from the radio; in more extreme cases, the artists were arrested. Although the government never formally banned any songs, denying access to airwaves was a powerful way to silence them. Jestina Mukoko, a former state media journalist, told me the state would give instructions on what they could do or say on national TV, including which songs were appropriate to play. After Mapfumo's music was effectively banned on radio and television, he was forced into exile. In a 2020 interview, Mapfumo, when asked about his relationship with the state, said:

> It is true ... They don't play my music on the radio there. Yet during what they called the Liberation Struggle, my music played a very big role. I supported them while they were still in the bush. And when they came back [into power], I thought, we are a great government, and we have a great president. I thought things were going to be rosy. Then after eight years, I noticed that there was a lot of corruption and that made me write that song. (Khan, 2021)

There were certainly some musicians from the older generation who continued to sing government praises, but their voices were lesser, and it was clear that their declining circumstances forced them to align more closely with the ruling party. More successful artists like Mtukudzi became more subtle, avoided criticizing the government, and sang about social issues without ever openly naming the cause of these social ills. In 2000, Mtukudzi's sound engineer spent four nights in jail after the government alleged he was shining a spotlight on Mugabe's portrait while the band played the hit "*Wasakara*/You Are Now Old." Since 2000, Zimbabwean artists have become very afraid to associate themselves with politics, and yet politics is life. Music is life and therefore it is inherently political. When they do sing about politics, all their jingles profess praise for the ruling party. The sounds are inauthentic.

The losses from deaths in the arts communities have also negatively impacted knowledge transfer and mentorship. Communities need elders: humans rely on knowledge and skill transfer from one generation to the next. Had the artists who died from HIV lived long lives, their art and voices would have matured and the global library would be richer. The younger generation of musicians may have been more vocal about politics if they had had examples to draw from. If contemporary musicians could engage with their ideals, they would not only copy their style as many have done with *jiti*, but they would have a rich resource to draw from on how to use their music to effect social change.

Opposition Leaders Were Dying

The loss of its leadership also weakened opposition politics. In this subsection, I examine ways in which the HIV pandemic negatively impacted representation. HIV disproportionately impacted the opposition MDC because most of its leadership was a lot younger and more urban.[5] Nelson Chamisa, who took over leading the opposition after Tsvangirai's death in 2018, recalled the early 2000s as an era with a "bit of death and hope" for the opposition. When I interviewed Chamisa about the impact of HIV on the opposition, he said he was just eighteen when the opposition was founded, too young to lead, but he realized his rise in the party was made possible because many in the leadership either left to go abroad or they died. Attending funerals became a major part of political campaigning, and it remains so. Zimbabwean political actors and their counterparts in South Africa realized the utility of campaigning at funerals, where people were already gathered to mourn.

This profile of opposition leaders and activists who were dying mirrored the profile of those decimated by the HIV pandemic in the general public. A six-country study by Chirambo (2004) found that in high-prevalence countries such as Malawi, Tanzania, Zambia, and Zimbabwe, there was a higher rate of attrition among members of parliament at the peak of the HIV pandemic. A striking finding from this research is that between 1985 and 2006, 60 percent of the by-elections that took place to replace MPs occurred following the death of an MP (Chirambo, 2004). Prior to this, there were hardly any by-elections. In Zimbabwe, the opposition MDC reduced ZANU-PF's parliamentary supermajorities in their first election during the 2000 parliamentary elections. In previous elections, ZANU-PF had won almost all the parliamentary seats. In 2005, they only won sixty-two to MDC's fifty-seven (out of 120 seats). Following that historic win, there were twenty by-

---

[5] During the coronavirus pandemic, the virus had a disproportionate impact on ZANU-PF politicians, who tend to be older and have multiple comorbidities.

elections between 2002 and 2005. Nineteen of those were caused by undisclosed illnesses only identified as short- or long-term illnesses. A critical by-election in 2003 was held to replace the seat of opposition founding member Learnmore Jongwe. Jongwe died in jail after he was arrested on suspicion of murdering his wife, whom he accused of adultery and infecting him with HIV.

Both MDC and ZANU-PF lost party members due to deaths; in fact, ZANU-PF lost 18 percent of its legislators and MDC only lost 11 percent. As HIV deaths continued to skyrocket, Mugabe announced six of his cabinet members had died of HIV and urged all his ministers to get tested (Voice of America Zimbabwe, 2012). However, the impact of those electoral losses was greatest on the opposition. ZANU-PF retained all eleven seats that became open after an MP's death. In all seven cases when a member death created a vacancy for an MDC seat, the party lost the seat to ZANU-PF in the by-elections. Although Jongwe died in jail, HIV led to his death in the sense that he was upset his wife had infected him with HIV. The MDC lost seats in both urban and rural constituencies. These MDC losses reinforced ZANU-PF's majority status, making it increasingly difficult for the opposition to challenge ZANU-PF's policies. By-elections are also costly in terms of financial and human resources.

High turnover among elected officials and the increased number of elections disrupted parliament business. The loss of some of the most vocal advocates in parliament had a negative impact on votes and citizen representation. It is possible that with more members of the opposition in parliament, ZANU-PF might not have pushed forward policies that allowed the rushed and disastrous land reform program. The same might also be said about Operation Murambatsvina, a gerrymandering eviction program that left over 700,000 citizens homeless. Although Zimbabwe is an authoritarian regime, it remains one that governs via parliament, which is why it is so often very difficult for citizens to demand reform. Many of the draconian laws passed by ZANU-PF were voted for in parliament.

In many cases, there is a façade of strong parliamentary debate. It is hard to know how people would have been influenced by the strong advocacy of Jongwe, Jabulani Ndhlovu, and Proud Mupandwa, whose deaths are often referenced as points that weakened the opposition. Had they not died prematurely, their voices might have slowed down some of the worst bills or made significant pushbacks on some of the worst policies.

The HIV pandemic resulted in costly and destabilizing by-elections. The high cost of elections already made participation difficult for the opposition, which had limited resources. Zimbabwean campaign finance laws restrict political fundraising. Parties only receive money for campaigns based on the proportion of their wins in the last elections. As a result, the opposition started out with less money than the ruling party, which received 100 percent public funding in the 2000 elections. The opposition did not qualify for funding in 2000 because it had not participated in the 1996 election. It would only be eligible to get funding ahead of the 2002 elections. Therefore, the opposition relied on the diaspora to fund its participation. However, the ruling party placed restrictions that made it illegal for Zimbabweans domiciled abroad to donate money to political parties. Chamisa, the current opposition president, said his party continues to find it difficult to manage the financial burden of runoffs. In the 2002 by-election to replace Jongwe, one of the few seats retained by MDC, Chamisa attributed the success to party recognition. In rural areas, ZANU-PF benefited from their strong networks and access to state funding, positioning them well to regain their seats.

Opposition losses mattered in government institutions, and they were also felt in communities. The death of Amos Mutongi cost the opposition an important swing seat. Rural areas are very difficult for the opposition to win, and when they do, the victory is often followed by excessive violence. Communities are sometimes willing to take the risk in hopes that the elected officials will raise their issues in parliament. The opposition never regained control of that constituency. Death is also exhausting. Although politicians perfected electioneering at funerals, death left communities fragmented and weakened.

Death of Educated, Young, Working-Class Urbanites

Chigwedere et al. (2008) estimated that the deaths of 330,000 South Africans from HIV during 2000–2005 translated to a loss of over 22 million years of human life. About 1.5 million Zimbabweans have died since the pandemic began. Using the Chigwedere estimators, Zimbabwe has lost 110 million years of human life, people in their prime whose political activism, engagement, votes, and voices would have likely changed the course of Zimbabwe's political trajectory for the better. In this subsection, I show how loss of life due to HIV damaged the political fabric of opposition politics because many of those impacted by HIV fit the profile of opposition voters. This contributed to ZANU-PF's ability to hold on to power against all odds.

The profile of those most impacted by HIV helps explain the pandemic's impact on politics. Most of those who contracted HIV were young, urban, working professionals or were working class. Many had high school diplomas, a first degree, and some postgraduate training. The men were likely to be older and the women younger. Young men and middle-aged women were not likely to be the ones passing on the illness to their partners. Part of this has to do with the euphoria and the liberalism of the 1990s.

One British survivor of HIV described the environment before HIV: "Life was a party before HIV arrived in London" (Lee, 2021). This is also how life in postindependence Zimbabwe has been described to me. The immediate postindependence era brought a new sense of personal freedom and many opportunities for the young to explore their sexuality and relationships beyond the traditional framework of marriage. There was a budding middle class that could afford luxuries like a car and going on holiday. Those who were young at the time called it a period of free love. In their newly independent state, they felt free to take advantage of what life had to offer. There was a high rate of rural-to-urban migration as young people sought opportunities that had been closed to them under colonialism. Cultural norms were also changing.

In Zimbabwe, it became more common for married men to have younger mistresses, the emergence of the "small house" phenomenon. The arrangement was made possible by colonial family structures in which most housing in cities was available to single men but rarely to single women. Once married, husbands would send their wives to live in the village while they continued to work in the city. Younger unmarried women, not just sex workers, had the independence that came from being employed, earning a salary, and living away from their ancestral homes. They were much more willing to experiment sexually than earlier generations. This explains the gender and age differences in who contracted the disease. In popular culture, music and television, for example, Mtukudzi's 1989 hit "Stick to One Woman," admonished men for having multiple partners and encouraged them to stay with one partner.

The profile of those infected by HIV is also the profile of active political participants, engaged democrats, and likely opposition voters. The average opposition voter is young, urban, educated, professional, and part of the working class (Dendere & Young, 2023). The high number of deaths among this age group had a destabilizing impact on the democratic movement, which was still in its nascent stages and only just finding its foot to fight long-term rule by ZANU-PF.

Politics requires a mature and educated citizenry. The death of educated urbanites weakened civil society engagement. Today, one talks of the youthful nature of the African population. The population is young because a whole generation of thought leaders died. A consistently young population cannot build strong political and economic institutions. Very young children and the elderly can do very little to build robust political systems.

In Victoria Falls, where I spent many months studying the impact of HIV on communities, the headmaster of the only government high school in the area told me most children from child-headed homes hardly made it to school. Education is not free, and most HIV orphans cannot afford tuition even when they are living with relatives. When they do attend school, their attendance is sporadic, especially among girls who become primary caregivers of younger siblings or ailing parents. In more extreme cases, young girls are forced into sex work to earn money. Vusa was only fifteen when I first met her in Victoria Falls at a local hotel where she was soliciting clients. Her parents died when she was only ten, leaving her in the care of her grandmother who now had more than ten orphans to care for. Vusa's parents had been working folks in Bulawayo before they got sick and returned to the village where they eventually died. Like most orphans, Vusa did not have the national ID that is required for her to vote. Even if she were able to get an ID, as a mother of three, she had no time for political engagement. Vusa and others in her situation are more susceptible to government manipulation during election time. A small bag of rice and beans goes a long way and does more for her immediate situation than promises of change from the opposition. Vusa had vague memories of her parents supporting the opposition, but she said supporting a political party did not interest her. If even a small fraction of HIV orphans feel as withdrawn from politics as Vusa, this translates to hundreds of thousands of young people who will not vote in elections and hundreds of thousands of voices that are not expressed.

HIV Was Exhausting Everyone

Fatigue from caregiving responsibilities due to a significant health crisis within an economic crisis can also cause citizen apathy and disengagement. One activist, Bella Matambanadzo, described the fatigue from the early days of the AIDS crisis as "arresting" and added, "We [her activist community] could not think or do anything else because most women left the movement to care for dying relatives. And the problem was that there was no end in sight. HIV took all our energy and time." Matambanadzo, a renowned journalist and photographer, spent most of the 1990s and 2000s advocating for gender equality, especially in property rights. She noted that as the HIV crisis deepened, more and more women left volunteer work and eventually the labor force to care for sick relatives. Immaculate, interviewed in Epworth in 2013, lost four of her eight older siblings to the pandemic. Care required for HIV victims was extensive and fell to women in the family, leaving very little time for much else. She detailed that care for one of her sisters who contracted the illness from her truck driver husband started early in the morning with feedings and bathing her. Once people became incapacitated by HIV, they would no longer be able to feed or bathe themselves. Most lost control of their body, necessitating constant baths and diaper changes. Caring for relatives was a twenty-four-hour job, as sick persons could not be left alone for long periods. While Matambanadzo and Immaculate came from different class backgrounds and lived in opposite parts of the city, they shared the same care burdens. They observed the same among the women in their communities. When I asked how caregiving changed political participation among women, Matambanadzo said, "Women are always asked to give up their interests for the greater good." She was referencing the fact that women in Zimbabwean societies often have to give up school or work opportunities if their presence is needed in service of the family unit. Participating in Zimbabwean elections is time-consuming. One must register or reregister if caregiving responsibilities have forced one to relocate. Registration centers are not easily accessible. In 2023, the average person had to travel 10 km to register to vote (Dendere & Young, 2023 working paper).

Rural Women Were Special

Another way that HIV/AIDS enabled ZANU-PF's survival is because of the high number of orphaned children. A major challenge for opposition politics in Zimbabwe is that young people are largely apathetic and refuse to participate in politics. Although Zimbabwean youth make up nearly 70 percent of the population, they are less than 40 percent of registered voters, and voter turnout among the young is even more dismal. Since 2000, the number of registered young voters has fallen far below expectations. The 2002 and 2012 censuses showed that 18–20 percent of eligible voters were between the ages of eighteen and twenty-two, but that age group is only 3 percent of registered voters. The age group twenty-three to twenty-nine years makes up almost 23 percent of eligible voters but is consistently below 12 percent of registered voters. Zimbabwe's young voters are missing from electoral participation. A common explanation is that the youth are just apathetic and uninterested, but I argue that lack of political education that would have otherwise come from solid family units has much to do with this.

While young voters are missing from electoral participation, older voters are overrepresented. ZESN (2013) reported that in the 2013 voter's roll, the government reported 5.82 percent of registered voters were over the age of eighty years old and census data reported that only 2.34 percent should be within this age group. It is not surprising that there is overrepresentation of older voters (Hodzi, 2014). Older rural voters tend to vote for the ruling party and younger urban voters support the opposition. Low political participation among youth directly benefits the ruling party. Youth in Zimbabwe face many barriers to political participation, as shown in Chapter 2. Understudied is the impact of growing up without parental guidance or influence toward civic engagement as most orphaned children took on caregiving responsibilities at a young age. An estimated one million children in Zimbabwe are orphans, and over 700,000 of them were orphaned by the HIV crisis (Daniel, 2021).

CONCLUSION: DEAD PEOPLE CANNOT VOTE

This chapter has shown that the exodus of millions due to HIV-related illnesses, death, and fatigue benefited Zimbabwe's ruling party, ZANU-PF. I expanded and modified Hirschman's groundbreaking theory of exit to include exit because of death, disease, and fatigue.

Hirschman considered exit a binary choice: someone is either present in or absent from a firm, organization, or state; if they are present, they are considered loyal. Exit is not a free choice for those who may face death or deprivation if they use their voice – sometimes, even if they do not – but it may not be easy to get travel papers and find a destination. Exit has the same effect on a regime whether the exit was freely chosen or compelled by the government. Exit also has the same effect if people, rather than moving to another country, die from disease or famine. The premature death of millions of voters in a short period of time affects electoral outcomes: They have no voice and cannot vote.

Hirschman did not consider another form of exit: disengagement from politics while remaining in the country. HIV/AIDS, like other terminal illnesses, demands a lot of attention from caregivers for an extended time.

This is a situation in which people have no real choice. Caring for one individual requires at least two others dedicated to the task because caring for sick individuals is a constant, never-ending job. In Zimbabwe, most of these were young women who sometimes quit work or school to become full-time caregivers. Most such caregivers are left with little energy for themselves, let alone for politics. They, and of course the patients they care for, become disconnected from the state and exit themselves from participation. Their voices become silent, but not because of loyalty or state action.

My research, which drew from Afrobarometer data collected in Zimbabwe from 1999 to 2023, UNAIDS Spectrum project data on HIV and migration from 1980 to 2023, and extensive interviews with families of HIV victims and survivors, showed that the ruling ZANU-PF party gained an HIV premium of between 1 and 3 percent in elections held between 2000 and 2013.

HIV did not discriminate between who contracted the illness and who did not, but it affected young, urban, professional and working-class people more. Unfortunately, this is the profile of those who supported the opposition party. As a result, HIV deaths and illnesses reduced political participation among opposition supporters. Moreover, as more elected politicians died from HIV-related illnesses, the opposition tended to lose seats in by-elections.

ZANU-PF also gained an advantage in the elections due to a weakened civil society. Musicians and artists who had served as critical voices against the government were passing away, leaving fewer voices to challenge the government. Additionally, the HIV pandemic increased the number of orphaned children who did not have the necessary political training or education to participate in politics as adults. This chapter has highlighted that a society weakened by the economic and social demands of HIV cannot sustain democratic growth.

4

Voting with Our Feet

When Voters Leave, the Regime Survives

> One problem with our politics is that over 80 percent of our professionals are out of the country. They are excelling out there (abroad), but their voices are missing here at home.
> —Ibbo Mandaza, July 2022 at Alex Magaisa's memorial

When my mother left Zimbabwe in 2000, she became the first person in my immediate family to live abroad. We thought it would be temporary, but my mother did not return home for twenty-four years. This is true for many Zimbabweans who left home and stayed away for many years. Between 2000 and 2004, when I started my first year of university in the United States, it felt like everyone we knew was leaving. After my mother emigrated, our home became an informal processing center for many people who wanted to go abroad. In a month, my sister assisted about fifteen people with their travel arrangements. Our family home was only five miles from the airport, so relatives and friends often stayed over before their flights. I was in high school at a boarding school, and it felt like every other friend's parent was leaving for the United Kingdom. Our teachers were leaving, too. Everyone was going to London. Our church in Hatfield, one of the first Black middle-class neighborhoods, was almost empty. At age forty-eight, my mother was on the older side of those who left. Most were young parents in their late twenties to early forties. People sold houses and furniture to buy a one-way ticket to England. Zimbabweans did not require a visa to enter the United Kingdom until 2003, so travel there was reasonably straightforward as long as one could purchase a ticket to London.

By the time I started graduate school in 2008, I had traveled to the United Kingdom over a dozen times. During each visit, I would join my mother at work, cleaning hotel rooms during the week and the houses of wealthy people on the weekend. At my mother's job, I noticed a shift. In the early 2000s, it was mostly Caribbean workers alongside us. By the late 2000s, there were a lot of Zimbabweans at the hotel. My mother helped hire two cousins, and there were about fifty in the end. However, by the 2010s, as the European Union made entry for Eastern Europeans easier, Zimbabweans were replaced by a new set of migrants.

I was interested in understanding how this migration affected politics in Zimbabwe. While socializing with Zimbabweans at events and beauty salons and assisting my cousin at care facilities, I noticed politics was a topic of conversation among everyone. Regardless of their tribal or regional backgrounds, their general sentiment was that Zimbabwe needed change. In the early 2000s, several online newspapers were launched. One important platform was newzimbabwe.com, co-run by an experienced journalist Violet Gonda, who had been forced to leave the country by Robert Mugabe's oppressive regime. These online platforms informed us about events in Zimbabwe and provided millions of expats a forum to discuss politics anonymously and passionately.

Zimbabwean migrants were going all over the world, not just to the United Kingdom. Hundreds of thousands were going to South Africa and other neighboring countries. The profile was similar: young, educated, and urban. Just as they did in the United Kingdom, Zimbabweans created social and political communities in South Africa. Creating these parallel political structures so close to home was a lot easier than in the United Kingdom. In recent years, Zimbabweans have continued to leave home, going to places further away, such as China, Russia, Poland, and Australia. Most migrants leave home to further studies in foreign lands because it is much easier for Africans to get student visas than other visa types. Still, others leave to find work or reconnect with family.

Although transnational engagement has positively impacted opposition politics by providing direct financial resources and lobbying foreign governments, the Zimbabwe African National Union-Patriotic Front (ZANU-PF) has continued to win elections. The exit of millions of voters, an estimated four million educated, passionate, and engaged citizens, has contributed to ZANU-PF's survival. Citizens living abroad can influence regime change, as they did during the liberation struggle and in long-ruling regimes like Gambia's, which lost power after its diaspora was able to vote out the incumbent. ZANU-PF has opposed extending the right to vote to those in the diaspora because the party argues that it would be disadvantaged because it believes that many who support the opposition are living in Western countries (Wellman, 2023). Many people I met in the diaspora who engaged with Zimbabwean politics, including my mother, have not returned home to vote. The two decades of Zimbabwe's political crisis have led people's commitment and passion to engage in politics to ebb and flow as their circumstances and the situation at home changes.

The exit of millions of Zimbabweans since 2000 has provided opportunities for the political survival of ZANU-PF and weakened the opposition. In this chapter, I add to Albert Hirschman's EVL by showing that the exit of millions via emigration bolstered ZANU-PF's survival by reducing votes for the opposition. Most migrants are young, educated urbanites. This is the profile of opposition voters, so their departure weakened opposition support and sustained the regime. Even though Zimbabweans abroad continue to speak up on political matters, their transnational activism does not much affect the outcome of elections. Zimbabweans who leave the country lose their right to vote unless they return home, which is expensive and time-consuming and would threaten their claims of asylum. If these voters had not left the country, the opposition would have received more votes and may have won some elections. Using multiple data sources, I demonstrate that ZANU-PF received a migration premium of 4 percent in 2000, 6 percent in 2002, 8 percent in 2005, 10 percent in 2008, and 11 percent in 2013.

POLITICAL EFFECTS OF MIGRATION

Individuals often migrate due to deteriorating political and economic conditions. They may feel compelled to leave their homes when they fear for their safety or the safety of their loved ones, or they may be incapable of sustaining themselves or realizing their ambitions in their home country (Davenport et al., 2003; Melander & Öberg, 2006). The United Nations estimates that at least 215 million people, 3 percent of the world's population, live outside their country of birth. The large number of people leaving their home countries has significant implications for politics in both receiving and sending countries. My work adds to the small but growing literature on the impact of migration on country-of-origin politics.

Research on migration has mainly focused on the economic implications of migration, such as the brain drain phenomenon and the impact of waves of immigrants on receiving country politics. Early work by economists argued that emigration could be detrimental to the sending country because it often loses skilled professionals. However, newer research shows the effects of brain drain might not be as dire as previously estimated.

However, little has been studied about the relationship between emigration and politics in the homeland. Some studies on political movements in regions such as the Middle East have shown that the involvement of young, urban, middle-class citizens with access to social media played a crucial role in toppling regimes (Beissinger, 2012; Papic & Noonan, 2011). However, when these voters exit the political process, their absence has negative consequences for the success of sociopolitical movements. Findings from other studies suggest the diaspora can contribute to economic growth and contribute to the development of strong democratic institutions in their home countries. In essence, the diaspora can remit democracy back home (Batista & Vicente, 2011; Docquier et al., 2011; Lodigiani & Salomone, 2012; Pfutze, 2012). These scholars argued that the diaspora can remit democracy because they are more likely to absorb the democratic beliefs of the host country, and they will influence the beliefs of their friends and family back home by exposing them to new beliefs on governance. The diaspora can also directly influence politics back home by sponsoring an opposition party or funding political revolutions, as in the Middle East during the Arab Spring.

Modern politics is no longer dominated by outright dictatorships that disregard and stifle elections. Instead, there has been an increase in electoral authoritarian regimes (Cox, 2009; Donno, 2013; Gandhi & Lust-Okar, 2009; Geddes, 2005; Way & Levitsky, 2002). Levitsky and Way (2002) defined these regimes as political systems under which "formal democratic institutions are widely viewed as the principal means of obtaining and exercising political authority" (p. 2). An important and unique characteristic of these regimes, including Zimbabwe's, is that they regularly hold elections. In most cases, the elections are marred by reports of violence and are seldom regarded as free and fair. Ruling parties consider these elections an important way to maintain their legitimacy.

Politicians in democracies and hybrid or semiauthoritarian regimes that hold regular elections depend on votes to stay in power. They get their supporters to dominate the polls and win elections. In nondemocracies, the ability to prevent opposition supporters from participating in elections also guarantees electoral wins. Hirschman (1970) proposed a dichotomy between exit and voice to convey how citizens unhappy with the domestic situation face the choice of emigrating (exit) or protesting and contributing to political change (voice). Undemocratic regimes may be quite happy to see their opponents leave. In Zimbabwe, the exit of would-be opposition supporters provided a much-needed lifeline for the vulnerable incumbent party.

Following Hirschman's EVL argument and building on the new literature, this chapter argues that when millions vote with their feet by leaving the country, it weakens the pro-democracy opposition parties and bolsters the regime. Exit is not the end of loyalty to a country. I use loyalty in more conventional ways than Hirschman did. Loyalty is an attachment to a space that leads one to continue participating even after exit. It is the attachment to the imagined community of a diaspora, to a place one may have never lived. This attachment leads one to use voice and advocate for change or improvement in that community. Individuals may express their loyalty to their home country by using technology to voice views on politics from abroad and sending remittances to families. I show that diasporas use their voice to demand the right to participate in elections from their host nations. However, the effectiveness of their voice is diminished by the authoritarian policies of the regimes back home.

The emigration of the citizens most likely to challenge the regime is bad for democracy. Kapur (2010) found that the exit of talented individuals diminishes the supply of citizens willing to bolster incumbent political regimes and run state institutions. In Zimbabwe, the loss of professionals had a huge negative impact on all sectors of society, including health and education. For example, Zimbabwe lost over 50 percent of its medical professionals (Chikanda, 2006). Voter exit also affects the demand for better political and economic institutions. According to Kapur (2010), the more educated (and internationally marketable) are often better positioned to exercise voice and press for changes in the status quo. Zimbabwe's activist and intellectual communities were greatly diminished as active citizens emigrated and those who remained were silenced by state repression.

Scholars of Zimbabwean politics have made similar arguments. Masunungure (2011) concluded that the mass exodus of Zimbabweans since 2000 has dampened the voice of people (p. 51). The profile of my sample of Zimbabweans in the diaspora supports this view. They were educated urbanites, a disproportionate percentage of whom were disaffected minorities, people with histories of active opposition support, or identifiers with opposition parties. In response to excessive use of political violence and a deteriorating economy, members of the Movement for Democratic Change (MDC) who had the means to emigrate left the country. Many individual cases can be invoked to support this. Tinotenda, aged 33, had emigrated in 2008 during the campaign for the bloody runoff elections. In his capacity as a security officer for the MDC, he claimed to have witnessed the death of his comrades and said he no longer felt hope that the situation in Zimbabwe would change. At the time of our interview in 2013, he had withdrawn from politics. The people in his Scotland networks knew nothing of his past as an organizer and took him for one of the many economic immigrants from Zimbabwe.

The insecure status of Zimbabwean immigrants in countries of settlement contributed to a trend toward disengagement with politics at home. This works to the benefit of ZANU-PF. Both those who had legal status and those in various stages of legalizing their stay in the host country asked me "Who sent you?" to ensure I was not sent by the ZANU-PF regime or immigration officials in the host country. Some of the people I interviewed for this study reported they became openly engaged in MDC politics simply because it was the surest route to secure papers, and engagement ended thereafter. Julie, a forty-five-year-old woman from Harare who was living and working in Washington, DC, said she had fled the increasing political violence in Zimbabwe in 2002 and came to the United States. She would not have been a vocal opposition supporter had it not been for the need to strengthen her asylum claim. Although an opposition supporter, she always felt her participation and vote choice were private. Like Julie, Blessing, a fifty-five-year-old hotel worker in England, recalled an incident in which more than ten of her housemates were victims of a Home Office deportation raid. Many of them had spoken to people who posed as being from a charity organization but were collecting information on behalf of the Home Office.

This body of theory and my interviews with evidence of the exodus and gradual disengagement of a politically active cohort of emigres demands a closer examination of connections with Zimbabwean electoral politics after 2000. After summarizing migration from Zimbabwe over recent decades, I analyze qualitative and quantitative data to show the ways in which emigration has contributed to the ZANU-PF regime's survival.

ZIMBABWEAN POLITICS AND THE CONDITIONS LEADING TO MASS EXIT

ZANU-PF has been in power since the country gained independence in 1980. The survival of ZANU-PF presents an interesting academic puzzle because the party survived the worst political and economic crises in modern history. Failing economies and violent political crises of less significant magnitude have been credited for the demise of other governing parties, such as in Mexico, Japan, Zambia, and Senegal (Magaloni, 2006; Posner & Young, 2007; Scheiner, 2005). How did ZANU-PF survive, and how did emigration contribute to its capacity to retain power?

In response to the economic and political crises during the 1990s, Zimbabweans had rallied behind the country's first viable opposition party, the MDC, led by trade unionist Morgan Tsvangirai. In late 1999, partly in response to increased urban strikes and riots and more vocal demands for land reform from war veterans, ZANU-PF proposed a referendum to change the country's constitution. The election asked voters to choose between a new constitution approved by Mugabe and ZANU-PF or to support Tsvangirai and his MDC's opposition to the constitution. Most Zimbabweans, especially urbanites, voted against the new constitution and ZANU-PF lost its first vote in over twenty years. It was a memorable moment, as Angie, interviewed in Scotland, recalled:

To be honest, I am not sure I voted before 1999. My husband and I had two little girls then, and we had just bought our home in Letombo Park. We went with our new neighbors to vote no on the constitution. It was electric. We stood in line for what felt like twenty hours, but we had no intention of going home. I voted again for MDC in 2002, right before we left.

Harare had the largest turnout, with 291,708 votes; the majority of Harare voters (218,298) supported the MDC position. Bulawayo also had a high turnout, 118,159, and most of them (90,422) also voted no. Even in predominantly ZANU-PF areas like the Mashonaland provinces, nearly half of those who turned out voted no on the new constitution (Electoral Institute for Sustainable Democracy in Africa, 2000). There was a lot of public excitement, especially among young urban professionals who had largely felt alienated from national politics.

The MDC had revived urban politics and the interests of young professionals like Angie, who suddenly had hope for change. In June of the same year, ZANU-PF lost its majority in parliament to the MDC newcomers. Zimbabwean politics appeared to be following democratic transition patterns seen in Senegal, where the dominant Socialist Party lost power to an opposition coalition in 2001; in Zambia, where the United National Independence Party lost power to the opposition Movement for Multiparty Democracy in 1992; and in Malawi where longtime leader Kamuzu Banda failed to extend his rule when his Malawi Congress Party lost to the United Democratic Front in the

1994 presidential elections. There was a general expectation that the winds of change ushering in democratic governance had arrived in Zimbabwe, and that the younger and popular Tsvangirai had the electoral support to topple Mugabe. In 2000, a lot of urbanites voted for the first time. In the years that followed, the MDC had more success than any other opposition party. But it could not oust ZANU-PF.

Since the unification of ZANU-PF and PF-ZANU in 1986, Zimbabwe had functioned like a de jure one-party state, with the ruling party winning over 98 percent of seats in parliament and at least 80 percent of the electoral vote (Sithole & Makumbe, 1997). In June 2000, the MDC won 47 percent of the parliamentary seats. This was the first time the unified ZANU-PF faced significant opposition from a party with widespread appeal. In the elections between 2000 and 2010, ZANU-PF's supermajorities declined sharply.

During this time, life was becoming increasingly difficult for citizens. Between 2000 and 2009, annual inflation rose to 516 quintillion percent – 516 followed by eighteen zeros. Zimbabwe's inflation surpassed the infamous German economic meltdown of 1923, when inflation reached 29,000 percent. Bricks of Zimbabwean dollars accompanied a trip to the grocery store for a loaf of bread. Prices were changing by the hour. Those seeking to leave Zimbabwe were forced to buy foreign currency on the black market as international airlines and other multinational companies refused to accept local currency (most of them left Zimbabwe altogether). Yet, the ZANU-PF regime remained in power. After thirty-six years, President Mugabe was finally ousted by his vice president, Emmerson Mnangagwa, via a military coup in November 2017. The regime's persistence over this turbulent history needs to be explained.

MIGRATION DATA COLLECTION

Beginning in 2000, as Zimbabwe's economic and political situation deteriorated, an estimated two to four million citizens emigrated, 15–20 percent of the total. What role did their emigration play in the survival of ZANU-PF? My initial plan was to send out electronic surveys to 1,200 Zimbabweans worldwide, asking them to respond to questions about political participation and voting intentions. This is the standard way of collecting political science data. I would have then used statistical tools to analyze the data and show various levels of statistical significance. I quickly learned that migrants, especially people who have escaped a brutal regime, are wary of electronic surveys. The Zimbabwean migrant population is difficult to study through large-scale surveys because respondents are suspicious of interviews. Many live in the shadow of their home country's regime and fear deportation from their host country.

Instead of surveys, I conducted ethnographic interviews with respondents selected through snowball sampling. The American Anthropology Association defines ethnography as a study of human behavior in a natural setting, where investigators must immerse themselves in the community. There is no set requirement for how long one must live in a community or how many interviews one must conduct. I used semistructured interviews with ten questions and lived in communities for three to six months. While ethnography is a well-established methodology, I had concerns about my positionality and the generalizability of my findings. I had discussed these in greater detail in Chapter 2.

I began planning for ethnographic fieldwork by looking at diaspora mapping work created by Pasura (2008) in the United Kingdom, Makina (2008) in South Africa, and Crush and Tevera (2010) in Canada. While migrants tend to move frequently from the places where they first landed, I knew they follow network patterns. I used similar methodologies to recruit interviewees in each location, with minor modifications to accommodate community differences.

I wanted my sample to improve on previous studies of Zimbabwean migrants, which had been less representative of host countries, racial groups, and ethnolinguistic communities. A lot was known about the experiences of Zimbabweans in London (Bloch, 2005; Kuhlmann, 2010; Pasura, 2010), but there was very little on the experiences and opinions of migrants in the United States and in South Africa other than in Johannesburg. I wanted my study to cover multiple countries and cities. I believed posing similar questions in a similar time frame to people in different host countries would add richness to this study. I could also learn whether there were fundamental differences in how the diasporas viewed the ruling party back home. When I began my work, I found the UK diaspora to be more active in transnational politics than those in the United States and South Africa. After the 2017 coup, the American diaspora became more vocal against ZANU-PF than those in the United Kingdom. At the same time, support for the regime back home grew and became more open.

Sampling Strategy

A colleague reading an early draft of my work asked whether I had considered just interviewing members of my family living in the diaspora.

This strategy has been used by other Zimbabwean scholars who fear retaliation. I briefly considered this, given that autoethnography is growing in popularity and it would get me past my fear of an intense recruitment scheme. But I wanted to get away from my immediate social network. In my strategy, the first person often had strong ties to someone I knew or were themselves very active in political conversations. I wanted more diversity in the pool so that I could learn about the views of Zimbabweans outside my circles. As I will show later, I had reason to be concerned about speaking primarily to individuals with close ties to the political communities.

To achieve my goal, I devised a three-stage snowball strategy to reach a stratified sample of 100 interviewees. In the snowball method, participants help a researcher reach additional participants. Snowballing increases trust between the researcher and participants because people tend to be more open to someone known within their community. My initial contact would talk to a potential participant on my behalf and ask whether I could have a conversation with them.

For my snowball strategy, I created a list of Zimbabwean community and church leaders in different countries with the help of people I knew. The existing connections helped me test my interview questions and map out immigrant locations, but I excluded them from the final respondent group. I would contact Person A, ask them five basic questions about their knowledge of the Zimbabwean community, and ask them to introduce me to Person B. I would ask Person B an additional five questions about political participation and networks, then Person B would introduce me to Person C. My final list of respondents was comprised of Person Cs, though where someone had died or I had an underrepresented community (e.g., White Zimbabweans and those above age sixty), I interviewed some Bs. I added another layer of Person Cs to the interview if I had an overrepresented community. In South Africa, I added Person B.1 when a neighborhood was quite densely populated with Zimbabweans, and I wanted more distance between Person A and Person C. In places with fewer immigrants (e.g., Stirling, Scotland), I sometimes ended up with multiple recommendations to the same Person C. In such cases, I added Person C.2.

Interview Process

My sampling strategy was intertwined with my interview process. The first interviews occurred in four countries – the United States, the United Kingdom, South Africa, and Zimbabwe – in 2013 and 2014, with subsequent rounds in 2017, 2020, and 2022. If I could not reach some respondents because they had moved or died, I recruited a new respondent from their family or community network or pulled someone from my list of Person Bs for an extended semistructured interview. I tried to find someone with characteristics similar to the original interviewee. In the years after the COVID-19 pandemic, I sometimes replaced face-to-face interviews with phone calls. Face-to-face interviews are richer in detail because people often communicate more with their facial expressions and are more open than on the phone. I had conversations with over 300 Zimbabweans about transnational politics. I also attended many community meetings, church meetings, and community functions in the United States, United Kingdom, and South Africa. These meetings and events provided additional information about communities.

PROFILE OF ZIMBABWEAN MIGRANTS

The profile of exiles is important for understanding how exit sustains authoritarianism because demographic factors influence political choice, which in turn influences the structure of the political scene. Zimbabwean emigrants are often considered middle-class risk takers, including opposition activists (Masunungure, 2011). When ZANU-PF was at its weakest, facing strong domestic and international opposition and overseeing the worst economic crisis in history, the exodus of millions of Zimbabweans alleviated pressures for change. In this section, I briefly describe the profile of opposition supporters in Zimbabwe and then discuss the profile of the migrants, showing similarities between the two populations.

I built the profile of opposition supporters from Afrobarometer surveys of Zimbabwean voters from 1999 to 2017. Of those who said they supported a political party, those who were young, educated, urban, and professionally employed were most likely to say they supported the opposition. These are the very groups most likely to emigrate. Most of the urban poor also said they supported the opposition. Among those who intended to emigrate, most said they supported the opposition. Most of those who demanded democracy also said they supported the opposition.

Profile of Opposition Supporters

I looked at the profile of MDC supporters from the full population of voters, not just those who identify with a political party. The trends are the same. Younger people are more likely to support the opposition than their older counterparts. The opposition has also had consistent support from the more educated voters, although in the peak years of Zimbabwe's political crisis, the opposition drew support across all education levels. The opposition support base is more urban than the support base of ZANU-PF. Opposition supporters tend to have professional skills. However, given the high unemployment rates in Zimbabwe due to the economic crisis, it makes sense that the party would attract a lot of support from unskilled people, who tend to be younger. There is a strong relationship between being an opposition supporter in Zimbabwe and demanding democracy.

Opposition Supporters and Migration Intention

Although Afrobarometer did not include questions on intent to migrate between 2000 and 2013, the patterns of who intended to leave the country were consistent with what I found in the diaspora. In 2017, nearly half of the Zimbabwean population (47 percent) said they intended to emigrate (see Figure 4.1). These numbers likely underestimate the sentiment of those who wish to leave. Zimbabweans tend to be unwilling to reveal their intentions to leave because some communities believe verbalizing these intentions would jeopardize or jinx their plans. Among those who have considered leaving the country, the majority (67 percent) supported the MDC, 59 percent were urbanites, and 57 percent demanded full democracy. Intent to emigrate was strongest among young voters. An estimated 62 percent of those aged eighteen to twenty-five have considered emigrating, while only 10 percent of those aged fifty-six and above have done so. The majority of those with postsecondary education (64 percent) also said they intend to emigrate, compared to only 14 percent among those with no formal education. Those who have experienced poverty were more likely to report intention to emigrate than those who have not. For those still in the country, the intent to emigrate is stronger than the plans to reach that goal. This is likely because most opportunities to leave the country are out of people's control. Still, those who support the opposition, older voters, urbanites and those with more money are likely to have made more solid plans to emigrate than younger voters who may not have as much money. The most popular intended destination among Zimbabweans is South Africa. It is the closest neighbor accessible by road and air, and the costs of moving to South Africa are also much lower than those to any other intended destination.

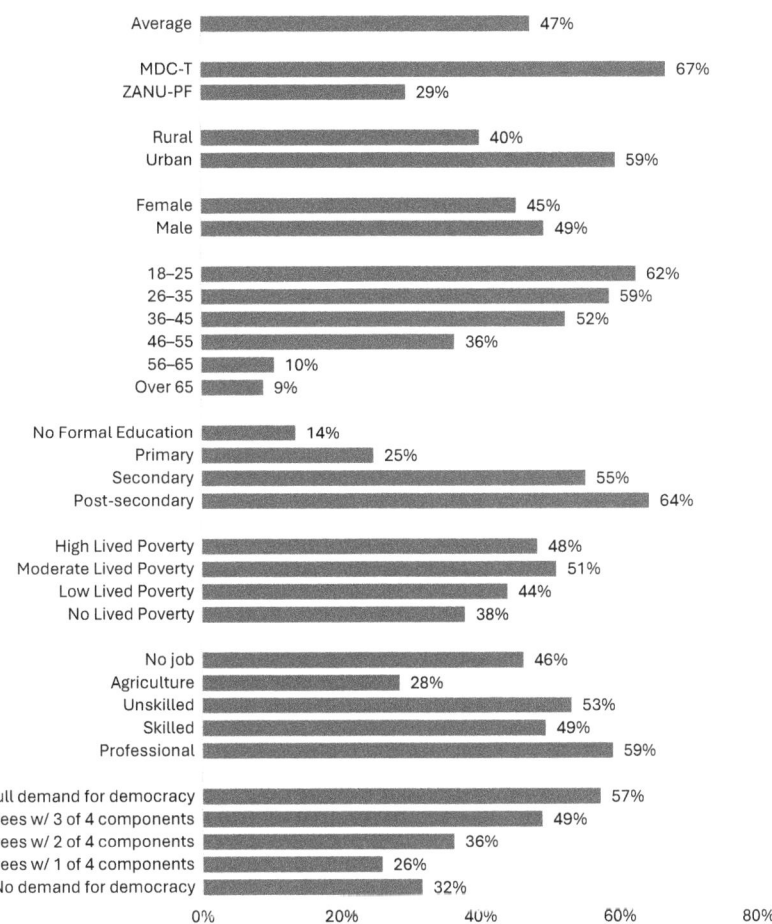

FIGURE 4.1 Considered emigration, at least a little bit. *Source*: Afrobarometer Round 7 (2017).

As I found in my interviews and consistent with findings from other scholars, the most common reasons for emigrating were economic. Most Zimbabweans (63 percent) reported they want to go abroad to find work, 18 percent reported economic hardship, 8 percent reported poverty, and 12 percent reported better business opportunities. By 2017, the proportion that identified political persecution was lower, but this was not because there was no longer any political persecution. Instead, economic hardships overshadowed any other motivations. As noted from the asylum data, hundreds of Zimbabwean refugees were still escaping their home country, albeit at a lower rate than before.

Profile of the Diaspora

The key demographic features of the opposition base in Zimbabwe closely match those of the respondents in my own survey. The majority in my survey were young adults: 68 percent were between the ages of twenty one and forty; over 70 percent of those interviewed were urbanites, having emigrated from Harare (57 percent) or Bulawayo (20 percent); 50 percent were male; and 60 percent were highly educated, with at least 20 percent holding a degree beyond the first bachelor's degree. This profile closely matches the profile of opposition supporters in Zimbabwe.

In terms of race and ethnicity, self-identification in the sample was 70 percent Shona, 21 percent Ndebele, and 9 percent White. This means the latter two categories slightly overrepresented their share of the population in Zimbabwe. Whites and Ndebele speakers have trajectories of political engagement and exodus in response to patterns of violent repression in Zimbabwe that explain their larger numbers within the diaspora. My sample had relatively few open ZANU-PF supporters – only seventeen individuals said they supported ZANU-PF, most of whom were male. Most of the returnees I interviewed, on the other hand, had joined ZANU-PF. An exception to this pattern was among young female returnees I interviewed, who had withdrawn from politics altogether upon returning home.

My sample can be summarized, therefore, as opposition-supporting young adults who were more likely to have higher levels of education or be a disaffected minority than the general population of Zimbabwe. As this cohort of Zimbabweans emigrated, the pool of politically energized urban opposition party activists declined in parallel. The MDC relied on urban support to win elections. The mass exodus of urbanites was likely to weaken the opposition in their urban bases, and it did. Suppose 100 people in Zimbabwe split a 50–50 likelihood of voting for ZANU-PF or the opposition. If 30 percent left the country and most of those who left supported the opposition, then the odds of winning would be greatly tilted in favor of ZANU-PF.

While the sample in my study was not randomly selected, it is similar to what Afrobarometer and other surveys have identified: an urban and youthful bias, though the middle-class status of migrants is less pronounced in the regional diaspora than in more distant European and global destinations. Zimbabwean political commentators and scholarly discussions of the diaspora have also argued that it was predominantly opposition supporters who left during this period (Hammar et al., 2010;

Pasura, 2008, 2010). A survey by Makina (2008) of 4,654 Zimbabwean migrants in Johannesburg, South Africa, showed that 58 percent identified political push factors as the main cause for emigrating and 83 percent identified the debilitating economy among a sample in which 51 percent were from cities (40 percent from Bulawayo and 11 percent from Harare). Recent data from the International Organization of Migration shows that most Zimbabwean migrants are young to middle-aged, many have some high school or university education, and most are from urban areas (Zanamwe & Devillard, 2018). Relative youthfulness is consistent with Pasura (2008) and Makina (2008) and is also a feature of broader Zimbabwean demography: the 2012 census showed 65 percent were under forty years old.

Most White interviewees in my sample had left in the early 2000s in response to a land reform policy that had turned violent. Black Zimbabweans from Matebeleland had a longer history of expulsion from Zimbabwe in the wake of the 1980s Gukurahundi massacres and thus had longer standing and better ties within the diaspora, which facilitated the migration of others after 2000. Like other studies of the Zimbabwean diaspora (McGregor & Primorac, 2010; Pasura, 2010), I found support for secession of Matebeleland to be significant, as evidenced by the flourishing of separatist politics under the banner of Mthwakazi. I attended a few meetings for these groups and concluded that the call for devolution was also an attempt to force the government to address the Gukurahundi itself.

During their time in the diaspora, many Zimbabweans continued to further their studies and improve on the professional skills they had prior to emigrating. When they emigrated, the majority of respondents had either a high school education (40 percent of my sample) or professional training such as a teaching certificate (20 percent). However, by 2013, most respondents reported having a university degree (56 percent). Once people completed their education, the next logical step was to find gainful employment to support themselves and their families. As the economic situation in Zimbabwe declined, the young who were just finishing high school and university were unable to secure employment and opted to leave the country in pursuit of better opportunities. Among the diaspora, those who furthered their education in the host country often became less engaged in Zimbabwean politics. In 2013, most of those in my sample who had high-earning jobs showed very little interest in returning home to vote.

In short, therefore, while my survey was not representative, it captured some key features of the broader diaspora: its oppositional character, urban origins, greater levels of education, and disproportionate populations of disaffected minority ethnic and racial groups. My argument about the impact of emigration on politics at home hinges on these features of the cohort of exiles who left after 2000.

MIGRATION REDUCES TURNOUT FOR THE OPPOSITION

In every election since 2000, even though absolute votes for ZANU-PF declined, support for the opposition was not high enough for it to win. ZANU-PF's survival largely results from its ability to manipulate electoral returns in its favor. The exit of millions of would-be opposition voters gave the ruling party additional ways to manipulate electoral outcomes to their advantage. In the 2002 elections, Tsvangirai narrowly failed to win the presidency. Turnout was high (55 percent), but MDC support had declined in urban areas and the ruling party had maintained a stronghold in rural areas. In 2008, the economy was at its worst as hyperinflation peaked, and another wave of emigration began just before the March 2008 elections. Turnout in that election was only 43 percent.

In my 2013 survey of the diaspora, 80 percent of respondents said they identified with the MDC. However, only 36 percent said they had taken the opportunity to vote in any election between 2000 and 2010. Among these, 80 percent supported the MDC. The 64 percent of respondents who had not participated in any election between 2000 and 2010 fell into three groups. Three-quarters of them, 49 percent of all respondents, said they had been too young to vote and then had left the country. These young respondents, now in their late twenties to early thirties, had never participated in the democratic process of voicing their preference for leadership and could not afford to return home to vote. A smaller group, 9 percent of the total, said they lacked interest in politics; upon further investigation, some of them were afraid to return to vote because of the risk of political violence. Ten percent of the nonvoters, 6 percent of the respondents, did not even have the option of returning home to vote: they were no longer considered citizens. I discuss the impact of citizenship laws in the next section on barriers to voting. This inability to vote in the diaspora ultimately benefited ZANU-PF.

BARRIERS TO DIASPORA VOTE BENEFIT ZANU-PF

Zimbabwean citizens living outside their country technically retain the right to vote, but they face the significant practical obstacle that

Zimbabwe does not permit external voting. The financial burden of returning home to cast a vote is high. Even for those who can afford to come back, the timing of voter registration and election dates is inconsistent. Furthermore, those who are not legal immigrants in their host country and those who have received asylum status risk not being able to return to their new home if they go back to Zimbabwe to participate in an election.

Established democracies make provisions for external voting so people who leave their country do not lose their right to vote. In Africa, the provision of a diaspora vote is increasingly common, with recent laws passed in Kenya allowing its diaspora to vote in presidential elections. However, the only way to vote in Zimbabwe is to go to the precinct where one is registered. The Zimbabwean government makes voter registration extremely cumbersome for urbanites and for those who travel about the country, which lowers turnout for the opposition.

Zimbabweans living abroad cannot vote from there, except for the small minority in diplomatic posts. The Zimbabwean diaspora has been lobbying the ZANU-PF government for the right to vote for the last two decades. Beatrice Mtetwa, the leading human rights lawyer in Zimbabwe, who has represented diaspora groups in many court cases against the government, says the constitution guarantees every eligible Zimbabwean the right to vote. However, the government has responded to that argument by saying they have no obligation to provide resources for people who are living outside the country.

The first of four court cases on the issue came in 2005, when a coalition of Zimbabwean residents in the United Kingdom filed suit against the government in the Zimbabwe Supreme Court (Case No. SC 22/05). The court dismissed the case, saying it lacked merit despite the constitutional provision of suffrage for all Zimbabweans, regardless of race, creed, or residency status at the time of an election (Tungwarara, 2005). Cases in 2011, 2015, and 2018 had similar outcomes. They were either dismissed without a hearing or the court reserved judgment. The multiple court rulings that denied the Zimbabwean diaspora the right to vote have had serious implications for the democratic process in the country. By preventing nearly two million voting-eligible citizens domiciled abroad from voting, ZANU-PF effectively disenfranchised a significant portion of the population. It is not unreasonable to suggest that the ruling party was fearful that if the diaspora were allowed to vote, they would cast their votes in support of the opposition, potentially bringing an end to ZANU-PF rule.

In 2012, during the constitution-making process, the Constitution Committee sought feedback from Zimbabweans living abroad. The diaspora requested three constitutional provisions: dual citizenship, devolution of power, and a diaspora vote. Dual citizenship is important for Zimbabweans who have established residency abroad but want to maintain ties with their homeland. The diaspora has argued they should not have to choose between their adopted homes and their country of birth. Dual citizenship and a diaspora vote provision would allow Zimbabweans to participate in the affairs of their homeland while living abroad.

However, the constitutional draft was silent on the issue of the diaspora vote, and opposition leaders backtracked on their support for it. MDC National Secretary Abedenico Bhebhe said in September 2012 that his party was tabling the issue of the diaspora vote because it feared ZANU-PF would rig postal votes. Bhebhe said his party's position was that the diaspora vote should be addressed later because it was unclear how the government would allow Zimbabweans outside the country, some of whom were illegal immigrants, to vote. The opposition also argued that a diaspora vote would advantage ZANU-PF in Southern Africa because neighboring states' governments were allied as liberation movements that would do anything to support each other in elections.

The MDC's 2012 position on the diaspora vote directly contradicted past statements by Tsvangirai, who had often supported it. In 2011, Tsvangirai, now prime minister in the unity government, had called for the restoration of the diaspora vote, which had been scratched from the books by ZANU-PF in the late 1980s because it feared the votes of exiled White Zimbabweans. Tsvangirai said, "The MDC believes that all adult Zimbabweans, regardless of their station either at home or in the diaspora, must be allowed to vote in the next and in any election if democracy has to assume its generic meaning out of today's political transition" (*The Zimbabwean*, 2011).

Since then, ZANU-PF has remained consistent in its opposition to the diaspora vote. Diaspora activists hoped the end of the Mugabe era would lead to a change in policy, but this has not been the case. In 2018 and 2023, the government shut down demands for the diaspora vote.

EXIT DAMPENS POLITICAL PARTICIPATION

In this section, I discuss in greater detail the ways that exit dampened political participation due to loss of citizenship, fear of returning home to vote, reduced transnational activism, and the time and financial pressures faced by the diaspora. The Zimbabwean diaspora faced these challenges at different times. In the early 2000s, the diaspora was more likely to vigorously engage in transnational activism. However, over the ensuing two decades, fatigue brought on by financial pressures and the time required for opposition politics reduced the activism of some opposition supporters.

Loss of Citizenship

A significant proportion of Zimbabweans in the country and living abroad lost their citizenship because of government policy. Zimbabwe's citizenship laws have been and remain highly politicized. During colonial times, the laws protected land ownership by the White minority rulers. In 1979, during the Lancaster Agreement negotiations, the constitution was amended to give citizenship by birth to children born of a Zimbabwean father, regardless of marital status, and to limit the transfer of citizenship of those born abroad to one generation. A child born to a Zimbabwean mother but a non-Zimbabwean father could not gain citizenship, regardless of how long the father had lived in Zimbabwe. The law was changed in 1996, but only for children born after that date (Manby, 2019). Those children would have reached voting age in 2014.

Daimon's (2016) extensive work on the politicization of citizenship by ZANU-PF shows that the government manipulated and abused descendants of emigrants for political gain. Between 1980 and 1996, the government allowed descendants of emigrants to participate in elections, but after the formation of the MDC, the government pushed for more stringent laws that required descendants of migrants to renounce their other citizenships to maintain a Zimbabwean one. The Citizenship Amendment Act of 2003 targeted White Zimbabweans as the only group that could be visually identified as foreigners. However, it also impacted poor urbanites and farm workers who traced their family lineage to neighboring Mozambique and Malawi. The law was meant to disenfranchise millions of Zimbabweans whom the government perceived as opposition supporters. Ahead of the 2005 elections, state media published multiple announcements from the registrar general reminding stateless Zimbabweans to regularize their status. It was ironic that the state considered them Zimbabweans even after rendering them stateless. My sample of interviewees undersamples the population impacted by these policies because most of them were White Zimbabweans and their farmworkers. Still, my interviews show how citizenship policies impacted individual citizens and their ability to participate in politics.

Zimbabweans like Immaculate, whose story was discussed in Chapter 1, were forced to denounce the Malawian citizenship they did not know they had because they were born and raised in Zimbabwe to a mother with clear Zimbabwean roots. Immaculate and thousands of others lost their right to vote until they could regularize their citizenship. Most White Zimbabweans like Peter, whom I interviewed in High Wycombe, United Kingdom, chose to claim British citizenship and renounce their Zimbabwean status. The United Kingdom modified its laws that limit claims to citizenship to one generation to accommodate White Zimbabweans. Peter had voted in every election since the 1960s but was no longer eligible to vote in his fifties and had to leave home.

I interviewed Baba Chido in Atlanta. He was a Black Zimbabwean born in the United States to two Zimbabwean parents who were studying there in 1978. When the new Zimbabwean government asked educated Zimbabweans to return home and take up positions, his parents left the United States and went back to Zimbabwe. Baba Chido moved to Zimbabwe when he was four years old, using his American passport, and he lived there until 2005. In 2005, he had the chance to go abroad, but Zimbabwean immigration authorities said he could not get a passport because he was not considered a Zimbabwean citizen. The new laws did not allow multiple citizenship. The authorities told him he had to either renounce his American citizenship and become a Zimbabwean citizen by heritage or face deportation to the United States. He chose to hold onto his American citizenship. As a result, he could no longer vote in Zimbabwe, nor could his American-born children, who were now of voting age.

Baba Chido was very active in Zimbabwean politics, and he often traveled back to his home country, where he owned multiple businesses and supported opposition candidates. However, despite his love for his country of heritage, he could not vote. His children, also passionate about Zimbabwe, could not contribute to their homeland either. This is a common problem for children born in the diaspora to Zimbabwean parents who did not have dual citizenship.

Lorraine, born in 1990 of two White parents, a Zimbabwean mother and British father, did not get a Zimbabwean passport until 2020. Her father had applied for British passports for his children when they were young. When he was forced to renounce his British citizenship, he did what most parents did at the time. He encouraged his children to retain the British passport and keep it a secret. At age eighteen, Lorraine, who was now studying in the United States, was technically required to renounce either the British or Zimbabwean ties, but she did neither. She kept her British passport and Zimbabwean ID. Lorraine was a determined voter, so although she did not technically have Zimbabwean citizenship, she used the ID she was allowed to have before age eighteen to vote. Others in the same situation told me they were too afraid to vote or be near a government office.

Even Zimbabwean lawyers are not immune to the abuse of citizenship laws. Marcia, a Zimbabwean-born lawyer, left in 2005, just before she was eligible to participate in her first election. At that time, she had a Zimbabwean ID and passport and considered herself a Zimbabwean by birth. In 2008, she returned home to vote and renew her passport. The registrar's office informed her that she was ineligible to renew her passport and national ID because she was, in fact, an alien, the term used for noncitizens. She was informed that she would need to renounce her Zambian citizenship before she could get new Zimbabwean identity documents and register to vote. Marcia could not vote in 2008 and spent the next three years fighting to regain her citizenship. She was finally able to vote in 2023. Many have not had their Zimbabwean passports or citizenship restored because the authorities ignore the 2013 constitution or demand large payouts.

In recent years, children born outside of Zimbabwe to Zimbabwean parents have been able to claim citizenship. However, the process to do so is complex and expensive. For instance, I had to travel from Massachusetts to the Zimbabwean Embassy in Washington, DC, to obtain my daughter's birth certificate forms. These forms can only be obtained in person from various Zimbabwean embassies. Once we had the forms, we sent them to Zimbabwe, where a relative used their network get the birth certificate issued. In 2023, when we traveled to Zimbabwe with our daughter, she was only issued a thirty-day visa despite having a Zimbabwean birth certificate. We immediately applied for a Zimbabwean passport, which cost $140. After her passport was issued, we returned to immigration to request that her visa be canceled. However, we were told it was not possible and that our daughter would have to return to America and fly back to Zimbabwe with her new passport or risk being deported. The government had no qualms about deporting even a three-year-old child. The consequences are even more severe for adult Zimbabweans who cannot prove citizenship. As a result, many people in the diaspora have chosen to relinquish their Zimbabwean citizenship along with their right to vote.

Fear of Returning Home to Vote

Most Zimbabweans who emigrated in the last two decades did so under extreme duress. This was a particular feature of my interviews with White emigres, former MDC members, and civic activists. Activists were forced to exit and silence their dissent out of fear of government retribution.

According to data from the UN Refugee Agency, at least 1.3 million Zimbabweans have applied for asylum or refugee status in other countries. Most of these individuals claim they left their homes due to fear of violence or even death because of their opposition political activities. The United Kingdom and South Africa have the highest number of applicants, but Zimbabwean asylees are present in almost every country. The United States processes many asylum applications, and I have provided professional testimony for dozens of cases. Not everyone who leaves the country out of fear applies for asylum. Many White Zimbabweans can secure British or other European passports, which negates the need for asylum. Others opt to study abroad. Still, 35 percent is a significant proportion of people who have left their homes in fear and put themselves through a harrowing refugee application system.

In my sample, 55 percent of the participants had applied for asylum upon arrival. However, 12 percent were still waiting for the outcome of their application. The rest had acquired permanent residency or citizenship in the host country. The asylee rate was oversampled in my survey, which can be attributed to most of my respondents being Black Zimbabweans who resided in the United Kingdom or South Africa.

Nobert, a taxi driver in South Africa, applied for asylum in 2007, but as of 2014, he was still waiting for his case to be processed. As a result, he was unable to leave South Africa. Individuals who apply for refugee status are not permitted to return to their country of origin. This meant that over one million Zimbabweans who had applied for asylum could not participate in elections between 2000 and 2013.

The asylum application process can be very lengthy. For instance, Juliet, an active MDC member in the United States who arrived after escaping a violent attack in 2002, waited eight years before her refugee status was granted. Gogo, a sixty-two-year-old woman in the United Kingdom, was in the system from 2000 to 2018. Rose, in the United States after being a victim of political gang rape, was lucky that her process took only two years. After seven years in the United States, she was granted citizenship.

Many of the asylum seekers I interviewed shared a similar sentiment: They have no plans to return to Zimbabwe even after obtaining citizenship and passports from the host country. Those still in the process of applying for asylum risk losing their refugee status if they return home. Other individuals who have obtained citizenship in the host country retain the fear that drove them to flee their homes.

White Zimbabweans and their farm workers were brutally violated in the full view of global media, forcing most of them to leave home. Carla, who participated in the research from Cape Town, revealed that it was two years before that her family had full details on how her father died. Peter, a hotel manager in High Wycombe, had never considered himself British. Still, he was grateful for family connections in the United Kingdom when his farm just outside Bulawayo was attacked. Their ranch, including more than 200 cattle, was burned to ashes. Peter walks with a slight limp – what he calls his parting gift from home. Their fear of participating in politics at home was underpinned by ZANU-PF's assault on White Zimbabweans that stripped them of their citizenship and property during this period. Mugabe would routinely give speeches arguing that White Zimbabweans had no claim to their country of birth. At the ZANU-PF congress in 2000, he said, "Our party must continue to strike fear in the heart of the White man, our real enemy" (Chinaka, 2000). ZANU-PF targeted White farmers who either had real financial ties to the MDC or were rumored to have given financial support to the opposition. Like most Zimbabweans, White farmers had hoped the opposition could turn the economy around. Some of them, like Mariah, whose family owned one of the largest tobacco farms, had stopped giving patronage to ZANU PF and directed support to the opposition. When I asked White Zimbabweans whether they would join rallies in the diaspora, they all said no. The situation has continued to change in response to economic and political events in Zimbabwe, including the 2017 coup. Still, the majority, especially older White Zimbabweans, would prefer to disengage from home politics altogether.

Targeted violence, hunger, and poor prospects for employment drive young Black activists away from home, ultimately forcing them to exit the political system. Simon, now a lecturer at a university in Cape Town, was a student activist at the University of Zimbabwe. The day he left home, he had no final destination in mind. He was twenty-three years old and single, and he said this made him feel more confident about exploring the region for opportunities. Like most young migrants, he worked a menial job for six months, in his case cleaning trains in Botswana.

As violence against Zimbabwean nationals increased, he paid smugglers to deliver him to Johannesburg, where he joined a commune of homeless Zimbabweans for a year. A journalist, Wali, left Zimbabwe after the government attacked independent media houses. He had the phone number of a colleague in Cape Town. They had previously discussed that if he needed to escape, his colleague would give him shelter in South Africa. Unfortunately for Wali and countless poor migrants, his friend was no longer reachable. The day Wali arrived in Cape Town, after failing to reach his friend, Wali slept on a bench at the terminus, where he was mugged and then saved by a group of semihomeless Zimbabweans who lived under a bridge. When we visited the bridge in 2013, we met at least twenty young Zimbabwean men strung out on various drugs.

Many migrants sold their belongings to pay for passage to the host country. Upon arrival, most Zimbabweans lived under a shadow of fear: fear that the situation at home would further deteriorate, fear of being deported by the host country, and fear that the long arm of ZANU-PF's secret police would find them and cause them harm. Wali, Simon, and others who had finally carved out a decent life for themselves in South Africa did not want to risk their stable situations by actively engaging in politics. Wali said he missed journalism but did not believe the ruling party would change its ways. He, like Simon and Peter, did not think diaspora voices could make a difference politically. Wali was more interested in raising funds to bring his sister to join him in Cape Town.

Ineffective Transnational Political Organizing

The average Zimbabwean migrant is a young, urban, educated risk-taker. This is also the profile of citizens able to use their voices to demand political change. Most Zimbabweans who left home in the early 2000s had been active members of their trade unions and engaged in protests. Of those who emigrated after the 2000 elections, 70 percent of the minority who voted said they had voted for MDC. Those who left before the formation of the MDC and those who were not yet eligible to vote at the time of emigration reported they would have voted for the opposition. Voting against Mugabe and his ZANU-PF was a strong act of defiance.

Zimbabwean emigrants had been active protestors against the ZANU-PF regime. Over 40 percent of those I interviewed had successfully sought asylum in a host country. Political refugees included teachers targeted for using their influential position to share opposition news in their spheres of influence. A teacher from a school just outside Bulawayo escaped

Zimbabwe with nothing but his passport and a small bag of clothes in 2002 after it was discovered that he had mobilized for the MDC in his constituency. A university professor in Cape Town had escaped Zimbabwe via Botswana, relying on a deadly human trafficking network after his life was threatened for his role in the student protests at the University of Zimbabwe. Many of these firebrand activists' political careers died a quiet and frustrating death after they arrived in the host country. Unlike those in other diasporas, who actively challenged host governments to become involved in the politics of their home countries, the Zimbabwean diaspora was largely silent.

Leaders of diaspora political groups like MDC UK/US, Zimbabwe Associations in the United Kingdom/United States, Nehanda Radio, Zimbabwe human rights nongovernmental organizations (NGOs), and ZimVigil are generally driven by political motivations. The involvement of their members has been more transient and tied to personal motivations. The MDC chairman in the United States expressed concern that demands for papers directly influenced their membership numbers. Most of its regular dues-paying members were individuals applying for asylum. ZANU-PF membership in the diaspora has also been shaped by the political conditions in the home country, but most ZANU-PF supporters have stronger ideological ties to the party. Until the shifts in November 2017, ZANU-PF members in the diaspora operated in fear of being identified with a party generally shunned in Western countries.

The Zimbabwe-based political parties have failed to build strong ties with the diaspora community, and there is weak membership in MDC diaspora factions. The average migrant between 2000 and 2010 fell into Pasura's (2008) definition of a *dormant member*, one who is not active and would not participate in protests but is highly interested and knowledgeable about the political system at home. Fear of immigration law enforcement in the host country and imagined ZANU-PF agents played an important role in migrants' lack of political action. Respondents also said they did not feel the MDC was interested in recruiting them for membership. Tsvangirai and the MDC leadership did not hold major rallies in the diaspora between 2000 and 2010. MDC diaspora offices were not officially recognized by the party until 2006. Charles, thirty-six, left Bulawayo in 2005, where he had been an active MDC youth organizer in his community. Charles said on arrival in the United Kingdom he had hoped to connect with other "brothers from the movement and strategize ways we could send money back home and other equipment to retaliate Operation Murambatsvina, but when I landed I couldn't feel the political energy. Everyone was tired. It was all about the shifts." Diaspora politics has been very fragmented, but there is great variation in this. Zimbabwe opposition politics in the United States has not been active, and Zimbabwe-based officials had their first US tours after the formation of the unity government. The US diaspora is more spread out than the UK diaspora and much more difficult to organize.

Continuing fissures within the opposition MDC party structures in the home country that began with the 2005 split and worsened following Tsvangirai's death in 2017 have had a negative impact on diaspora political activity. Migrants tend to settle in areas where there is a large population of their social network. Zimbabwean migrants, except those who emigrated primarily for education or work opportunities, tend to live near family or friends from home, so the diaspora is loosely divided by regional ties. Ndebele MDC activists interviewed in the diaspora revealed that many in their community felt the split within the MDC had occurred along tribal lines. Vucha said, "Most of us where really shocked that Tsvangirai had fallen out with Gibson Sibanda, it felt as though Ndebele contributions are not appreciated." In the United States, the MDC office in Washington, DC, was run by Ndebele officials who had facilitated asylum for hundreds of Zimbabweans. An MDC official in Washington said, "We will keep working with the party, but most of our people feel a little disappointed." Many Ndebeles I spoke to felt more than a little disappointed. Although they did not support the secessionist movement Mtwakhazi, they felt detached from Zimbabwean politics. In South Africa, those who speak Ndebele had an easier time with assimilating and took extra efforts to claim a South African identity because of xenophobic attacks against foreigners. In the end, a combination of poor party mobilization by the party and fear of the state (host and home) resulted in very weak transnational activity.

Migrant Financial Pressures

The diaspora was aware of the twin crises happening in Zimbabwe. In the mid-2000s, the Zimbabwean government had become more repressive. Many in the diaspora had family members who were directly affected by the government's draconian rules, including the infamous Operation Murambatsvina, which left nearly a million residents in cities homeless. The political crisis resulted in a more immediate and tangible economic crisis. The twin economic and political push factors that had forced more than two million people into exile could not be addressed immediately.

Zimbabweans living abroad have kept close ties with Zimbabwean politics, their family, and friends by regularly communicating through phone calls, emails, and social media. The political and economic conditions that forced people to leave home remained an important line of conversation. The diaspora received phone calls when the cost of bread went up and when the government bulldozed their homes. Most respondents said they clearly remembered that family members impressed on them the importance of staying safe and sending money home as soon as possible. This was true for adults and young people who emigrated between the ages of fifteen and twenty-five. The pressure to remit money was very high. Over 60 percent of Zimbabwean households received remittances (Bracking & Sachikonye, 2006; Chikanda, 2005).

When Zimbabweans arrived in the host country, their first order of business was finding a job so they could remit money back to their families. One woman, who was working as a nurse in Scotland, said that upon arrival from Zimbabwe she had thought she would have time to relax. She was shocked when her cousin told her she had two hours to shower and go to her first shift at a nearby gas station. In Zimbabwe, she had worked as an office administrator, so she had no retail industry experience, but she was informed that she needed to pay back her ticket, contribute to room and board, and send money back home. The average migrant had sold their property in Zimbabwe to purchase their ticket, benefited from various crowdsourcing initiatives, or both. Upon arrival, there was an expectation that individuals would repay the £800–1,200 spent on their ticket and to contribute to the public funding pool for future migrants.

No Time for Activism

The study of mental fatigue among immigrants is new and beyond the scope of this study, but migrants often face multiple burdens. The dual political and economic push factors have severe implications for transnational politics. The African diaspora has been credited with providing the financial support needed for political transitions in the home country. In the Zimbabwean case, diaspora members, especially those in the United Kingdom, joined opposition parties and their dues were remitted back home to support the ongoing fight for democracy. Zimbabwean transnational politics was never nearly powerful or influential enough to oust Mugabe, who was forced out by his own party in 2017.

A thirty-three-year-old MDC activist named Jerry, who I interviewed in Glasgow, Scotland, said he was surprised by how quickly his political aspirations ended once he arrived in the diaspora. When he arrived in Glasgow in 2005, a friend picked him up from the airport and took him to his home. His friend's group was one of the first to resettle in Scotland, away from the hustle of greater London. Upon arrival, Jerry shared his experiences of the hardship caused by Operation Murambatsvina and the destruction in high-density areas in Mbare and Epworth. However, instead of asking how they could help the people back home, his comrades asked him what kind of job he preferred to have.

Jerry had assumed that he would begin organizing strategies to overthrow ZANU-PF. However, his brothers-in-arms told him the diaspora was about making money, and they needed to work to survive. The monthly government subsidy for refugees was not enough to cover their bills, so they had to hustle. Jerry's political career ended the day he arrived in Scotland. Over the years, he would rise in MDC local membership, but the activism was different. They spent most of their time preparing fellow Zimbabweans for asylum applications. They raised money for the party from membership cards sold to desperate asylum seekers. They participated in demonstrations at the embassy, but he said this was not activism but performance activism. Many passionate activists have traded politics for survival.

In the early 2000s, a group of Zimbabweans in Portland, Oregon, formed Zimbabweans in the United States (ZUSA). The organization aimed to provide a meeting place where the diaspora could discuss politics and the economy and find practical ways to help people in the home country. There were multiple ZUSA outfits scattered around the United States, with those in large Eastern metropolises boasting the largest numbers. The model for ZUSA was borrowed from community groups popular with the West African and Caribbean diasporas. Their organization met once a month, rotating locations among member houses. The group was predominantly Ndebele. The groups discussed politics, but challenges with securing legal status and family problems often dominated meetings. The brutality of the ZANU-PF regime was always at the back of people's minds, but the immediate challenges of settling in a new country and sending money home often took priority.

MIGRATION REDUCED VOTES FOR THE OPPOSITION

It is much more challenging to capture migration data than death rates. Countries usually survey people at borders to determine the number of migrants, but collecting data from all ports is not always feasible and some do not enter using legal routes. The number of issued visas may indicate how many people enter a country, but it is unreliable because not everyone who gets a visa enters or leaves the country at the end of their visa. Census data is helpful but expensive, and it is collected less frequently. Moreover, migrants keep moving beyond their first destination. In developing countries with scarce resources and borders that are more porous, capturing migration data is even more problematic. Zimbabwe is a perfect example of this trend. Most Zimbabwean migrants went to South Africa, where many remain undocumented. Therefore, available data is likely to underestimate the actual population of Zimbabweans living abroad. The International Organization for Migration reports a broad range for the Zimbabwe migrant population, ranging from two to four million.

To ensure consistency in my analysis, I have once again relied on the Joint United Nations Program on HIV/AIDS (UNAIDS) Spectrum model to estimate the number of people who exited the country due to migration. The migration data used in this model were collected from multiple sources, making it one of the most trustworthy sources for migration data in Zimbabwe. The Spectrum data capture the annual population of migrants over time and allowed me to analyze consistent data. However, the data are not perfect. The Spectrum data underestimate the population of migrants and overrepresent certain provinces. It is highly unlikely that Midlands has experienced the same rate of migration as Harare. Moreover, migration data were not reported between 1983 and 1992 (see Figure 4.2), during which Zimbabweans certainly emigrated. As someone whose mother was a cross-border trader traveling to South Africa from the 1960s until 1999, I can attest that many women who do such work sometimes use unconventional methods to get their visas. The lives of their families depended on their ability to cross the border to do their work; often, they cannot afford to wait.

In this section, I use available migration data from the UNAIDS Spectrum project for voting-eligible Zimbabweans. I assume that if they had been able to vote, they would have done so at turnout rates consistent with the overall population. To determine what proportion of migrants would have voted for the opposition, I drew on data from the asylum database, Afrobarometer, and my surveys. At least 35 percent of Zimbabweans have applied for political asylum, claiming they left home due to the threat posed by their support for the opposition party. The Afrobarometer surveys did not ask questions about intention to emigrate during the peak years of migration; hence, I rely solely on my surveys to

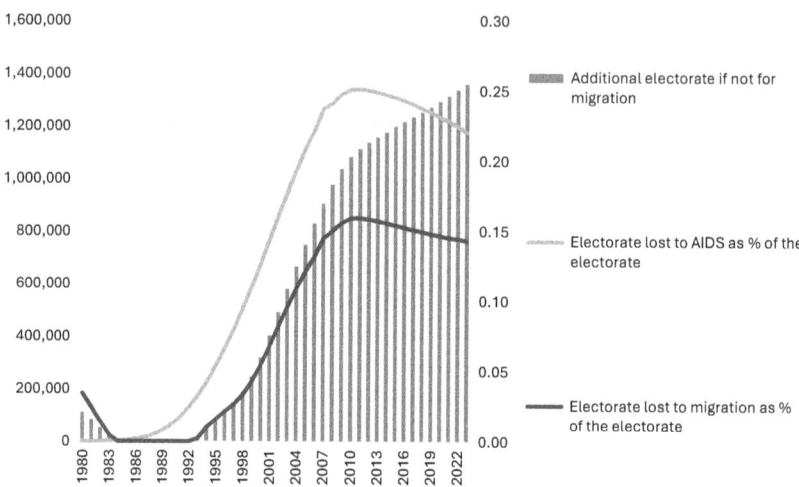

FIGURE 4.2 Total outward migration from Zimbabwe, 1980–2022. *Source*: Data from UNAIDS Spectrum model.

estimate how migrants would have voted had they not left between 2000 and 2013. I estimate that 85 percent of migrants would have voted for the opposition. This figure likely underestimates the proportion that would have voted for the opposition. Among those I interviewed, only 17 percent indicated support for the ruling party, but I recognize that my sample of 100 interviewees is too small to be generalized to the entire electorate.

To calculate the exit premium from migration, I multiply the alternative electorate (the total of those who migrated) by the turnout in the election to calculate the number of additional voters. I then assume that 85 percent of the additional votes within each province would have gone to the opposition. In formal terms, the calculation is:

Additional votes for Party X = migrants × turnout × 85%.

To illustrate this in round numbers, say that 100,000 citizens in a province emigrated by a particular election. If turnout in the actual electorate was 80 percent, then I assume an additional 80,000 Zimbabweans would have voted in that election if they had not migrated. I assume 15 percent of the migrants would have voted for the ruling party and 85 percent would have voted for the opposition because migrants are disproportionately more likely to support the opposition. In that province, that translates to 68,000 votes for the opposition and 12,000 for the regime – a net margin of 56,000 for the opposition. By repeating this across electoral districts, I calculate each election's net gain for the opposition. If this had happened, perhaps the regime would have stolen the election through violence or fraud, but the migration exit premium, like the HIV exit premium in Chapter 3, allowed ZANU-PF to survive without being more ruthless.

By 2000, around 319,539 migrants had left the electorate (see Table 4.1). If their turnout were consistent with that of actual voters, then an additional 162,519 votes would have been cast – 24,378 for ZANU-PF and 113,763 for the opposition. This would have resulted in an increase of 4 percent in opposition returns, which would have marginally changed the seats received by the opposition.

By 2002, the total number of people who had exited the electorate was estimated to be 491,907 (see Table 4.2). Assuming that the turnout was consistent with the real population, an additional 295,199 would have voted, 44,280 for ZANU-PF and 250,920 for the opposition. The net gain to the opposition would have been 206,664, which would have increased its share to 48 percent. This would not have been enough to force a runoff, but it would have bolstered the opposition for the next election.

By 2005, the total number of people who had exited the electorate was estimated to be 749,650 (see Table 4.3). Assuming that the turnout was consistent with the real population, an additional 357,227 would have voted, 53,584 for ZANU-PF and 303,643 for the opposition. The net opposition gain would have been 250,059, which would have increased opposition returns by just under 8 percent, likely changing the number of seats won by the opposition. Most of the migrants probably came from opposition-supporting districts and more of their votes would have benefited the opposition.

By 2008, the migrant population had grown to 16 percent of the electorate (see Table 4.4). Nearly a million eligible voters had left the country, decreasing the total number of people who voted in the election. Assuming that the turnout was consistent with the real population, an additional 462,622 would have voted, 69,393 for ZANU-PF and 323,835 for the opposition. This would have increased the opposition returns by 11 percent, which would have been enough to change the outcome of the heavily disputed 2008 election. The opposition led by Tsvangirai would have crossed over the runoff threshold.

By 2013, the migrant population had grown to well over a million people, 38 percent of the electorate (see Table 4.5). Assuming that turnout was consistent with the actual population, an additional 639,716 would have voted – 95,957 for ZANU-PF and 543,758 for the opposition. This

TABLE 4.1 *2000 parliamentary elections**

Province	Votes cast	Migrated electorate	Additional voters	ZANU gain	Opposition gain	Exit premium
Midlands	350,505	45,723	27,224	4,084	23,141	19,057
Matebeleland South	159,579	18,107	11,654	1,748	9,906	8,158
Matebeleland North	147,828	23,002	14,035	2,105	11,929	9,824
Masvingo	286,741	41,256	23,748	3,562	20,186	16,624
Mashonaland West	246,783	34,122	14,554	2,183	12,371	10,188
Mashonaland East	278,221	31,109	16,066	2,410	13,656	11,246
Mashonaland Central	247,953	26,119	15,660	2,349	13,311	10,962
Manicaland	272,909	43,354	19,664	2,950	16,715	13,765
Harare	394,073	42,121	12,966	1,945	11,021	9,076
Bulawayo	171,669	14,626	6,947	1,042	5,905	4,863
Total	2,556,261	319,539	162,519	24,378	138,141	113,763

Note. Data from UN Spectrum, ZEC, ZESN; *Only parliamentary election. Healthy electorate = Not sick or healthy enough to vote because on ART, per Spectrum; Exited electorate = Dead or too sick to vote (not on ART), per Spectrum; Additional voters = Alternative electorate multiplied by turnout.

TABLE 4.2 2002 presidential elections*

Province	Votes cast	Migrated electorate	Additional voters	ZANU gain	Opposition gain	Exit premium
Midlands	418,024	31,136	56,738	8,511	48,228	39,717
Matebeleland South	162,179	27,208	17,463	2,619	14,844	12,224
Matebeleland North	175,935	34,644	24,382	3,657	20,725	17,068
Masvingo	372,095	62,471	44,748	6,712	38,036	31,324
Mashonaland West	322,641	51,067	27,676	4,151	23,525	19,373
Mashonaland East	349,565	46,638	29,380	4,407	24,973	20,566
Mashonaland Central	300,613	39,318	27,811	4,172	23,639	19,467
Manicaland	355,954	65,436	37,569	5,635	31,933	26,298
Harare	412,935	62,395	19,814	2,972	16,841	13,869
Bulawayo	162,616	21,593	9,619	1,443	8,176	6,733
Total	3,032,557	491,907	295,199	44,280	250,920	206,640

Note. Data from UN Spectrum, ZEC, ZESN; *Only presidential election. Healthy electorate = Not sick or healthy enough to vote because on ART, per Spectrum; Exited electorate = Dead or too sick to vote (not on ART), per Spectrum; Additional voters = Alternative electorate multiplied by turnout.

TABLE 4.3 *2005 parliamentary elections**

Province	Votes cast	Migrated electorate	Additional voters	ZANU gain	Opposition gain	Exit premium
Midlands	311,003	144,603	73,912	11,087	62,825	51,738
Matebeleland South	107,667	40,100	16,359	2,454	13,905	11,451
Matebeleland North	144,444	51,329	27,885	4,183	23,702	19,520
Masvingo	319,178	93,187	53,524	8,029	45,495	37,466
Mashonaland West	286,576	74,975	34,192	5,129	29,063	23,935
Mashonaland East	285,844	68,622	33,379	5,007	28,372	23,365
Mashonaland Central	272,217	58,199	35,319	5,298	30,021	24,723
Manicaland	338,813	96,870	50,130	7,519	42,610	35,091
Harare	347,043	90,518	23,465	3,520	19,945	16,425
Bulawayo	108,065	31,247	9,063	1,359	7,704	6,344
Total	2,520,850	749,650	357,227	53,584	303,643	250,059

Note: Data from UN Spectrum, ZEC, ZESN; *Only parliamentary election. Healthy electorate = Not sick or healthy enough to vote because on ART, per Spectrum; Exited electorate = Dead or too sick to vote (not on ART), per Spectrum; Additional voters = Alternative electorate multiplied by turnout.

TABLE 4.4 *2008 presidential election**

Province	Votes cast	Migrated electorate	Additional voters	ZANU gain	Opposition gain	Exit premium
Midlands	341,787	214,098	118,424	17,764	100,661	82,897
Matebeleland South	119,183	50,821	21,631	3,245	18,386	15,142
Matebeleland North	151,112	65,285	34,366	5,155	29,211	24,057
Masvingo	316,245	119,058	63,146	9,472	53,674	44,202
Mashonaland West	255,161	94,535	35,944	5,392	30,552	25,160
Mashonaland East	292,734	86,512	40,116	6,017	34,099	28,081
Mashonaland Central	316,245	73,764	48,689	7,303	41,385	34,082
Manicaland	369,098	122,743	64,993	9,749	55,244	45,495
Harare	313,995	112,442	25,553	3,833	21,720	17,887
Bulawayo	96,685	38,608	9,758	1,464	8,295	6,831
Total	2,572,245	977,866	462,622	69,393	393,228	323,835

Note: Data from UN Spectrum, ZEC, ZESN. *Only presidential election. Healthy electorate = Not sick or healthy enough to vote because on ART, per Spectrum; Exited electorate = Dead or too sick to vote (not on ART), per Spectrum; Additional voters = Alternative electorate multiplied by turnout.

TABLE 4.5 *2013 election**

Province	Votes cast	Migrated electorate	Additional voters	ZANU gain	Opposition gain	Exit premium
Midlands	323,704	188,991	109,609	16,441	93,167	76,726
Matebeleland South	109,629	64,734	33,627	5,044	28,583	23,539
Matebeleland North	148,902	83,519	52,091	7,814	44,277	36,464
Masvingo	314,752	153,054	96,205	14,431	81,774	67,343
Mashonaland West	245,512	120,257	63,645	9,547	54,098	44,551
Mashonaland East	288,791	109,944	65,923	9,889	56,035	46,146
Mashonaland Central	228,581	94,030	67,299	10,095	57,204	47,109
Manicaland	348,953	156,662	93,703	14,056	79,648	65,592
Harare	311,386	140,230	41,656	6,248	35,407	29,159
Bulawayo	84,917	47,824	15,958	2,394	13,564	11,170
Total	3,378,320	1,159,244	639,716	95,957	543,758	447,801

Note: Data from UN Spectrum, ZEC, ZESN; *Harmonized election. Healthy electorate = Not sick or healthy enough to vote because on ART, per Spectrum; Exited electorate = Dead or too sick to vote (not on ART), per Spectrum; Additional voters = Alternative electorate multiplied by turnout.

would have increased the opposition returns by 447,801 (11 percent), which would have been enough to change the outcome of the 2013 election again in favor of the opposition.

The diaspora had many reasons to be pleased with the opposition. Under the national unity government, the opposition stabilized the economy. Each political party was assigned ministries to manage. MDC received the finance and education portfolios. The economy steadily improved as Tendai Biti, the MDC finance minister, introduced the use of American currency. In the diaspora, people felt more hopeful that the economy would improve under the MDC, which would reduce the financial burden on themselves. Many people did not go home due to the various costs associated with returning home to vote. They still expressed great disappointment that the MDC had not done better in the 2013 elections.

CONCLUSION

Authoritarian regimes have been reluctant to expand voting rights to citizens living abroad (Lafleur, 2013). Zimbabwe does not allow such citizens to vote, which disenfranchises the estimated two to four million Zimbabweans who by now are living abroad. Most of these Zimbabwean emigrants could not return home to participate for fear of political violence or because of the high costs associated with travel. Zimbabwean transnational voting is also limited because many migrants have not legalized their status and live in fear of deportation.

The massive wave of emigration from Zimbabwe was sudden. Most of them had not made long-term plans to emigrate. Most anticipated returning home soon to participate in politics (Pasura, 2008, 2010). Vucha, an activist teacher, explained:

> I never thought I would leave Zimbabwe. I was a teacher just outside Bulawayo. My entire family – my brothers are all here with me – we are educated. We went to the UK. We are a family of professionals. I owned a house and a car. But they were targeting teachers, and accused us of conscientizing rural folks, so I left.

While the massive wave of emigration in the early 2000s was not explicitly a ZANU-PF strategy, the party benefited from the exit of MDC supporters. Whether forced or voluntary, the exit of a large cohort of young, educated, professional, urban, risk-taking Zimbabweans like Vucha and his six brothers, who have been unable to participate in elections since 2000, contributed to ZANU-PF's hold on political power.

The migration of millions of Zimbabweans benefited the ruling party. As might be expected from Hirschman's theory on the impact of exit, voice, and loyalty on politics, when voters vote with their feet, their exit changes the political outcomes of the country they leave. Their exit does not necessarily mean the end of voice, but it becomes severely muffled, especially for those who cannot go home and vote. Migration benefits authoritarian regimes in countries like Zimbabwe, where external voting is not allowed.

I analyzed these patterns using data from Afrobarometer and the UNAIDS Spectrum project, which cover Zimbabwe from 1999 to 2023 and HIV and migration from 1980 to 2023, respectively. I interviewed ten Zimbabweans living in four countries: the United Kingdom, the United States, South Africa, and Zimbabwe. My research indicates that ZANU-PF enjoyed an exit premium of 4–10 percent in elections between 2000 and 2013. The large waves of outward migration disproportionately affected the opposition because most of those who left matched the profile of its supporters: young, urban, educated, and in the professional and working classes.

Over the past twenty years, ZANU-PF has restricted political participation by Zimbabweans living abroad by prohibiting voting from overseas. Apart from these legal barriers, the diaspora cannot vote due to the high cost of returning home, and some do not have the legal status to be able to return home and vote. In Chapter 5, I will demonstrate that the remittances the diaspora sends home while having a positive impact on individual lives also dampen political participation of receivers thus bolstering ZANU-PF rule.

5

Remittances and ZANU-PF Survival

In the previous chapter, I discussed how the demographics of immigrants in the United Kingdom changed over time. At first, there were more people from the Caribbean than from Zimbabwe, but then the number of Zimbabweans increased. Later, more Eastern Europeans started immigrating. Despite their differences, they all had a common practice: on Fridays after work, they would go to the bank or Western Union to send money home, consistently remitting about 80 percent of their pay every week. I befriended a young woman in her twenties who worked part-time at a hotel. Her aunt had advised her to keep only £20 for her weekly expenses and send the rest back home to Zimbabwe. To save on living expenses and be able to remit more money home, most migrants shared a room with friends.

The cash foreign workers sent home as remittances kept our immediate and extended families alive. As Zimbabwe faced its worst financial crisis – inflation was over 79,600,000,000 percent and rising – those with family members abroad had access to money for basics. Rarely would the money go toward building a home; mostly, it was spent on food, tuition, and health care. While the diaspora was not developing the country by building skyscrapers, they invested in their families. This investment reduced citizen demands on the government.

After being impressed with the impact of remittances, I began to consider its political implications. Over the years, the diaspora's relationship with their home country's politics has evolved, ranging from passionate involvement, hopeful expectations, and enthusiastic anticipation to complete exhaustion. However, during the first decade after leaving Zimbabwe, it seemed almost every Zimbabwean I met was talking about politics. The conversation was the same among Ndebeles, Shonas, and those from urban or rural backgrounds: something must change. In the 2000s, there was a burst of online newspapers like newzimbabwe.com, run by veteran journalists who had been forced out of the country by Robert Mugabe's brutal regime. The online papers kept us abreast of events at home and provided the millions living far from home an avenue to discuss politics passionately but anonymously. Transnational engagement and remittances positively impacted opposition politics by providing direct financial resources and lobbying in foreign countries, yet ZANU-PF continued to win elections. I wondered whether the remittances that over four million Zimbabweans living abroad sent home had bolstered the regime.

In this chapter, I offer a detailed explanation of my fourth modification of Hirschman's EVL. I argue that remittances can function as a type of loyalty that strengthens a regime. I argue that diaspora remittances sustained the authoritarian ZANU-PF regime in three ways. First, migrants' pressure to remit money home reduced their capacity to participate in elections. Second, remittances dampened the political participation of receivers. Finally, remittances benefited the government because the regime could skim taxes and direct funds to its narrow base of supporters.

The chapter is divided into several parts. First, I provide a brief overview of the literature on remittances. After that, I illustrate the flow of remittances from the early 2000s to 2022. Next, I use longitudinal data from Afrobarometer to show the profile of remittance receivers and the impact of remittances on their political actions, including voting, protesting, and contacting political officials. Receivers are more likely to be young, urban, educated, and opposition supporters. They are more likely to engage in nonvisible political activities, such as contacting a political official, but less likely to vote or join a protest.

The impact of remittances on an individual level is discussed through an in-depth analysis of five case studies of individuals and their families in Zimbabwe, along with data from multiple sources. The economic pressures associated with being a low-income immigrant, their often-insecure legal status, and significant financial obligations to family in Zimbabwe have changed some of the diaspora's perceptions about home politics over time. During the early stages of the crisis in Zimbabwe, parents of young adults used remittances to discourage receivers from getting involved in politics, as political violence was on the rise. Parents who had managed to escape the oppression of ZANU-PF wanted to protect their children from becoming targets. However, over the years, senders hoped their family members might become more involved and that change would be brought by their participation. They hoped such changes would reduce the burden on themselves. These findings are based on a small sample size and may not be representative of all diaspora experiences; nevertheless, they support findings from larger Afrobarometer surveys.

REMITTANCES AND THE POLITICS OF THE COUNTRIES OF ORIGIN

According to a 2023 World Bank report, global remittances have grown from about $2 billion in 1970 to an estimated $669 billion (Ratha, 2024). Despite the pandemic that caused economic disruptions for most families, the flow of remittances has increased, exceeding foreign aid and foreign direct investments (FDI) to developing countries. Net global remittances, which are almost three times the development aid provided to developing countries, continue to play a crucial role in preventing poverty in these nations. In 2023, remittances flowing into Sub-Saharan countries, including Zimbabwe, increased by 1.9 percent to $54 billion (World Bank, 2023).

The impact of migration on both the economics and politics of the destination and origin countries is complex. Some economists believe brain drain, which results from the loss of skilled migrants, is harmful to countries of origin. However, other analysts argue that migration can have positive effects. For instance, Abduvaliev and Bustillo (2020) found that in post-Soviet countries, a 1 percent increase in remittances led to a 0.25 percent decrease in poverty. Bukari et al.'s (2021) research on the impact of remittances on Ghanaian families supported earlier findings by Adams and Cuecuecha (2013): families receiving remittances are more likely to avoid poverty than those who do not receive them. Additionally, Gao et al. (2021) observed that remittances can be used for development purposes rather than just consumption. Meanwhile, studies such as Song et al. (2021) and Ferdaous (2016) have reported conflicting results, suggesting remittances can increase income inequality between the rich and the poor. Although my research primarily focuses on the impact of remittances on political behavior, my findings can help clarify the complex relationship between remittances and income inequality. In the last chapter, I show that those who emigrate are often young, educated, and middle class. Therefore, it is reasonable to assume that well-off families will receive more remittances. There is a growing interest and literature on the relationship between remittances and political institutions in the sending countries (Abdih et al., 2012; Escribà-Folch et al., 2015). This literature expands traditional migration studies that focus on the economic impact of emigration on the sending countries. The literature on the relationship between remittances and democracy is split almost evenly between scholars who argue remittances advance democracy and those who argue remittances are bad for democracy.

Some studies suggest the diaspora can contribute to economic growth and positively impact the development of strong democratic institutions in their home countries. Essentially, the diaspora can promote democracy back home (Batista & Vicente, 2011; Docquier et al., 2011; Lodigiani & Salomone, 2012; Pfutze, 2012). Scholars believe the diaspora can promote democracy because those who have left are more likely to adopt the democratic beliefs of the host country. Then, they will influence the beliefs of their friends and family back home by introducing them to new beliefs on governance. The diaspora can also directly impact home politics by supporting the opposition or funding political revolutions, as was seen in the Middle East during the Arab Spring. Escribà-Folch et al. (2015) argued that remittances reduce electoral support for authoritarian regimes because they mitigate the impact of clientelism and patronage politics.

On the other hand, large flows of remittance money into a poor, politically unstable country have been shown to have the same debilitating effects on democratization as the natural resource curse and aid revenue (Abdih et al., 2012; Tyburski, 2014). Natural resource curse scholars have found that when governments have access to large sums of nontax revenues, they can use those funds to buy political support and repress the political participation of opponents (Boas et al., 2014; Gettleman, 2011; Morrison, 2009). D. Moyo (2009) argued that instead of voting for African leaders, Africans should vote for one of the many aid agencies that sustain African lives. D. Moyo (2009) argued that the huge flows of aid into African countries foster corruption and dependency. With regard to the impact of remittances on African politics, work by Dionne and Inman (2014) supports my finding that remittances suppress voting behavior but can increase political activities like contacting a political official. In more democratic and wealthier countries, remittances can improve democratic policies (Bearce & Park, 2019; Williams, 2017).

Due to data challenges, it is difficult to establish a clear causal link between remittances and increased democratization or stabilized authoritarianism. However, this study aims to explore how remittances affect politics in unstable, poor regimes. Sending money often leads immigrants to exit the political space, receiving money can dampen receivers'

Remittances into Zimbabwe

participation, and large sums of free money can provide a lifeline for authoritarian regimes dealing with an agitated citizenry.

REMITTANCES INTO ZIMBABWE

The puzzle at the heart of this project is how ZANU-PF managed to maintain power through the worst economic crisis in Zimbabwe's history. According to economic voting literature, voters tend to vote against the incumbent if the economy is not doing well (Anderson, 2000; Lewis-Beck & Stegmaier, 2007). However, I show that remittances from the diaspora provided a financial lifeline for the struggling regime. Those receiving money from abroad did not tend to protest or vote against the regime but rather withdrew from the political process. While most Zimbabweans were unemployed, between two and four million were employed outside the country and regularly sent back money.

When the Zimbabwean economy was at its worst, remittances played a vital role in rescuing the government and its citizens. Although there are no exact figures for the amount of money flowing into the country as remittances, available data suggest that since 2000, remittances have made up over 10 percent of the annual GDP (see Figure 5.1). With over a quarter of the adult and working-age population living and working abroad, almost 60 percent of households in Zimbabwe rely on remittances as their primary source of income.

The official data on the flow of remittances into Zimbabwe is incomplete because some of these transfers are not tracked. Figure 5.2 illustrates

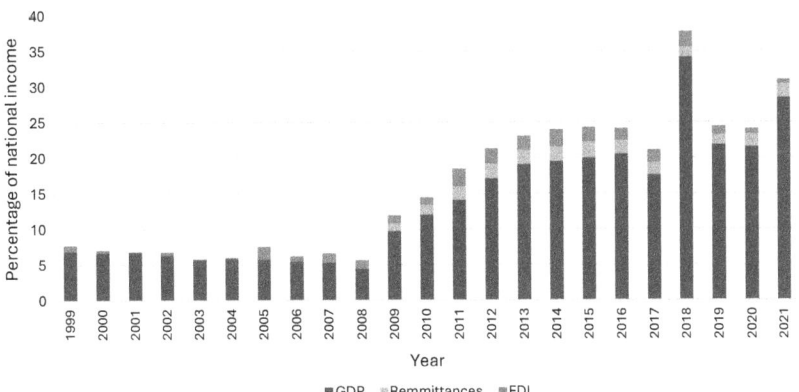

FIGURE 5.1 Zimbabwe sources of income, 1999–2012: GDP, remittances, and FDI.
Source: Data from World Bank.

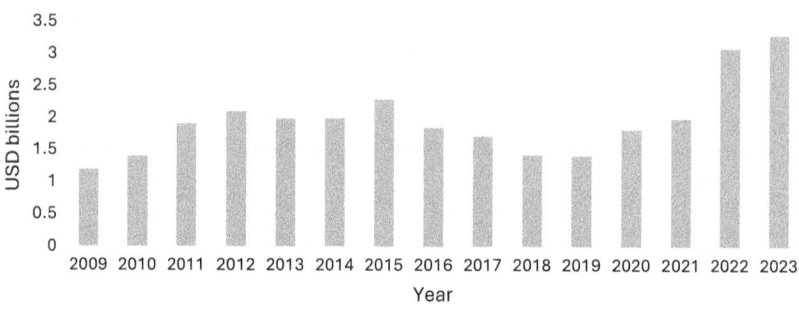

FIGURE 5.2 Zimbabwe personal remittances received. *Source*: Data from World Bank.

that before 2009, the World Bank had no formal data on remittances, even though migrants had been sending money back home. This was not because remittances were not being sent but because the government had implemented policies that forced people to use less formal transfer methods. Once formal transfers resumed, official data became available, but the data do not account for all transfers into the country. The Zimbabwean government claims annual remittances to the country have averaged $1 billion over the last decade. In some years, remittances made up 4–10 percent of the GDP; in others, as shown in Figure 5.1, they have exceeded FDI. According to World Bank data, remittance receipts accounted for a higher percentage of the GDP between 2009 and 2013, when inflation was at its highest.

Zimbabwe's staggering inflation and constant currency changes make it difficult to have an accurate picture, but there is no denying that remittances have been a substantial part of the national economy. Conservative estimates from 2000 to 2016 indicate remittances comprised over 14 percent of the country's GDP (Karombo, 2022). Meanwhile, revenue from agriculture, Zimbabwe's main source of income, has declined, as have returns from FDI (see Figure 5.3). Remittances have been the only consistent source of revenue for Zimbabwe, providing the struggling ZANU-PF government with a crucial financial cushion to sustain their rule. Unlike FDI and donor aid, remittances are not conditioned on the government's behavior.

In 2016, officials from the Reserve Bank of Zimbabwe reported FDI had fallen by 23 percent to $421 million since 2014, while remittances almost doubled to $835 million in the first half of 2016 (Mhanga & Ndebele, 2016). These figures include only formally reported transfers

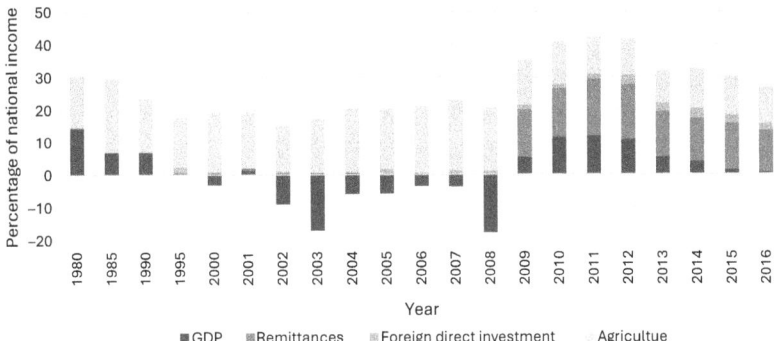

FIGURE 5.3 Zimbabwe economy: GDP, remittances, FDI, and agriculture, 1980–2016.
Note: Percentage of the national income generated from GDP, remittances, direct investment, and agriculture.
Source: Data from World Bank.

in years where data is available. The actual growth in remittance transfers is likely greater. As economic and political conditions in Zimbabwe got worse, more migrants remitted money home. These remittances funded the survival of ZANU-PF. At a time when the country was not producing any goods for export, the ZANU-PF regime had a steady foreign currency income. Figure 5.3 shows the impact of remittances, which became the second major source of national revenue after agriculture as the economy declined.

Although remittances have had a positive impact on Zimbabwe's economy, they have negatively affected its politics. The ZANU-PF government found a way to tax remittances and channel the money into the struggling government. To do so, the government increased taxes on remitting agencies such as Western Union and MoneyGram. In 2005, the government even banned all international remitting agencies to force the diaspora to send money via the Central Bank of Zimbabwe. However, this plan failed, and the diaspora resorted to black market trading to send money back home. The government realized it could not tax the black market and relicensed the remitting agents – but with a condition. Until 2008, all money remitted to Zimbabwe could only be issued in Zimbabwean dollars, which were worthless due to hyperinflation.

In the early 2000s, a few hundred Zimbabweans settled in the United Kingdom and set up transfer offices where Zimbabweans in London could go and hand over cash. This was before transfer agencies like Western Union had opened offices in Zimbabwe. The Londoners would notify someone in their Harare office that the sender's family members would be coming to collect the cash. At first, people would get the remittance in Zimbabwean dollars, but as inflation skyrocketed, people received their transfer in British pounds.

Around 2004, the government banned Western companies, including news agencies like BBC and CNN and formal transfer companies like Western Union. The government was aware that the diaspora was remitting a lot of money into the country, and it hoped to capture the wealth with their programs through the Zimbabwe Reserve Bank. However, people did not trust the government, and the programs did not have much uptake. A transfer agency program initiated by the government, HomeLink, was promoted by Reserve Bank Governor Gedion Gono as a safe way for the diaspora to channel their remittances into the country (New Humanitarian, 2005). Before the launch of HomeLink in 2004, Gono traveled to the United States and the United Kingdom to sell his program to the diaspora. *The Herald* (2004) defined the program: "The new money transfer system was put in place to facilitate the transfer of funds from Zimbabweans living abroad, many of whom want to send money home to help their families or to invest for when they eventually return home themselves." The cash-strapped central bank opened foreign bank accounts where the diaspora could deposit funds to be remitted to their families or to purchase a property. Before the establishment of HomeLink, less than $1 million was transmitted via the government, but soon after its launch, more than $61 million was transmitted via the Reserve Bank in 2004 (Zanamwe & Devillard, 2009). The increase in remittances coming through HomeLink was primarily because the government had banned other international agencies during that time.

The HomeLink project aimed to help Zimbabweans living abroad purchase a house in their home country. In early 2023, World Remit, a money transfer agency, approached me to partner with them on data collection. The project required me to contact fifty Zimbabweans who had made remittance transfers in January 2023 and gather their opinions on the agency. In return, World Remit would provide me with tallies of those individuals' transfers. One of the remitters had sent money at least eight times a month, so I contacted them and asked why. I inquired whether they were involved in a construction project, as most people who remit money tend to be trying to build a home. The respondent, Chiedza, a doctor and young mother of two, laughed and said, "I am building, not a house, but my relatives." That was my aha moment.

Before the HomeLink program was established, the Zimbabwean diaspora had limited access to money transfer agencies. HomeLink allowed Zimbabweans living abroad to borrow money from the Reserve Bank to build homes for themselves and their families back home. The government was also anxious to address the 1.5 million housing unit backlog. Within the first year of the program being established, the government reported that more than "2,000 Zimbabweans living abroad have bought considerable properties back home. A total of USD 55 million was generated in Zimbabwe through the HomeLink initiative" (*The Herald*, 2004).

However, HomeLink faced opposition from some in the diaspora, who argued that the government was desperate for ways to channel foreign exchange into their empty coffers. The opposition MDC also heavily campaigned against HomeLink among the diaspora. HomeLink did not work very well for several reasons, but the top two were corruption and lack of buy-in among the diaspora.

The ban on money transfer agencies had a negative impact on the daily lives of Zimbabwean citizens. For instance, when a friend of mine was accepted into a scholarship program in the United States Achievers Program (USAP) that helped high-achieving, low-income students apply to top universities worldwide, her family could not afford even a one-way ticket abroad. My mother agreed to help and offered to purchase my friend's ticket to attend college in Connecticut. However, when my sister went to collect the money from Western Union, she was told that the government had banned them from remitting foreign exchange. My sister refused to accept Zimbabwean dollars, knowing that inflation made them worthless and all airlines had banned them. My sister spent the next month going to the Reserve Bank governor's office every morning to ask him to change the policy regarding foreign exchange at Western Union. The governor, impressed by my sister's determination, gave us the needed foreign exchange himself. It was a mix of US dollars and British pounds. The ban on money transfer agencies lasted for about a year and had a significant impact on Zimbabwean citizens' daily lives.

Things do not always work out. Just before the ban was lifted, Kundai, who was studying in the United States, sent money home to pay for his father's treatment. His father had become acutely ill and needed urgent care. The hospital refused to admit him unless his family could pay the full fee in US dollars. Kundai begged the doctor to treat his father, even offering to send double the payment via Zambia or South Africa. They refused, and Kundai's father died. Kundai, who had spent the last of his savings on his father's care, could not travel home for the funeral. Kundai's experience is a typical story of migrant heartbreak because of government failure.

The Zimbabwe government could ignore demands for change, thanks to the availability of remittances. It knew Zimbabweans would receive support from their friends and family abroad, including money and basic goods like rice, bread, cooking oil, and fuel. Government hospitals now accept payments through Western Union or other transfer agencies. As a result, the government had no incentive to provide welfare for millions of Zimbabweans who were struggling due to poor economic policies. For instance, they did not have to change their economic policies, such as the Indigenization Act, that were hurting the economy. Moreover, while the government could not tax the citizens residing in the country because most of them were unemployed, they could tax those working in high-paying jobs abroad. The government would speak negatively about those living in the diaspora, but they benefited from their exit. Essentially, voter exit was a gift for ZANU-PF.

WHO IS SENDING MONEY?

Zimbabwean migrants are often more willing to discuss money transfers than politics. During my interviews, I noticed a significant change in the tone of the conversation when I transitioned from political questions to questions about remittances. For instance, in one of my early interviews, I spoke with a woman, Gogo, who was in her sixties. Initially, our conversation was not going well because she was reluctant to talk about politics. Two of her children were MDC activists, and one had been severely beaten during the elections. She attributed her family's poor outcomes to politics. However, when I asked her about remittances, she went to her bedroom and brought out a large box. Inside were over two decades worth of Western Union transfer receipts. Despite the rise of online transfers, she continued to use physical stores for more than twenty years. During this time, she sent over $100,000 to her family. As a domestic worker, Gogo sent an average of $500 per month to her adult children and extended family.

On average, Zimbabweans interviewed for this project said they remitted at least $100 a month. By the time these interviews took place, the amount being sent home had declined for a number of reasons, in particular the declining global economy. In earlier studies, people were sending back as much as $500 a week (Bracking & Sachikonye, 2006;

Maphosa, 2005; Tevera & Chikanda, 2009). According to the International Fund for Agriculture, in 2008, when the Zimbabwean economy was at its worst, the diaspora remitted nearly $361 million, and that number doubled in 2009 (Murithi & Mawadza, 2011). By 2012, diaspora remittances made up to 40 percent of the local GDP, reaching almost $1.4 billion (Makina, 2012). The receipt of remittances sustained the reeling economy, allowing those who remained at home to continue purchasing local goods and services. Most families, urban and rural alike, depended on support for everyday basic commodities from their family members in the diaspora (Bracking & Sachikonye, 2006). Bracking and Sachikonye (2006) found that one in three families in both rural and urban areas were receiving some financial support from a family member in the diaspora. Most families tie their survival in the last decade to the receipt of remittances from the diaspora.

In 2020, I collected more remittance data from a broader pool of respondents. I expected that remitting behavior would have been dampened by the pandemic, but this was not the case. Regardless of income, participants were likely to remit once or twice a month. Big senders are more likely to remit once a month. People who sent less than $500 were likely to remit between one and five times a month.

Most of those who participated in my study were sending money home. Sending money home is the typical behavior of most migrants. Senders are elders like Gogo or very young people who were born abroad or migrated when they were still children. Sending money home is an important part of the diaspora culture. Unless otherwise noted, the information described here is from data I collected during 2013–2021. The sample size for my remittance data is larger than for the interview data because, in 2021, I ran an online survey on remittances that yielded over 200 responses. Zimbabweans were very comfortable completing online surveys that were just about remittances. I combined these results with data collected in my interviews. The group sending the most money was thirty-five- to forty-year-olds, who made up 25.7 percent of the participants. I chose age thirty-five as an arbitrary marker of young versus old: 32.2 percent were younger, and 67.8 percent were older. Older participants were likely to take the survey and admit sending money home.

Most of the senders were professionals. The top three sending sectors were business, administration, and economics (29.3 percent); science, technology, medicine, engineering (STEM), research, and academia (14.4 percent); and students (undergraduate and graduate) and fellows (11.5 percent).

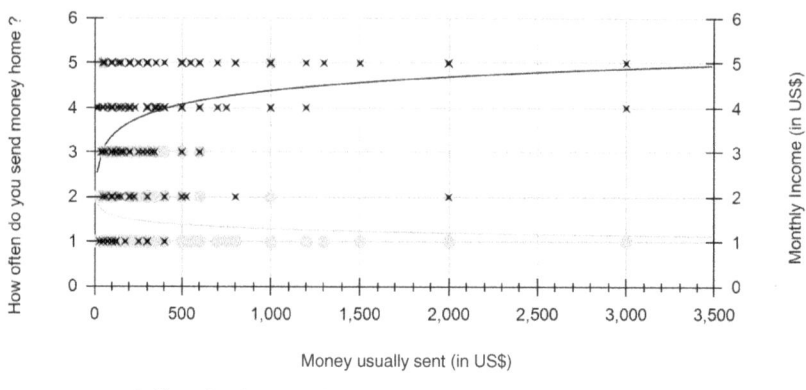

FIGURE 5.4 Scatterplot of money usually sent.
Source: Data from Dendere surveys in 2022.

Most survey and interview participants reported remitting at least twice a month (see Figure 5.4). Big senders, those who sent over $3,000 a month, were more likely to remit once a month unless the money was to fund a construction project. Construction projects were typically family homes. Building a single-family home costs from $40,000 to $80,000 in most neighborhoods. Most formal transfer agencies do not allow individuals to make very large transfers, forcing people to send money more frequently.

About half the people I interviewed had built a home in Zimbabwe or been part of a building project. Attachment to home ownership is very strong among Zimbabweans because it has always been a marker of middle-class status. Those in the diaspora feel strongly that having a home is a physical sign of their wealth and hard work. The pull of home ownership is so strong that even people as young as nineteen immediately felt a strong urge to build a home for those in their home country. Chido arrived in the United States as one of the more than 300 young people who have benefited from the USAP, which helped high-achieving students from low-income families apply to top universities in the United States. As my friend mentioned, most of these young people came from families that did not own a home. Rebecca Mano, the founder of USAP whom I spoke to in Harare, estimated that over 90 percent of her students start a home-building project shortly after they arrive in the United States for their undergraduate studies.

One example is Chenyai, a young woman orphaned with her five siblings at a young age. They bounced from one relative to another and never had a home. When she started her first job in a financially lucrative industry, she built a beautiful five-bedroom house for herself and her siblings. Chenayi said the building process was fairly easy because she had very low financial expenses in the United States and her brother, who was managing the remittance flow for the project, was very trustworthy.

Sometimes individuals fail to complete building projects due to competing demands on their financial resources. Building projects take an average of five years to complete because family members in Zimbabwe redirect the financial resources to other needs. In most cases, the diversions are due to a genuine need, such as when Rudo, thirty-six, was forced to pause working on a home for her parents after her father became ill. His hospital bills were very high, and Rudo, whom I spoke to in the United States, said she could not fund both needs.

However, sometimes the diversions can be cruel. Makanaka, a nurse in Scotland, nearly had a heart attack when she returned to Zimbabwe after almost a decade of sending nearly $80,000 to construct her home. On her first visit home, she asked to visit the construction site. She did not expect everything to have been done to perfection. She had heard stories of diaspora people swindled by builders, but she was convinced her case was different because her husband and mother were handling the project. The house had been built. It was beautiful from the pictures she shared with me, but it was not in her name. It was in the name of her now ex-husband, who had married her younger sister. Not even her mother saw anything wrong with this. When I asked her whether she would consider returning home to vote, she said that after this experience, Zimbabwe was no longer her home. Interestingly, she has continued to send remittances to her mother, who provides for her sister's financial needs.

People who sent less than $500 would remit between one and five times a month. Smaller senders often primarily send money to meet everyday needs such as food, electricity, rent, and tuition. Big senders are also sending for these needs, but they have other goals or can meet needs beyond everyday expenses. When we met in Cape Town, Victor, forty-five, worked as a gardener. From his small salary, he could not send much cash to his mother, who was caring for his three children and six of his late siblings' children. His mother was in a polygamous marriage, so she would also need to share whatever resources she received with the senior wife and any children in that home. Victor would remit $100 to cover tuition and healthcare, then send food and other provisions that could be ferried by bus drivers or traders known as *malaicha*. Victor would often send six months' worth of groceries, including food and detergent; in

2008, at the height of inflation, they were sending perishables like meat. Simba, a *malaicha* I interviewed in Cape Town, said sometimes he ferried goods worth tens of thousands of dollars, from groceries to car parts and technology equipment.

Who Is Receiving Money?

The government and transfer agencies do not have data on how many individuals directly receive remittances. This is likely because there is great variation in the self-reported numbers of receivers. When I asked the diaspora how many people directly benefited from remittances, the numbers varied from five to twenty. In the 2009 and 2006 Afrobarometer surveys, 31 percent and 27 percent, respectively, said they were receiving remittances from abroad. When I asked the same question to a subset of respondents in Victoria Falls, 16 percent said they were receiving remittances from abroad.

A quarter of the population was out of the country, and about a quarter reported receiving remittances. I was interested in the profiles of receivers and their relationships to senders. Most senders remit to close family (direct beneficiaries): their spouses, parents, or children. Most senders have between one and four direct beneficiaries. Direct receivers often receive money directly from transfer agencies in the formal or informal sectors.

Profile of Receivers and Their Political Actions

Afrobarometer surveys in 2009 (4), 2014 (6), and 2017 (7) that asked questions about remittance receipt provide the profile of receivers and how remittances influenced their political behavior. In each of those years, respondents were asked: How often, if at all, do you receive money remittances from friends or relatives outside of the country? In 2009, respondents were asked about various types of remittances, including food and clothing, but in 2014 and 2017, they were only asked about money.

In 2009, about 30 percent of the country was receiving remittances at least once every year (see Figure 5.5). Those who supported the opposition were more likely to receive remittances than supporters of the ruling party. Most receivers lived in urban areas and receipt was split almost evenly between men and women, to the advantage of women. The youngest people, those eighteen to twenty-five, were more likely to receive remittances, while those forty-six to fifty-five were the least likely to

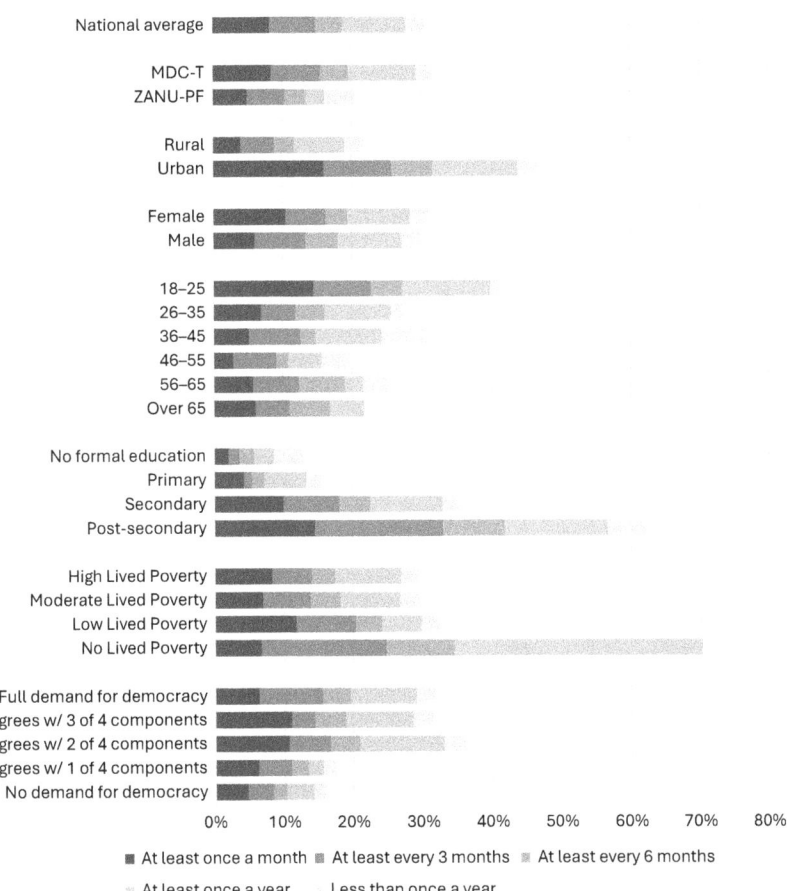

FIGURE 5.5 Profile of remittance receivers in 2009. *Source*: Afrobarometer, 2009.

receive remittances. Those with a postsecondary education were also more likely to receive remittances, while those with no formal education were the least likely to receive remittances. Well-off citizens were more likely to receive remittances than those living in high poverty. Those who demanded democracy or agreed with at least two components of democratic rule were more likely to receive remittances than those who did not demand democracy.

In 2009, Afrobarometer asked which type of remittance people received (see Figure 5.6). Most voters received money more than any other kind of remittance, and they were likely to receive money more frequently. Receipt of food remittance was also popular. This makes sense because 2008 and 2009 were two of the worst economic years in

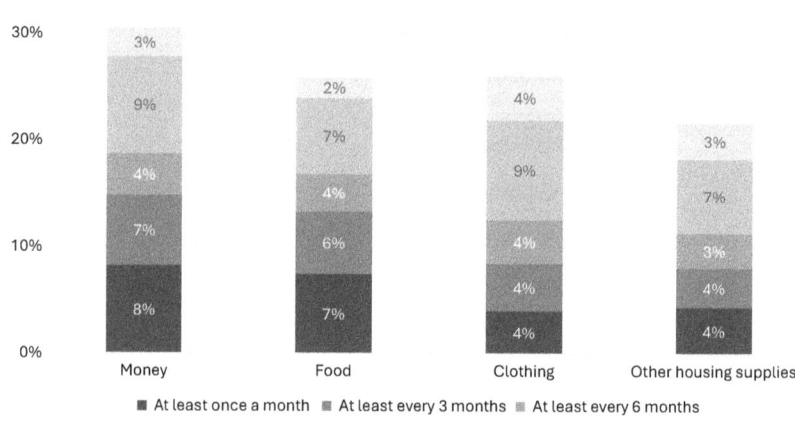

FIGURE 5.6 Type of remittances in 2009.
Source: Afrobarometer, 2017.

Zimbabwe. Grocery stores were empty, so even those with access to money could not always buy what they needed. As I show in the next section, Zimbabweans, especially those in South Africa and other neighboring countries, would remit food to their families, including meat and cheese. Receipt of clothing and other housing supplies was not nearly as common as money and food.

By 2014, when my interviews took place, the proportion of Zimbabweans receiving remittances was slightly lower than 30 percent, but this is probably because in 2014, the Afrobarometer only asked about receipt of money (see Figure 5.7). The profiles of those receiving support from family members abroad remained the same, with those in the opposition, urban areas, women, the young, and the well-off being more likely to receive remittances than other groups. The proportion of the well-off receiving remittances had dropped from almost 70 percent to just under 40 percent. This is likely because those in the middle class were more likely to emigrate and move with their families. A notable difference in 2014 is that more than 40 percent of professionals and the highly educated were receiving remittances, and they were doing so more frequently than everyone else. Those who demanded democracy were still more likely to receive remittances than those who did not.

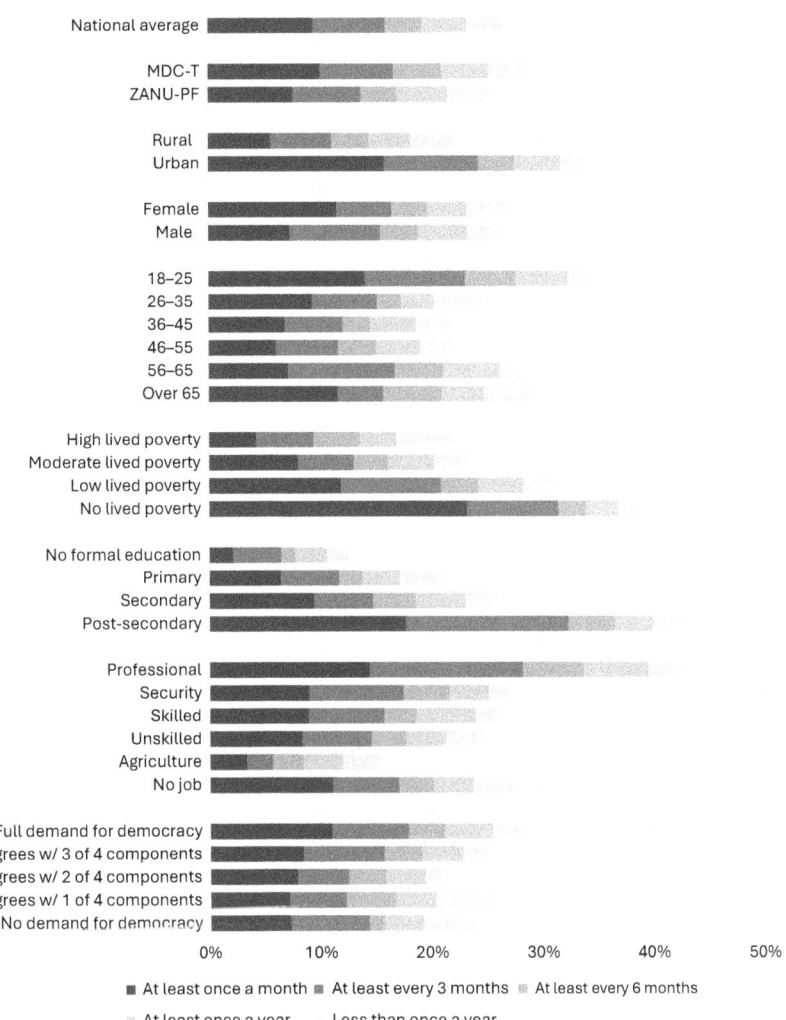

FIGURE 5.7 Receiving remittances 2014.
Source: Afrobarometer, 2014.

In the early surveys, respondents were asked: How often, if at all, do you or anyone in your household receive money remittances from friends or relatives living outside the country? In 2017, Afrobarometer asked the question slightly differently. Respondents were asked: Considering all the activities you engage in to secure a livelihood, how much, if at all, do you depend on receiving remittances from relatives or friends living in other countries? The way the question was asked changed the pattern of

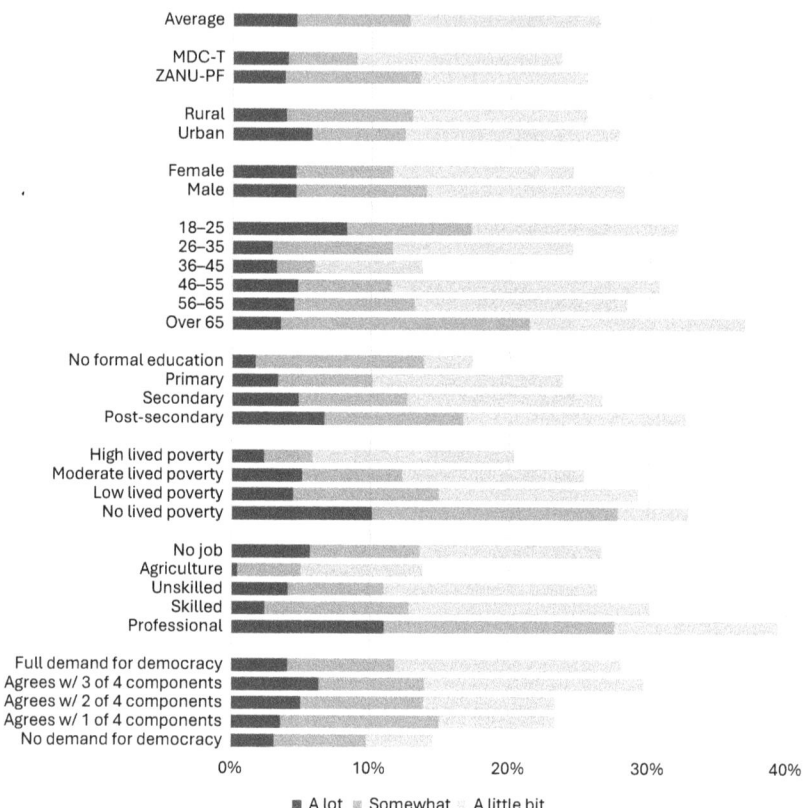

FIGURE 5.8 Receiving remittances 2017.
Source: Afrobarometer, 2017.

responses (see Figure 5.8). The question was aimed at explaining dependency on remittances for livelihood and not just the receipt of remittances. Men, ZANU-PF supporters, the elderly, and professionals reported some dependence on remittances to secure a livelihood. The proportion of Zimbabweans who said they depended on remittances either a lot, somewhat, or a little bit was much lower than in previous years. Only 25 percent of women and 30 percent of men reported receiving remittances to meet any of their needs. This was also the first time more men reported receiving remittances than women.

Impact of Remittances on Political Participation

Afrobarometer also asked a series of questions on political participation. In this subsection, I discuss how the receipt of remittances impacted the likelihood of receivers to engage in various political activities. Zimbabweans receiving remittances are slightly less likely to engage in politics that those who do not. As I will show in my analysis of interviews with senders and their receivers, attending a community meeting is very public and something people concerned about political violence might choose not to do. Also, community meetings tend to happen more in rural and poor communities. Most receivers are not in these communities; when they happen in their communities, they are too busy or uninterested to attend the meetings.

Afrobarometer data do not show much difference between those who receive remittances and those who do not in their likelihood to raise an issue. This is likely because of the option to raise issues online, which is very popular among those who are middle class, young, urban, or more educated.

There was no notable difference between receivers and nonreceivers in the likelihood of attending a protest. This question had a high refusal-to-respond rate (70 percent), so it is difficult to interpret. Zimbabweans tend to be afraid of attending protests. Protests are rarely successful in Zimbabwe because the government responds to protests by sending soldiers with instructions to shoot.

Those who receive remittances are more likely to engage in safe or non-visible activities, such as contacting an elected official or the media (see Figure 5.9). This is likely because these activities are relatively low risk.

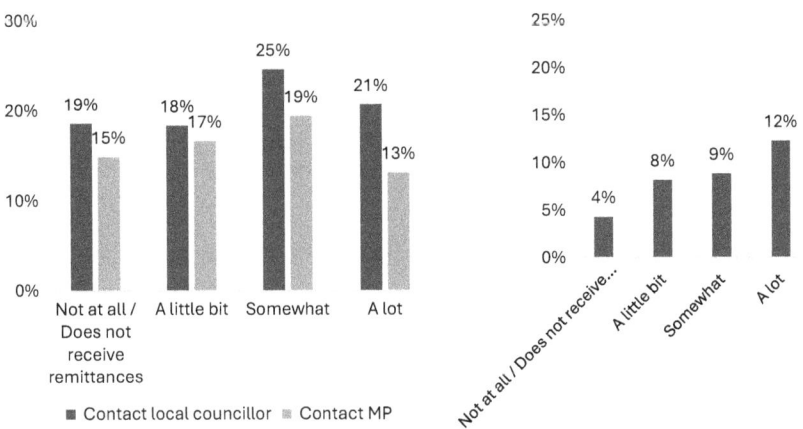

FIGURE 5.9 Contacting elected officials or media at least once.
Source: Afrobarometer, 2014.

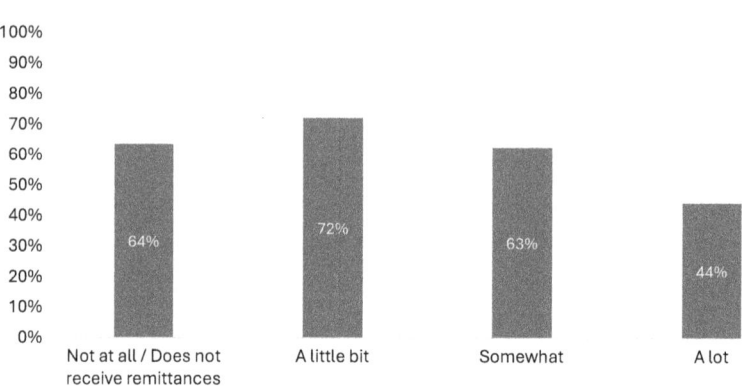

FIGURE 5.10 Voted in most recent election.
Source: Afrobarometer, 2014.

When it comes to voting, those who receive remittances are less likely to vote than those who do not receive remittances (see Figure 5.10). Dionne and Inman (2014) found that those dependent on remittances were more likely to engage in soft political activities but might not vote. This was particularly true in authoritarian and poor countries.

In the next section, I use the stories of five families of individuals I interviewed in the diaspora to illustrate the flow of remittances and how receipt of remittances impacts political behavior at the individual level. The most important part of the remittance story missing from large-scale surveys such as the ones discussed above might be that while one to four people directly receive money, the number of indirect beneficiaries ranges from eight to thirteen. To better understand the flow of remittances, I traveled to Zimbabwe to speak with receivers. I wanted to see how remittances impacted their family, social, and political lives. Their stories are not representative of the behavior and attitude of all receivers, but they provide important insight into how some individual perspectives.

THE IMPACT OF REMITTANCES ON SENDERS AND RECEIVERS

In this section, I discuss how remittances affected the families of five respondents. During my diaspora interviews, I asked individuals if they could introduce me to their families for further interviews. While most were eager for their families to be interviewed, obtaining consent from the families back home proved challenging. Respondents often told me their families were hesitant to engage in political conversations. This was not surprising: most Zimbabweans are fearful of discussing political matters. As discussed in Chapter 2, Zimbabweans tend to be suspicious even of large-scale surveys such as Afrobarometer. As a result, I assume there are differences between the families that agreed to be interviewed and those that declined. Except for one family, all of those who agreed to be interviewed resided in gated communities in the more affluent parts of the country. Perhaps they felt more secure behind the large walls surrounding their homes.

This group of individuals had more success helping their relatives move abroad than others who were interviewed. This could be the reason why they exhibited higher levels of frustration and exhaustion with the Zimbabwean system. Many family members who were interviewed were young, and younger Zimbabweans tend to disengage in politics and show frustration with the economic situation in the country. However, despite these nuances, the patterns in their stories were not too different from those found in the more representative Afrobarometer surveys. The recipients saw no point in demanding better resources from the government because remittances served as a financial cushion to meet their basic needs and sometimes luxuries. As a result of their proximity to the diaspora, some recipients saw leaving (exit) as the most viable way to better their circumstances. Their exit will add to the population of voters lost to emigration.

Samson, United Kingdom

Samson was a fifty-eight-year-old man who had lived in the United Kingdom since 2000. He regularly sent $800 to his three adult children and one young brother who lived in Zimbabwe. Over the last ten years, he had sent a total of around $96,000, which is about $9,000 per year. This is a lot of money – more than double the annual income of most families in Zimbabwe. Economists might assume this money helped Samson's family escape poverty and start businesses. However, such analysis does not take into account how the money was actually used. Figure 5.11 shows Samson's remittance network.

Families in the developing world are not always just nuclear families. Samson sent money directly to four family members, not just his immediate family. He usually sent the whole $800 to his oldest daughter, who then gave some of the money to the others. This helped reduce transfer fees. Most transfer agencies charge $10 for each transaction under $500 and more for higher amounts. Transaction fees also vary with the location of the recipient.

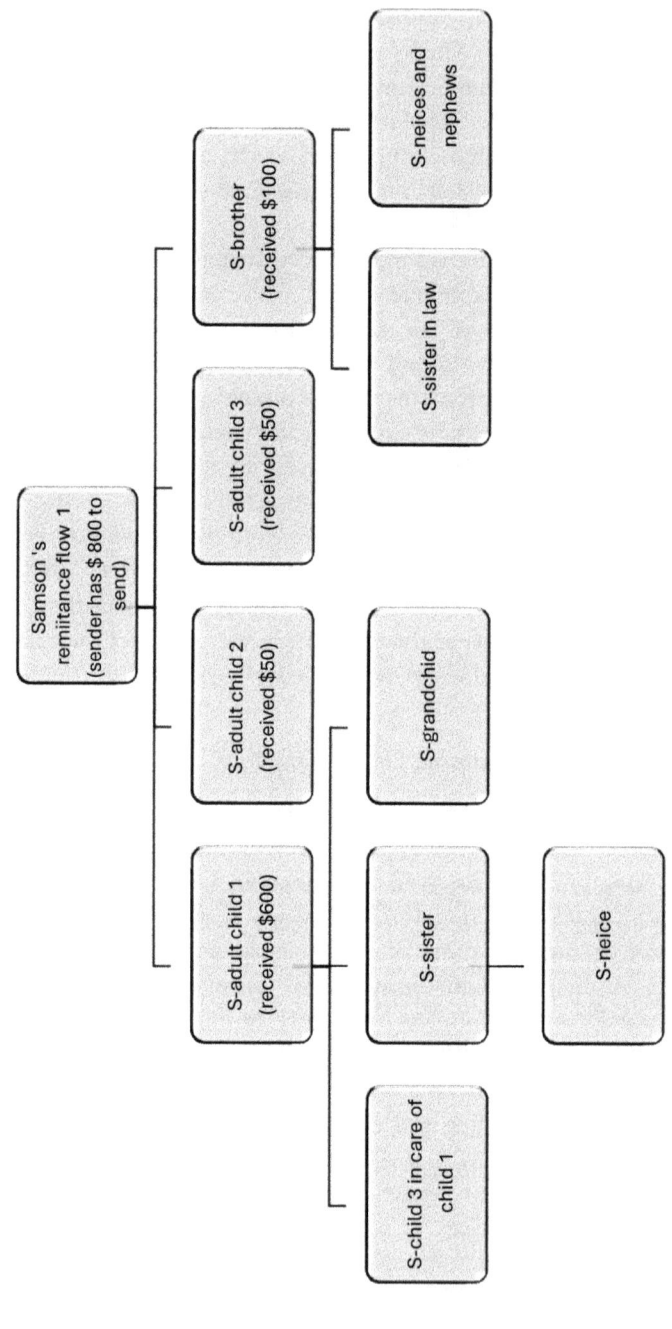

FIGURE 5.11 Samson.
Source: Dendere interviews.

Samson generally allocated $600 to his oldest daughter to assist her with most of his affairs since he left Zimbabwe. His eldest daughter was self-employed, and hence her income was not consistent. This situation was unusual because generally adult children are the ones who emigrate and have the responsibility of caring for their aging parents and younger siblings. The oldest daughter was a single parent of three school-age children and was also responsible for her youngest school-going sibling. Most of her funds were assigned to tuition and other education-related expenses for Samson's youngest child and two grandchildren. The eldest daughter took care of Samson's sister, her two adult children, and their three minor children. The major expenses included healthcare costs for the ailing sister and tuition fees for the school-age children.

Samson sent money to his two adult children as well as his older brother. His children received only a small amount, as they and their spouses worked in the formal sector. Samson believed in treating all his children fairly. He also worried about the unpredictable economy and wanted to ensure his children had a safety net in case they lost their jobs. His brother was laid off from work in the late 1990s and had been unable to find full-time employment. He recently got married and had two children under the age of ten. Because Samson's brother was the oldest male in the family, Samson felt responsible for supporting him in case of any family emergencies or events. For instance, his brother stood in for him at his children's weddings and family funerals, and those responsibilities required access to funds.

The remittances Samson sent his family had a positive impact on their immediate and long-term economic needs. However, the effect of these remittances on national economic growth is not easy to determine. Samson was frustrated that the money he sent did not fulfill the majority of his family's needs. He worked as an airport janitor in London and lived in a cramped apartment, but he still felt his family did not benefit from his hard work. He believed poor politics in the country contributed to this situation. Samson discouraged his daughter from entering frontline national politics due to concerns for her safety.

Samson's attitude toward political participation was similar to that of many parents in the diaspora. The safety of his children was more important to him than political commitments. Before emigrating, he had seen his friends being beaten up or abused by the state, and he did not want his children to face the same fate. When asked whether he encouraged his children to vote for democracy, he said living in the United Kingdom had convinced him that voting could be safe, and he wanted the same for his children. He enjoyed voting himself. To show his pride in participating in politics, he showed me a pile of vote notifications he had kept over the years. Although he no longer believed that voting alone could remove ZANU-PF, he still encouraged his family, especially the men, to vote. He had had more hope before leaving the country, but now that was gone.

When I met Samson's daughter in Harare, she expressed her gratitude for the money her father sent but mentioned it was not enough. The money barely covered the basic needs of their immediate family because they also had to support relatives who were facing financial difficulties. Unlike other families, they had not been fortunate enough to have any family members emigrate. One of Samson's older brothers was deported when he tried to join Samson in the United Kingdom. This deportation caused major emotional and mental challenges for the brother, who was unable to find stable employment to support his family.

Samson's family did not seem to be significantly affected by the remittances he sent or his appeals for them to vote. While their lives had improved slightly thanks to the extra income, they still felt they were struggling and did not believe politics would solve their problems. Samson's eldest daughter was determined to emigrate to the United Kingdom and was working to get a nurse aide certification so she could join her father there. Meanwhile, his youngest child planned to attend university in South Africa if she passed her high school exams. Only two people in the household were registered voters.

Many young people in Zimbabwe, particularly those with family members living abroad, are determined to leave the country. Nurse aide courses have become another way for the government to profit from the crisis. In 2021, when I checked in on Samson's daughter, she was attending a nurse aide course at a local university along with hundreds of other young people who were hoping to emigrate. Each student pays around $500 for the certification and an additional $3,000 to the agency that assists with migration. The COVID-19 pandemic had an adverse effect on healthcare sectors in Europe. The National Health Service in the United Kingdom was in urgent need of healthcare professionals. Samson's daughter hoped to emigrate with her children, and she was encouraging her brothers to consider leaving as well. When asked whether they would register to vote in case of an election before they left, she said she would consider it, but she doubted she would return home to vote once she left. When I visited one of the nurse aide classes with Samson's daughter, I was struck by how crowded the rooms were with young people eager to leave the country. I asked a few people whether they were registered voters, and they replied in the negative. Many young people have a great desire to leave the country, and politics takes a back seat.

Indeed, only the oldest daughter had voted when I checked in with the family in 2023 following the elections. At that point, her paperwork to leave for the United Kingdom had been approved, and she said she would not be able to face her father if she did not vote. The rest of the family did not vote. They are not alone. Although young voters between eighteen and thirty-five make up over 60 percent of the eligible voting population, less than 30 percent of that age group voted.

Maria, United Kingdom

Maria emigrated from Zimbabwe to the United Kingdom in 2004. She had been working as an accountant in Harare prior to emigrating. Maria's sister, who was already settled in the United Kingdom, sponsored her relocation. Maria left behind her husband and two children. They had agreed as a family that she would settle in the United Kingdom, and, once her immigration papers for permanent stay in the United Kingdom were finalized, she would send for the rest of her family. At the time of the interviews, Maria had been in the United Kingdom for nine years and only recently received approval for a permanent stay. The two children she had left as toddlers were now teenagers. Her financial situation had drastically improved, largely because she had finished her nursing degree and was now employed full-time. Maria was regularly sending $1,200 per month to her family back home. She was sending $800 to her husband and their two children. Although her husband was employed full-time, they had decided to send their children to a more expensive private school and employ a full-time nanny. Figure 5.12 shows Maria's remittance network.

Maria also remitted money to her widowed mother, who still cared for her younger siblings – one a university student and another a single mother of two children. Maria sent money directly to her mother. She felt the additional cost of transfer fees was negligible to avoid the potential family conflict if her husband found out how much she was giving her mother. I found that most women would hide from their husbands the true amount of their remittances to their families. Maria's mother also received remittances from Maria's older sister in the United Kingdom. Maria's sister sent their mother a much smaller amount because her husband and children were now residents of the United Kingdom, and they did not have much disposable income.

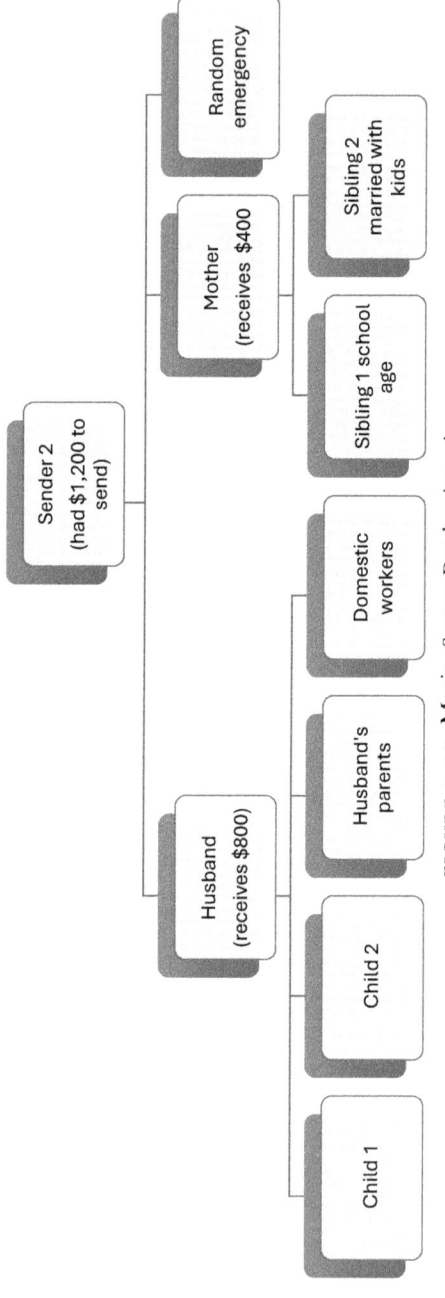

FIGURE 5.12 Maria. *Source:* Dendere interviews.

In Maria's case, remittances substantially impacted her family's socio-economic status. They were able to build a home in a nicer part of Harare, and her children were attending schools she "would have never dreamed of." Maria reported that she and her husband often discussed politics. Her husband strongly supported the opposition MDC party in principle, but he was unlikely to join in public political activities. He did not attend rallies. Maria had been involved in opposition politics in the United Kingdom. Her earlier involvement had less to do with her loyalty to the political party and more with the fact that she had applied for refugee status in the United Kingdom. However, over time she became more engaged in Zimbabwean and Scottish politics and had real interest in contributing to change in both countries.

When I met Maria's husband, he said he was committed to joining her in the United Kingdom, but he was worried that the quality of life for their children would decline. He was a registered voter, and I saw him at the polling station in the 2013 election. At the time, their children were too young to vote, but they were eligible to vote in the 2023 election. One of the children was a very committed opposition activist on social media. The other did not say whether she would vote; she was more concerned about leaving the country to study abroad. Maria received her British citizenship in 2023 but did not manage to vote, and she was unsure whether she would travel to vote in 2028.

Frank, South Africa

In 2020, during the peak of the COVID-19 pandemic, I collaborated with filmmaker Rumbi Katedza to gather more information on remittances. I created a survey that we shared on social media and through email lists to Zimbabweans all over the world. Our focus was to investigate the impact of the pandemic on remittance behavior. As part of the project, we invited volunteers to be interviewed for the documentary *Transactions* (Katedza, 2022). Frank was one of the 200 survey respondents and our only volunteer for the documentary. Frank resided in Cape Town, South Africa, where he had lived since 2009. He came from a family of four siblings, three of whom live abroad; two in the United Kingdom and the eldest sister in Bulawayo, Zimbabwe. Frank's entire family, including his mother, agreed to be featured in the documentary. It was one thing to agree to interviews. Telling their story on film for the world to see took a lot of courage from the family. The film exposed the high cost of remittances on family relationships, not only for the senders, but also for

Frank's older sister KiKi, who felt guilty about her inability to make financial contributions to the family.

The documentary opens with Frank on a video call with his mother. Frank is reassuring his mother that he will send the money he promised earlier the same day. MaMlilo, his mother, responds that now that he has sent money, they will have a proper Christmas. However, this financial gift is not enough. She goes on to request funds for the grandmother and herein lies some of the family tension. It is not enough to help their mother, but the children must cater to a growing and never-ending list of needs from their mother on behalf of the extended family. The mother is a small business owner, but because the economy is not doing great, most of her needs are met by remittances from her children.

In Bulawayo, the second largest city in Zimbabwe, KiKi is the eldest sister and works as an HIV counselor. However, her salary is very low, and she struggles to pay her monthly rent of $35. Kiki's only hope is to obtain a passport and leave the country, like many other young Zimbabweans who are determined to raise enough money for a passport and ticket. Kiki takes viewers on a tour of the city, which appears to be deserted due to the pandemic. Most young people in Bulawayo cross into South Africa illegally by swimming through the crocodile-infested Limpopo River. Kiki's siblings are worried that if things do not improve for her, she may also try to make this dangerous journey. They urge her to stay at home, but KiKi feels guilty that she still depends financially on her younger sister, Portia.

Portia has been in the United Kingdom since 2015, initially on a visitor's visa, but then decided to continue her studies while working as a carer for the elderly. Although it is a challenging job, it gives her enough flexibility to pursue her studies and enables her to send money home. Portia divides her remittances among her mother, two cousins, and her sister KiKi. Frank's family in Zimbabwe does not feel that demanding better resources from the government is useful because they believe the government is unresponsive. They rely on remittances instead.

Vongai, United States

When I met Vongai back in 2011, we were both graduate students. Vongai had emigrated to the United States through a different path than most students, as her mother used to work as a domestic worker for a White American couple stationed in Zimbabwe for their jobs. When Vongai finished college, the couple sponsored her visitor's visa to the

United States. There was no formal plan for how she would continue her studies, but as Vongai said, "They made a plan." Figure 5.13 shows Vongai's remittance network.

Living in the United States on a visitor's visa was not easy for Vongai, as she could not work legally. Hence, she had to do much under-the-table work as a nanny, cleaning houses, and caring for the elderly. This was very challenging for a young person with the goal of furthering her studies. Whatever plan they made worked, because a decade after she arrived in the United States, Vongai was enrolled in a prestigious graduate program at a time when very few Black women were studying computer science. Later, she got a lucrative job at a tech company.

This discussion focuses on remittance flows during her early years in the United States. By 2022, when we had our last conversation, although she was still based in the United States, she had bought a beautiful home in an upmarket neighborhood for her mother. Her father had passed away a few years before. She had also started multiple businesses that employed her siblings, and one of her sisters was living and working in the United States.

Vongai and her twin brother were the second oldest children in a family of seven. After they came to the United States, the expectation was that Vongai would take over the family's financial expenses, including food, tuition for her six siblings, tuition for her oldest sister's two children, utilities, and transportation. Neither of her parents had worked a formal job, so they did not even have small pensions to subsidize their expenses. Her mother continued to do some trade work as a street vendor selling sweets and vegetables, but traders are often raided by the city council. Every few months, the city council announces a clean-up process that essentially ends with the council confiscating trade wares from vendors. Vongai worried about her mother's safety and discouraged her from doing trade work.

On average, Vongai was remitting $700 directly to her mother. In the beginning, she would remit to her father, but unfortunately, he would sometimes use the money for his private needs and not cater to the family. Vongai had many conversations about this with her father. She told me her father felt poverty was emasculating him and being given a budget by his daughter was insulting. He could no longer join his friends at the pub because he was dependent on his child. Vongai understood this. Many parents in the area in which she grew up were dejected. I visited Vongai's family multiple times during this study. The first time, I witnessed the difficult poverty the family was living in. Her father, once a tall and proud

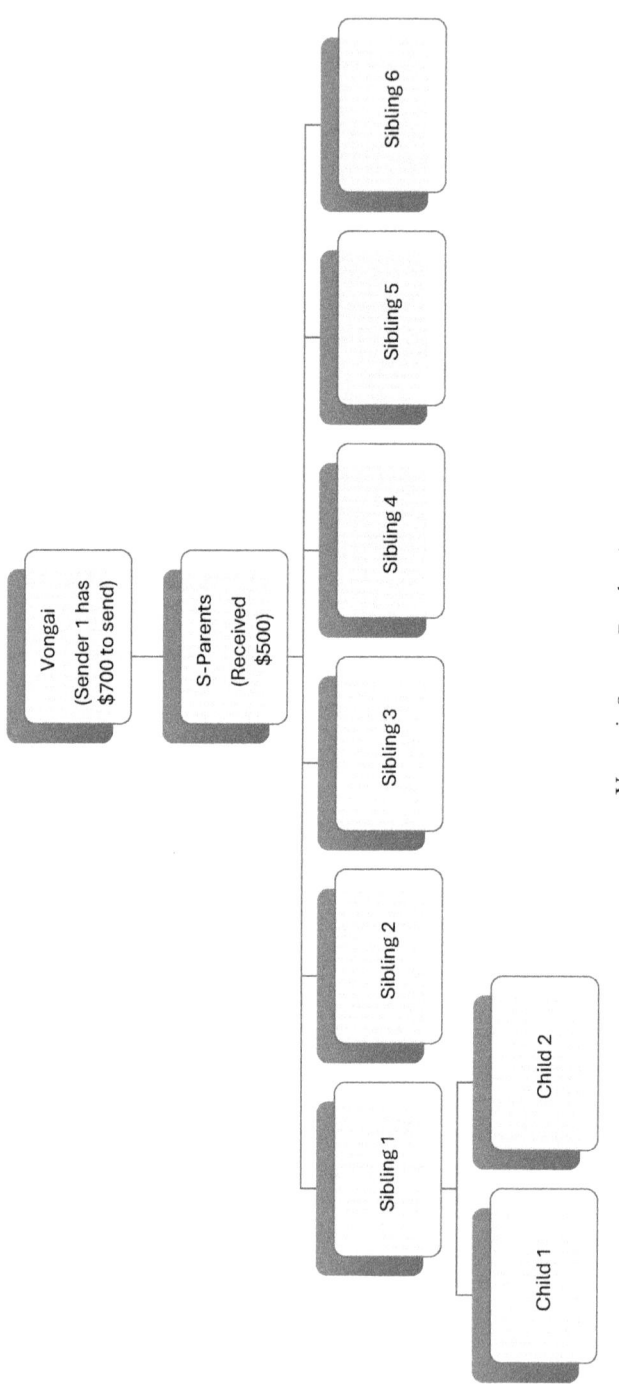

FIGURE 5.13 Vongai. *Source*: Dendere interviews.

man, had a permanent frown on his face. He could not understand why Vongai was failing to do what the child of their neighbor who was in the United Kingdom had done for the family. The neighbor had multiple children in the United Kingdom who had made major renovations to the home, and the family did seem to have a lot of extra cash for things like alcohol. Meanwhile, Vongai could barely afford her remittances. She was taking out large student loans to cover the cost of caring for her family back home.

When I asked Vongai if she had been able to go home between 2002 and 2016, she said no. She could not afford the flight. Indeed, her parents discouraged her from coming home. They said the money for the ticket could be better spent on the family's expenses. Vongai is not the only migrant who faces such tough choices. Many people work hard to send money home but could not make the choice to go home because their families would get upset about the wasted resources. This meant Vongai and many in her situation could not afford to go home and vote.

Before she was able to return home and start her businesses, Vongai had failed to encourage her family to start a small business. Some recipients of remittances have started small businesses, but many, like Vongai's family, either start businesses that quickly go under or they are not interested. Nearly everyone I interviewed had tried to start a small business with family back home, but most gave up as relatives failed to run the businesses without additional financial investment from the family abroad. One time, Vongai sponsored her twin brother to start a chicken-rearing business at their home. After the brother made his first sales, he bought himself one of the latest phones. Vongai was quite heartbroken, but she was determined not to give up. Vongai sent funds so her sister could upscale her hair braiding business. When I met her older sister, she was determined to make it work. Hair braiding did not earn a lot of money, but it was consistent. Vongai's sister had worked out that women in their area spent an average of $7 each month getting their hair done. Her goal was to get at least ten clients a month. She was eager to relieve pressure on Vongai. Unfortunately, the national economy was unstable. The cost of everyday expenses was going up and her earnings were not consistent. She told me that one way to know that an economy is failing is that women give up on getting their hair done.

Unfortunately, Vongai's sister died during childbirth. The hospitals in their area were asking pregnant women to bring needles, buckets of water, bandages – pretty much anything required for delivery. Vongai's sister had all the required items, but the clinic was not equipped for C-section deliveries. A procedure that is done routinely in most countries was not available. She was in labor for thirty-four hours before she and her child died. Vongai bore the cost of the funeral. I happened to be home at the time. I felt strongly obligated to help. Their family had given me a lot of their time for their project. I also understood that an additional unexpected $1,200 expense was a lot to handle for a graduate student.

Vongai was unable to go home for the funeral because she did not have the money. I have spoken to many in the diaspora who missed out on attending funerals for loved ones, including children, because of the cost associated with travel and in other cases the fact that they did not have legal status that would allow them to return. In our early years, Vongai would tell me she was too tired of trying to survive to care about politics. After I visited her family, I understood what she meant. The emotional toll of remittances, worrying about family members, and the million possibilities of what could go wrong took up energy that she could have directed to politics. This also explains why her brother, who was now married with children of his own, had not been active in politics. He said he had no time for politics, but I think what he and others who say that mean is that their primary needs have not been met and therefore they cannot participate in politics. Poverty and emotional stress force people to exit the political space.

The story is different for Vongai's younger siblings. They were too young to vote during the 2013 and 2018 elections, but they told me they were very excited about the 2023 election. Their mother was worried about their enthusiasm and online activism, but I noticed her worry has been less intense since they moved to the upmarket area. One of the younger siblings was such a strong opposition supporter that she aggressively responded to me on Twitter when she thought my comments had attacked the opposition. We laughed when she later wrote me privately to apologize. This work is hard, and circumstances in Zimbabwe are so often depressing that I take any opportunity to laugh. Unfortunately, the two young ones who were still in Zimbabwe were not able to vote because the 2023 election date was announced after they had left to start college in the United States. Vongai and the other sister, completing her studies in the United States, also failed to return home to vote because the election date was announced late, giving voters less than three months to plan for travel.

Rudo, United States

I first met Rudo in the United States in 2013. At the time, her two children were in Zimbabwe, as were her parents and her one living sibling.

By 2021, when we had our final conversation, her youngest child had relocated to join her, and her parents were living and working in the United States part-time. During the almost twenty years that she had lived alone in the United States, she had remitted at least $2,000 per month. When she first arrived, remittances were almost 80 percent of her paycheck, but as she increased her earnings, the proportion of her income that went to remittances declined to about 20 percent, which is still high but more manageable. Even with one of her children and her parents now living with her on at least a part-time basis, she still sent a lot of money home. Figure 5.14 shows Rudo's remittance network.

On average, she sent about $2,000 a month. Rudo said she almost always preferred to send money through formal transfer agencies. She would make about five transfer transactions per month. Her oldest child, who was parenting her youngest child, received about half the transfer. At some point, Rudo started remitting directly to the youngest child, a choice that created tensions between her children. She also sent funds directly to her brother, who lived in a different city, and to her parents. She often needed to make an emergency transfer to one of the direct recipients or to someone new. Making multiple transfers is very costly. She spent about $100 just on transfer fees. Rudo's oldest daughter, brother, and parents had multiple dependents they supported using the money Rudo sent. Most of the dependents were children of Rudo's late siblings. Rudo said she lost three of her siblings to HIV and to injuries made worse by the failing health system.

In Zimbabwe, I spent time with Rudo's two children and her parents. At Rudo's insistence, none of Rudo's family members were vocally active in politics, but all the adults were registered voters during the 2018 election. They had not voted in the previous elections, partly due to fears about violence and partly due to what I call middle-class apathy. Rudo's daughter said voting felt like a waste of time. This sentiment is widespread among middle-class urban youth but not among working-class urban youth. Voter turnout in affluent neighborhoods is often abysmal, while it is much higher in working-class areas. The attitudes of contemporary middle-class youth are in direct contrast to those seen in Rudo's days as a student at the University of Zimbabwe. Many had been active in politics and continued to engage after entering the labor force. When I asked Rudo why she thought her daughter had a different attitude about politics, she said it had to do with resources. During her daughter's university days, Rudo had made sure her daughter's needs were fully met.

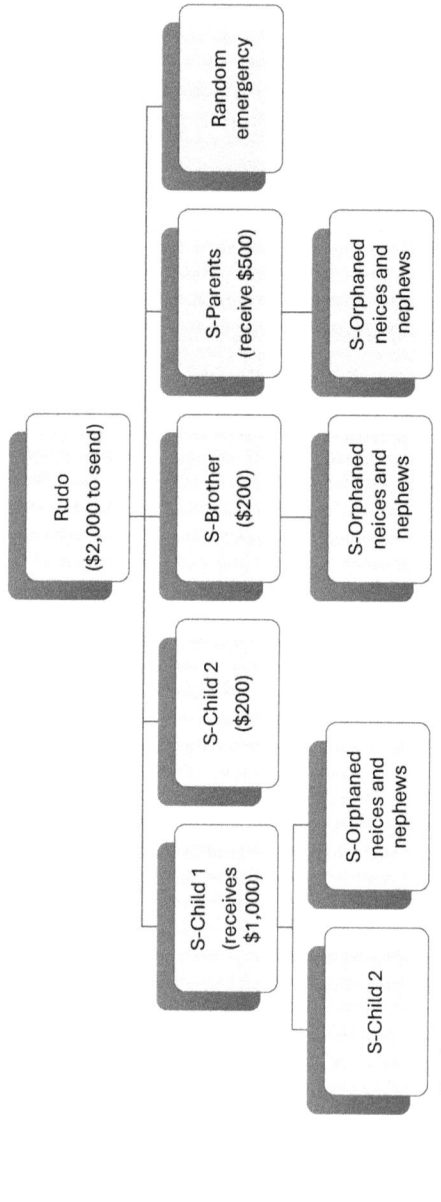

FIGURE 5.14 Rudo.
Source: Dendere interviews.

Rudo said that before 2018 she worried that if encouraged, her parents might vote for ZANU-PF. Rudo's mother said she would have never done so, but they always felt that it was important to appear to support the government for the safety of their children. Even Rudo's grandmother, who lived in a rural area when I met her during one of her visits to the city, said she did not support the ruling party, but in Mashonaland Central, where they lived, surveillance was very high. Rudo's *gogo* asked me to show her videos of a young activist who was spreading protest messages on social media. Gogo, while grateful for the financial support and the message to advocate for change via the polls, did not feel she could vote for the opposition without getting into trouble.

Remittances and Political Opinion

Rudo was among many diaspora Zimbabweans who traveled home after the coup to celebrate Mugabe's ouster in 2017. She said the post-Mugabe period felt hopeful, and since then she had been working very hard to encourage her family members to vote. Rudo added me to one of the community groups on WhatsApp, where Zimbabweans in the United States discuss politics and community events. Since 2018, people in the group have been more vocal about asking family members to register to vote and linking remittances to these requests.

I asked members of this group to share their experiences with directly asking receivers to register to vote. A member based in Florida said, "I have struggled to get them IDs because they were trying to give excuses not to register." This response was met with much agreement in the group. One dissenting voice responded:

If you ask people back home to register, they will register. Or they will give an excuse not to register and let you solve that problem [that's stopping them from registering]. So it's either you solve that problem for them, or you stop sending the cash, and they will solve it themselves. But absolutely, you do have sway over their registration status if you exercise it.

For this responder, requests to register to vote should be accompanied by tangible or actionable benefits for the families back home. Others felt, as Rudo did, that because most remittances are going to support elderly parents, there is not much that can be done to leverage remittances for votes. A small group advocated cutting people's remittance access until they showed their registration slips.

I know from experience engaging on this matter that Zimbabweans are unlikely to do this. Most people view this as punishing innocent family members. Indeed, after the 2018 election, when I tweeted that I was frustrated that family members I was sending remittances to had not voted, I was accused of wanting to impose sanctions on loved ones. My tweet had been intended to provoke engagement. More than 100 people responded that they strongly disagreed with this view. Others felt very strongly that tying remittances to voting was not any different from the authoritarian behavior of the ruling party.

Even the opposition has argued that the diaspora should not tie remitting behavior to voting behavior. However, the conversations in the more than twenty diaspora WhatsApp groups I have joined over the years suggest that those living abroad want people back home to register to vote and to eventually vote.[1] For individuals like Rudo, the economy back home must improve so they can finally start their lives in Zimbabwe.

CONCLUSION

Remittances add up to billions of dollars, which is why some scholars argue they should significantly impact voting behavior. However, as shown by the examples of Samson, Maria, Frank, Vongai, and Rudo, the direct impact on individuals varies greatly. For some receivers, remittances and encouragement from senders increase their likelihood of voting. Other senders remit fear and discourage their families from going out to vote. Remittances may detach receivers from everyday failures of the government so much that they decide not to vote. Dambisa Moyo (2009) asked the same question in her controversial book *Dead Aid*: Why should Africans vote for their leaders instead of for the NGOs funding their lives?

Remittances and Quality of Life

Without the massive inflow of remittances into Zimbabwe, many more people would have fallen into deep poverty. At the family level, remittances have improved most people's quality of life (Acosta et al., 2009;

---

[1] In Zimbabwe, the voter registration process is very cumbersome. In 1980, the new law was that anyone born in 1980 or before was automatically registered to vote. By 1998, when the 1981 babies became eligible to vote, they had to register but the conditions were unclear. In 2017, the government deleted the voter's roll and demanded that every single citizen register again. The requirements were cumbersome, and the government did not have a set registration period. Thus, everyone abroad would have needed to return home in 2017 to reregister.

Adams & Cuecuecha 2013). Many who would not have owned homes do, and children who would not have finished school have been able to complete their studies. Moyo and Nicolau's (2016) study of the impact of remittances by Zimbabwean teachers in South Africa showed a more than 200 percent increase in household wealth. As with the people I interviewed, many of the teachers who left Zimbabwe before owning a home now do. This is also consistent with the impact of remittances for receiving households in Timor-Leste, who were able to participate in important cultural ceremonies because of remittances (Wu & McWilliam, 2023). In Nepal, individual families that received remittances had better mental health outcomes after experiencing a natural disaster (Tachibana et al., 2019). Focusing on the lack of development at the national level underplays the improvement in the lives of individual receivers. On the whole, remittances have been a critical lifesaving mechanism.

The cost of political participation does not outweigh those benefits in healthcare and education. Still, many who benefit from remittances have reduced their willingness to advance themselves and participate in politics. Bollard et al. (2011) argued that remittance inflow relaxes family budgets. In some contexts, this enables the outsourcing of labor, which allows children to go to school; in other contexts, as shown by Gao et al. (2021) in the Kyrgyz Republic, households that received remittances fared poorly on human development. Remittances are possible because voting-age adults have left the country, leaving, in most cases (including Zimbabwe), young children and the very old. The cost of remittances is that democrats are not there to raise young democrats. This echoes an impact of HIV: democrats died and are not there to raise their children to be democrats.

The socioemotional and political impact of remittances has not been well studied, but evidence from Mexico's ghost towns shows negative outcomes for youth raised in the absence of fathers who have migrated to the United States (Silver, 2014). Honduran migrant families are reported to have experienced higher rates of separation because of migration, and family reunification is not always possible after a long period of separation. In the Zimbabwean case, most women living away from their husbands reported their husbands had married second wives and no longer wished to relocate. One husband told me his wife made enough to provide for the family and he was better suited to remain in Zimbabwe, where their children would grow up without worries about racism. He neglected to mention that he could also enjoy the benefits of having multiple partners and use the money from his wife to support them.

Some of the children of migrant parents I have interviewed since 2013 have struggled to cope with adulthood away from their parents. Although useful for education and healthcare, remittances also provide extra money that reduced their willingness to further their studies or find jobs. It is difficult for people who are removed from society to find any reason to participate in politics. Thabani and Z were brothers living in an affluent Harare area. Their mother paid their rent, which had gone up from $500 in 2013, when we met, to $1,200 in 2018. Neither of them worked. They were thirty-six and thirty-seven, each married with two children. Their mother, a nurse in the United Kingdom, left when they were just thirteen and fourteen years old. Her attempts to relocate them to the United Kingdom failed. When they were minors, their father, who remarried shortly after their mother moved to the United Kingdom, would not relinquish their documents. Thabani and Z said he was worried about losing remittances, so he did not want to leave. Before their mother went to the United Kingdom, Z was a straight-A student who wanted to become a doctor. After his mother left, his grades plummeted – partly because he missed his mother and partly because he was living with their father and his new family and had money to spend that was not tied to how well he did in school. Their father did not reprimand him because he did not want to upset their mother, and their mother did not either. Mothers living away from their children often feel guilty about their absence and use money and gifts to counter it.

Remittances and Political Engagement

When I asked Z and Thabani whether they would vote, they said their lives were not connected to politics. I was interested in their views as parents of young children. Did they not want a different system for their children? They felt strongly that their votes would not change politics. They were not alone in feeling this way. Most children of senders did not seem as agitated by the political situation as their poorer peers. The children of migrants who relocated to join their parents were more likely to show interest in the politics of the country than their peers back home.

In 2022, I met Kuda, twenty-four, in Liverpool, where he was working after finishing university. He said he was determined to return to Zimbabwe to vote in 2023. He had not been back to Zimbabwe since he came to the United Kingdom when he was eight years old. He introduced me to his Zimbabwean British friends, many of them first-generation migrants who were all eager to return home. They all sent money home to whomever their parents wished: grandparents, cousins, aunts, and uncles. There is a second-generation impact of remittances. Like many Zimbabweans, they did not vote as they failed to meet the tight voter registration deadline. Their experiences as young Black people in a country that is not always kind to Black people stirred in them the desire to see their homeland improve. Their friends at home did not have the same motives. But home is easier to love from afar, where one is not faced with the daily assaults of a failing state. Mavita, twenty-two, was studying in South Africa when we met. His father paid for his tuition and sent him money regularly. He had been changing his degree every few years, and it was unclear when he would graduate. Monash, where he was studying, is known as where diaspora children go to discover themselves. Sometimes the discovery can take many years. I also sense young people are broken apart by not being with their families, and, as they age, it dawns on them that they might never live in the same spaces as their parents. That is a difficult realization.

Each time family members go to collect money sent by a relative living abroad, they are reminded of what is missing. An aging mother told me that although remittances had made her life better, she was also starting to accept that she would never see her daughter again. If she did, the daughter would likely be in a coffin. The mother was talking about the fact that most Zimbabweans, and migrants in general, return home in death. The 2022 death of renowned academic, lawyer, and political advisor Alex Magaisa at only age forty-five brought to the forefront a truth about Zimbabwean politics: Many of the people who left home will not return to participate in politics. Magaisa had served as an advisor to Morgan Tsvangirai and kept a weekly blog where he broke down the complex political conversation for ordinary people. Magaisa died of heart failure. At his funeral, many of his friends spoke of the strain diaspora life takes on people as they strive to provide for themselves and their families back home.

The fact that Zimbabwe receives billions in remittances is evidence that something has gone wrong. Outward migration from Zimbabwe rivals that of countries at war. In that sense, one can argue that the country will feel the negative effects of a war-like situation. Decline in political participation is one of the more obvious effects of exit. When voters no longer credit the government with the good things in their lives, they might check out of politics completely. Escribà-Folch et al. (2022) argued that when remittances meet needs, voters will have space to support the opposition. This argument ignores that voters receiving remittances might not want to risk their lives in authoritarian states where the regime uses violence as a tool for repression or voter mobilization. Indeed, that is what Vongai's mother told me. She said it was too scary to risk their lives when they were finally living well.

Meanwhile, Vongai's friend, who was still living in the old area and struggling, said she had no option but to keep voting. She said that, unlike Vongai's mother, she did not have a daughter living abroad to fall back on. She was more diligent about the small earnings from the business she started with a loan from Vongai's mother. She was running a successful chicken business from her home. I asked why she thought her small business had taken off while others had failed. She said it was because her friend Vongai gave her low-interest loans when she was starting up. She also said she had more to lose if the business failed, so she had been willing to work more and longer hours than her friends who had children abroad.

Poor urban youth with no prospects of leaving the country are more likely to engage in politics by attending rallies than their counterparts who do not receive remittances. In Victoria Falls, where I conducted a small survey, the youth who did not get remittances were much more likely to go out and protest. Less than 10 percent of those who said they received remittances reported participating in politics by attending rallies. The majority did not. Afrobarometer findings are consistent with what I learned from interviews in Zimbabwe.

That said, the overall population's willingness to attend rallies is low because the government uses violence against citizens when they choose to get involved. One reason Vongai's mom cautioned her children against political participation was because one of their neighbors had their house burned down after they were suspected of supporting the opposition. In the next chapter, I conclude the book by explaining the ways in which the loss of voice and citizen exit have contributed to authoritarian survival.

6

Connecting the Dots

Voice, Exit, Loyalty, and Regime Survival

In 1999, a team of trade unionists, lawyers, academics, nurses, and other professionals met in Harare to found the Movement for Democratic Change (MDC; P. Alexander, 2000; Dorman, 2016; LeBas, 2013). Conditions in Zimbabwe were ripe for an opposition win. Citizens were ready to vote for an alternative to the twenty-year rule of the Zimbabwe African National Union – Patriotic Front (ZANU-PF). Young MDC supporters would soon be seen all over the major cities handing out red cards to send the message that it was time for ZANU-PF and its leader, Robert Mugabe, to be sidelined. Yet, ZANU-PF managed to survive for two decades and more.

The survival of ZANU-PF has received a lot of attention from academics who argue the regime survives because of its use of violence (Basedau et al., 2007; Bratton, 2011; Maringira & Gukurume, 2022; L. E. Young, 2019), vote rigging (Lewanika, 2023; Mvundura, 2020; Ndakaripa, 2020), patronage politics (Mabweazara et al., 2020; Mpofu & Ncube, 2023; Oosterom & Gukurume, 2022), cooption of the opposition (Ndawana & Hove, 2023; Sachikonye, 2012), and support from the military (Masunungure, 2011; Ndawana, 2020; Tendi, 2020). I have shown that in addition to these tools, ZANU-PF benefited from an unlikely source of political relief: the exit of millions of Zimbabwean voters from the political system due to death, illness, and migration.

DEATH, ILLNESS, AND MIGRATION AS EXIT, VOICE, AND LOYALTY

Since the founding of the MDC, ZANU-PF has benefited from the myriad of tools available to authoritarian regimes, including violence and election manipulation. In this book, I have argued and shown that the exit of millions due to death, illness, and migration also bolstered the regime. The opposition galvanized support all around the country, even in rural strongholds of the ruling party. But the MDC was handicapped by a perfect storm that hit its voters most. More than a quarter of the population exited political processes due to HIV, dead or too sick to participate, or by leaving the country. In other words, ZANU-PF benefited from an HIV and migration exit premium and from an inflow of remittances that muted opposition.

My explanations for ZANU-PF's survival are anchored by my expansion and modification of Hirschman's theory of exit. I include death and severe illness as forms of exit that excluded would-be voters from participation, permanently or as long as the illness went untreated. Death and severe illness also end voice. When people die prematurely, their political voice dies with them. When people are very sick from an illness that ravages their bodies and faculties, they can no longer meaningfully engage in political discourse. I also show that loyalty to a country and political voice do not end with migration. Migrants can show their loyalty by sending remittances and use their voice, albeit at a reduced level, by speaking up on issues impacting their home country (Abduvaliev & Bustillo, 2020; Ahmed, 2017). Still, loyalty and voice are not as impactful in authoritarian regimes where every vote is needed to effect change. Remittances sent as a show of loyalty and commitment to families left in the home country also dampen political participation because they provide a safety net for people who would otherwise agitate for change because of economic hardship.

THE DEAD CANNOT VOTE

When the MDC was formed in 1999, the timing was right for a change in government. In hindsight, 1999 was the last year of normal politics. Although the political and economic situation was tense, the overall situation was relatively calm, and the excitement brought on by the founding of the MDC indicated change. However, between 2000 and 2005, HIV-related deaths reached their highest peak (Lopman & Gregson, 2008). One of the largest government hospitals was issuing over 2,500 death certificates a week during that period. For legal and socialcultural reasons, they were not allowed to name HIV-related illnesses as the cause of death, but as professionals, they knew HIV was killing thousands of people weekly. Most of those who were dying were young, educated urbanites, the same demographic that supported the opposition. HIV was destroying communities the same way it targets white blood cells. HIV was forcing not only infected voters out of the political system but also their caregivers and, eventually, their children, who were often left to be raised in poverty by aging grandparents or in underresourced care homes. An entire generation of activists, including musicians and community leaders, was also taken by HIV, silencing their voices (Barz & Cohen, 2011). The dead cannot vote or voice their voting preferences, but many would have likely wanted change if they could. Two million more voters would have substantially impacted election outcomes because the gap between the ruling party and the opposition was always less than 50,000 votes in elections from 2000 to 2013.

The dead are forever lost to the political system. Children who would have otherwise been raised in middle-class families with a firm grounding in civic education and the importance of voting lost that opportunity. Zimbabwe had an estimated two million orphans living in orphanages. Orphanages are primarily focused on ensuring children have access to shelter and food. Access to education was limited for most children in orphanages. These children did not grow up witnessing their parents vote or engage in politics. Many of them later did not vote or participate in civil society because those opportunities were never presented to them, and they never learned how to. The story of Jabulani in Chapter 4 is worth recalling. Jabulani's eleven children, whom he educated with the hope that they would have a brighter future, all died from HIV, leaving him to care for more than a dozen grandchildren, some of whom were born with HIV. Had their parents lived, these children would have had better lives. Their grandfather was poor and struggled to feed them. Some of the girls turned to prostitution as a path out of poverty. Their only interaction with politics was the knowledge that they were poor and the government had done nothing for them. There are millions of such young people.

ZANU-PF manipulated the HIV crisis in their favor as they did with other health crises, like cholera (Chigudu, 2020; Chikanda, 2007). As opposition MPs died in office, ZANU-PF invested heavily in special elections, allowing them to snag opposition seats. While ZANU-PF also lost MPs to the crisis, they never lost any seats in special elections to replace the deceased officials. ZANU-PF also used the crisis to redistrict voters. The government claimed its 2005 clean-up operation in poor urban areas that left over 700,000 displaced was designed to alleviate the HIV crisis. This was not true. They wanted to move urbanites away from opposition voting centers. The peri-urban areas where the government resettled those who lost their homes in the clean-up operation became ruling party strongholds where people depend heavily on the government for survival. Each election cycle, the government dangles promises of land and other benefits to poor people who have no choice but to hope for the best.

Not Voting with Their Feet: Migration Dampens Voice

While HIV was ravaging the nation, voters had opportunities to leave the country (Crush et al., 2015). In the early 2000s, Zimbabweans became aware of opportunities to work in the United Kingdom. The first to go were groups of medical professionals. Their exit further harmed the healthcare system, which was barely functioning under the weight of the HIV crisis. Other professionals, including teachers, also began to leave the country in waves. Health professionals and teachers had anchored Zimbabwe's most significant trade union subgroups. Throughout the 1990s, they organized sit-ins and protested the regime. Trade unions offered a vibrant voice against government misrule. Migration slowly chipped away at this as thousands, eventually hundreds of thousands of professionals left the country. The MDC leadership heavily depended on functioning trade unions for their activities. The founding president of the MDC, Morgan Tsvangirai, had been the Zimbabwe Trade Union (ZCTU) president, and it was at the 1999 ZCTU congress that they voted to create a political wing of the trade union.

Available data shows that at least 1.2 million Zimbabweans have left the country. It is generally accepted that if everyone were accounted for, at least four million have emigrated, and the numbers continue to rise. The majority of those living abroad show strong support for the opposition. The profile of those who have left the country – young, urban, educated professionals – is also the profile of those who support the opposition and would likely advocate for change. Across seven Afrobarometer surveys, most opposition supporters were young adults of working age, urban, educated, and professional. The ruling party's support base tended to be older, rural, and less educated. Most of those I interviewed and those who told Afrobarometer that they lived abroad share these profile traits: young, educated, urban, working class, and professionals. This group is also likely to demand full democracy.

Zimbabwe does not allow external voting. Citizens living abroad must return home to vote (Wellman, 2021). ZANU-PF has been clear that it has no interest in allowing the diaspora to vote. It argues that ZANU-PF officials cannot campaign in Western countries. Yet, it has also refused to expand the vote to the African countries where most migrants are domiciled. The ruling party is aware that most of the diaspora supports the opposition. It also understands that most in the diaspora face multiple pressures on their finances and will be unlikely to travel home and vote. The diaspora vote would bolster the opposition vote in significant ways. While a majority of the diaspora say they support the opposition, less than 30 percent of them routinely return home and very few are willing to spend the financial resources to travel to vote.

Participation requires individuals to be present and able to engage in politics. When voters are physically absent because they have emigrated or face economic barriers, their voice is silenced. As a result, democracy becomes compromised. Authoritarian regimes survive when they can manipulate voter participation or create barriers to citizen engagement. Some forms of manipulation are easily observable, such as physical violence, but other insidious opportunities occur when the country faces a health and economic crisis. Between 1999 and 2009, ZANU-PF managed to survive and retain power during Zimbabwe's most challenging political and financial circumstances. The chaotic environment gave a lifeline to ZANU-PF's authoritarian capacity to suppress opposition by limiting the opposition's opportunities to challenge its rule. ZANU's ability to mobilize the different forms of violence was made possible by multiple crises, which forced an estimated two million to leave their homes.

ZANU-PF Benefited from an Exit Premium

In this subsection, I once again draw on HIV and migration data from the UN Spectrum project of voting-eligible Zimbabweans to show the combined impact of the exit premiums on Zimbabwean elections from 2000 to 2013. I assume that if those who were critically ill, those who died, and those who emigrated had been able to vote, they would have done so at turnout rates consistent with the country's population.

To calculate the total exit premium from HIV and migration, I added the additional votes from each for each political party, as shown in Chapters 3 and 4. I then subtracted additional opposition votes from additional ruling party votes to get the net opposition vote or the ruling party premium. In formal terms, the calculation is:

Exit premium = (Opposition gain − ZANU gain)/Votes cast

To illustrate this in round numbers, say that the additional voters from HIV and migration for ZANU-PF were 100,000 and 150,000 for the opposition. Then, the ZANU-PF exit premium in that election would be

50,000. In other words, the opposition would have had 50,000 more net votes had not been for the exit premium.

The total exit premium for ZANU-PF between 2000 and 2013 ranged from 4 percent to 12 percent. As summarized in Table 6.1, the proportion of registered voters grew from 5,288,804 voters in 2000 to 5,695,706 in 2013. Over the same period, the proportion of additional voters – those lost to exit – increased from 744,598 to 1,251,163 voters. This loss of voters had a huge impact on political outcomes in Zimbabwe at a time when votes mattered the most.

In the 2000 parliamentary election, the total number of votes cast across all nine provinces was 2,556,261. Had Zimbabwean voters not exited, ZANU-PF would have received 290,671 more votes and the opposition 453,927. The exit premium for this election was 5 percent. The opposition would have gained more votes in seven of the nine provinces. This may have changed the distribution of parliamentary seats in the provinces where the opposition had more gains than the ruling party.

In the 2002 presidential election, the total number of votes cast across all nine provinces increased to 3,032,557. Had Zimbabwean voters not exited, ZANU-PF would have received 392,766 more votes and the opposition 591,568. The exit premium for this election was still 5 percent because of the substantial increase in total voter turnout. Even when the opposition was doing well and increasing votes across the board, the ruling party was still benefiting because of voter attrition due to exit. By 2002, HIV prevalence was increasing, as was emigration. To win, the opposition would have needed all the potential voters to stay healthy, alive, and in the country to combat the rigging and electoral manipulation used by the ruling party.

The 2005 elections came at a time when the situation in the country was continuing to deteriorate. The HIV crisis was made worse by growing inflation. At the time, Zimbabweans thought inflation was at its worst, though it would get worse, as I have discussed in the book. In the 2005 parliamentary election, the total number of votes cast across all nine provinces decreased to 2,520,850. The number of additional voters increased to 1,043,878. Had Zimbabwean voters not exited, ZANU-PF would have received 482,504 more votes and the opposition 561,374. The exit premium for this election would have been 2 percent. In the next election, the exit premium would be much higher.

By 2008, the economic situation in Zimbabwe had completely deteriorated. Inflation was at its worst, reaching twelve-digit levels. The country

TABLE 6.1 *Summary of impact*[a]

Election year	Registered voters	Votes cast	Additional voters	ZANU gain	Opposition gain	Total exit premium
2000*	5,288,804	2,556,261	744,598	290,671	453,927	163,256 (5%)
2002**	5,607,795	3,032,577	984,334	392,766	591,568	198,802 (5%)
2005*	5,658,624	2,520,850	1,043,878	482,504	561,374	78,870 (2%)
2008***	5,611,304	2,572,245	1,251,163	405,514	845,649	440,135 (12%)
2013***	5,695,706	3,378,320	1,251,163	716,241	940,165	223,924 (4%)

Note. Data from UN Spectrum, ZEC, ZESN; *Only parliamentary election; **Only presidential election; ***Harmonized election.
[a] Other voters excluded because Zimbabwe voter's roll has many missing voters, especially young urbanites.

was still reeling from the impact of the 2005 Operation Murambatsvina, which ravaged HIV healthcare centers and displaced almost one million people, mostly urbanites. Even so, the opposition, although divided, was very popular. Even as political violence and repression were increasing, the opposition made significant inroads into rural areas. Yet, they failed to win an election that was largely expected to be theirs. As discussed in Chapter 1, the ruling party had many tools in the election rigging toolbox, but the loss of voters to exit played an undeniable role in their survival. In the 2008 presidential election, the total number of votes cast across all nine provinces increased slightly to 2,572,245. The total number of additional voters increased to 1,251,163, largely because of increased numbers of Zimbabweans leaving the country. Had Zimbabwean voters not exited, ZANU-PF would have received 405,514 more votes and the opposition 845,649. The exit premium for this election was 12 percent.

Although the electoral situation in Zimbabwe changed a lot between 2008 and 2013 due to the unity government, there was still a small exit premium for ZANU-PF. In the 2013 presidential election, the total number of votes cast across all nine provinces increased slightly to 3,378,320. Although exit from HIV had declined, Zimbabwe was still experiencing high levels of outward migration. The total number of additional voters increased to 1,656,405. Had Zimbabwean voters not exited, ZANU-PF would have received 716,214 more votes and the opposition 940,165. The exit premium for this election was 4 percent.

Remittances Bolster Ruling Parties

Research on the impact of remittances on the economies of receiving countries shows a mixed pattern depending on the type of country. In very poor countries, remittances pull families out of poverty, but they are unlikely to lead to development at the national level. In mid-level economies and countries where the government has more control of the flow of remittances, they can contribute to development at the national level. The small but growing research on the impact of remittances on political outcomes has also shown mixed results. Receivers are more likely to engage in politics in more stable regimes than in unstable countries like Zimbabwe. In Zimbabwe, remittances have contributed significantly to helping families weather the failing economy, but they have also given receivers room to disengage from politics. In other words, some Zimbabwean senders have remitted fear, not democracy. Zimbabwean receivers have largely disengaged from politics, especially public-facing actions like protests and rallies. Admittedly, public-facing political participation comes at a high cost, but Zimbabwean remittance receivers also vote less than those who do not receive remittances.

Remittances, which comprise almost 10 percent of Zimbabwe's GDP, play an important role in the economy. During one of his legendary rants, Mugabe responded to concerns about the failing economy in Zimbabwe by challenging international reporters to try to sleep on the highway. Mugabe was arguing that the country was not under financial strain because, as far as he was concerned, the highway was packed. Zimbabwe experienced inflation worse than Germany between the world wars, and the government did not increase welfare for the most vulnerable during that period. Instead, the government continues to demand payment of foreign currency for health care and education. The government knows Zimbabweans living abroad will continue sending money to support their families back home. Those abroad are unlikely to stop sending money home even if it means the receivers will continue to disengage from politics.

BEYOND ZIMBABWE: OTHER FORMS OF LONG-RULING REGIMES

Although the world has become more democratic and more countries have passed both the first and second turnover tests, many authoritarian regimes still exist. This book is primarily about those that have ruled for a long time. Some democratic regimes, such as India, South Africa, Botswana, Italy, and Japan, have spent a long time under the rule of single parties. In democracies, longevity is sustained by support from the people and anchored in democratic tenets. In Zimbabwe, China, Russia, Vietnam, Eritrea, and other authoritarian regimes, long-serving parties survive by limiting free and fair participation. Exit via migration, illness, and death are also higher in such states and benefit the ruling regime even though they might not always experience the same types of exit.

Migration is not going to stop. There are regular stories in the media about hundreds of migrants who have lost their lives trying to escape tough economic and political conditions back home. This is particularly true for young Africans who are risking it all on treacherous trips via unwelcoming countries in North Africa, where unlucky people might die or end up enslaved (Achtnich, 2021; Syed Zwick, 2022; Tonah & Codjoe, 2020).

Over six million people have either been internally displaced or forced to leave Sudan since 2023. In Sudan, the pattern of migration is similar to that of Zimbabwe. Those who can leave tend to be young, educated, middle-class citizens who can afford to flee war (van Moorsel & Bonfiglio, 2023). They are spending thousands of dollars to make it to safety. Exit, especially of vocal pro-democracy activists, will impact the politics of a stabilized Sudan. Pro-democracy activists claim the government is targeting them; because of that, many have fled for their lives (Nashed, 2024). Without their voices demanding change and holding the government accountable, democracy will likely not come, just as it has not in Libya, where thousands of pro-democracy activists, the young and educated, fled the country and have not returned (Achtnich, 2022). The ouster of Muammar Gaddafi did not bring democracy to Libya; instead, the failed political and economic systems encouraged mass migration out of the country.

In many countries where thousands are fleeing war, even higher numbers of citizens, especially women and children, are dying. The combination of war and disease is lethal to the growth and stability of nations. The Democratic Republic of Congo (DRC), an authoritarian state not much better in its politics than Zimbabwe, will continue to sink deeper into undemocratic rule. Its current government is using the same toolbox of rigging and election engineering to win elections, and it is also benefiting from the massive exit premium of an estimated six million who have died or fled the country since the start of the most recent conflict. The DRC has been at war since the 1960s, but the recent waves of ongoing conflict began in 2012. Since then, over seven million have been displaced. Just since 2022, more than 700,000 have been displaced. The majority of these, about 72 percent, are living in refugee camps (United Nations Refugee Agency, 2024).

In March 2024, Russian state media announced that Vladimir Putin had won the presidential election with at least 88 percent of the vote (Edwards, 2024). Putin uses many strategies to stay in power, including intimidation and silencing of opponents. Still, the forced exit of an estimated five million Russians who have left the country since the start of the war has contributed to his win. Putin appears not to mind having all these young liberals leave the country; if he did, he would have sealed the borders. Ukraine's future as a democracy is also at risk because of the exit of millions who have either died or been forced to emigrate because of the war. Democracy thrives when the majority of citizens are able to use their voices and actively participate in elections.

The literature on the political impact of emigration, especially on young democracies like Ghana and struggling ones like Nigeria, is still small. Still, all evidence points to serious trouble as more young, educated, professional people exit their countries. While more than 90 million Nigerians were eligible to vote in the 2023 elections, less than a third of them did. Government policies make it difficult for young people, especially those in urban areas, to participate. Many people look forward to *japa*, the colloquial word for going abroad.

As more people are living away from home, the money they send home is also increasing. India, the biggest recipient of remittances, $125 billion in 2023, has made significant strides in encouraging the participation of their diaspora in politics and business (World Bank, 2023). In turn, remittances have greatly impacted development, especially for poor families (Bastiaens & Tirone, 2019; Noushad et al., 2022). Mexico is the second largest receiver of remittances, receiving almost $61 billion annually. Mexico's politics, although more democratic, faces some of the same challenges as Zimbabwe. In Mexico, remitters have been credited with remitting democracy to families back home, and their diaspora has found ways to be more engaged in politics back home by voting and running for office (Burgess, 2016; Danielson, 2017; Duquette-Rury, 2020). Mexico and India are more democratic; thus, it is much easier for remitters and their recipients to engage in pro-democratic politics. Ethiopia, Bangladesh, and the Philippines also receive a lot of remittances, but their democratic impact has been minimal. Most of the funds in poor and less democratic countries meet everyday needs such as health care, education, and food. Politics in those countries is undemocratic and, just as in Zimbabwe, remittances have bolstered the ruling regimes. Studies by Ahmed (2013), Hassan and Rahman (2015), Zerihun (2020), and Zewdu (2014) have shown that authoritarian regimes can leverage foreign aid and household remittances to finance patronage and extend their rule.

Deinla et al. (2022) found that experiences with COVID-19 and politics in the host countries made Filipino migrants more interested in politics back home. However, they argued their study was too small to provide generalizable data. After analyzing data from 156 countries, Islam and Lee (2023) found that remittances support democratic outcomes in countries with better social and governance policies. The study of the political impact of remittances on political outcomes remains small and uneven – some regions have been better studied than others – and the subject would benefit from more research, especially in harder-to-access countries.

Exit works with all the other tools that authoritarian parties use to hold onto power, such as violence and gerrymandering. Still, exit provides a significant premium often overlooked in regime survival studies. Large waves of voters exiting due to death, illness, or migration also pose challenges for democracies, especially younger ones. Democracy works best when all voices are represented.

There are no easy solutions because often, as I have shown in the Zimbabwe case, those who leave home are fleeing unfavorable conditions. It would be unfair to force people to remain in countries where they do not feel safe or cannot be the best versions of themselves. Still, there is room for the diaspora and its supporters to continue using their voices and leveraging remittances to demand better politics in the countries of origin as part of the policies of host countries. Pro-democracy actors, including international organizations and civil society, have an opportunity to counter the push factors of migration by increasing development aid to vulnerable countries. If more people were less vulnerable, they could participate more fully in democracy, and fewer people would take such risks to leave their homelands.

References

Abdih, Y., Chami, R., Dagher, J., & Montiel, P. (2012). Remittances and institutions: Are remittances a curse? *World Development*, 40(4), 657–666.

Abduvaliev, M., & Bustillo, R. (2020). Impact of remittances on economic growth and poverty reduction amongst CIS countries. *Post-Communist Economies*, 32(4), 525–546. https://doi.org/10.1080/14631377.2019.1678094

Achtnich, M. (2021). Bordering practices: Migrants, mobility, and affect in Libya. *American Ethnologist*, 48(3), 314–326. https://doi.org/10.1111/amet.13030

(2022). Waiting to move on: Migration, borderwork and mobility economies in Libya. *Geopolitics*, 27(5), 1376–1389. https://doi.org/10.1080/14650045.2021.1919626

Acosta, P. A., Lartey, E. K., & Mandelman, F. S. (2009). Remittances and the Dutch disease. *Journal of International Economics*, 79(1), 102–116.

Adams, R. H., & Cuecuecha, A. (2013). The impact of remittances on investment and poverty in Ghana. *World Development*, 50, 24–40. https://doi.org/10.1016/j.worlddev.2013.04.009

Agadjanian, V., & Zotova, N. (2012). Sampling and surveying hard-to-reach populations for demographic research: A study of female labor migrants in Moscow, Russia. *Demographic Research*, 26(5), 131–150.

Ahmed, F. Z. (2013). Remittances deteriorate governance. *Review of Economics and Statistics*, 95(4), 1166–1182.

(2017). Remittances and incumbency: Theory and evidence. *Economics & Politics*, 29(1), 22–47. https://doi.org/10.1111/ecpo.12086

Aldrich, J. H. (1993). Rational choice and turnout. *American Journal of Political Science*, 37, 246–278.

Alexander, J. (2021). The noisy silence of Gukurahundi: Truth, recognition and belonging. *Journal of Southern African Studies*, 47(5), 763–785.

Alexander, J., & McGregor, J. (2013). Introduction: Politics, patronage and violence in Zimbabwe. *Journal of Southern African Studies*, 39(4), 749–763.

Alexander, P. (2000). Zimbabwean workers, the MDC & the 2000 election. *Review of African Political Economy*, 27(85), 385–406.

Amoateng, A. Y., Kalule-Sabiti, I., & Oladipo, S. E. (2015). Psycho-social experiences and coping among caregivers of people living with HIV/AIDS in the North-West Province of South Africa. *South African Journal of Psychology*, 45(1), 130–139. https://doi.org/10.1177/0081246314556566

Anderson, C. J. (2000). Economic voting and political context: A comparative perspective. *Electoral Studies*, 19(2–3), 151–170.

Arriola, L. R. (2009). Patronage and political stability in Africa. *Comparative Political Studies*, 42(10), 1339–1362.

Bamfo, N. (2005). Term limits and political incumbency in Africa: Implications of staying in power too long with references to the cases of Kenya, Malawi, and Zambia. *African and Asian Studies*, 4(3), 327–356.

Barz, G., & Cohen, J. M. (2011). *The culture of AIDS in Africa: Hope and healing through music and the arts*. Oxford University Press.

Basedau, M., Erdmann, G., & Mehler, A. (2007). *Votes, money and violence: Political parties and elections in Sub-Saharan Africa*. Nordic Africa Institute.

Bastiaens, I., & Tirone, D. C. (2019). Remittances and varieties of democratization in developing countries. *Democratization*, 26(7), 1132–1153. https://doi.org/10.1080/13510347.2019.1604689

Batista, C., & Vicente, P. C. (2011). Do migrants improve governance at home? Evidence from a voting experiment. *The World Bank Economic Review*, 25(1), 77–104.

BBC. (1980, March 4). *Mugabe to lead independent Zimbabwe*. http://news.bbc.co.uk/onthisday/hi/dates/stories/march/4/newsid_2515000/2515145.stm

Bearce, D. H., & Park, S. (2019). Why remittances are a political blessing and not a curse. *Studies in Comparative International Development*, 54(1), 164–184. https://doi.org/10.1007/s12116-018-9277-y

Beissinger, M. R. (2012). *Who participated in the Arab Spring? A comparison of Egyptian and Tunisian revolutions*. Princeton University Department of Politics. www.princeton.edu/~mbeissin/beissinger.tunisiaegyptcoalitions.pdf

Bicego, G. J., Boerma, T., & Ronsmans, C. (2002). The effect of AIDS on maternal mortality in Malawi and Zimbabwe. *AIDS* 16(7), 1078.

Blair, D. (2002). *Degrees in violence: Robert Mugabe and the struggle for power in Zimbabwe*. Continuum International Publishing Group.

Blessing-Miles, T., Alexander, J., & McGregor, J. (Eds.). (2014). *Politics, patronage and the state in Zimbabwe*. Weaver Press.

Bloch, A. (2005). *The development potential of Zimbabweans in the diaspora: A survey of Zimbabweans living in the UK and South Africa*. United Nations Publications.

Boas, T. C., Hidalgo, F. D., & Richardson, N. P. (2014). The spoils of victory: Campaign donations and government contracts in Brazil. *The Journal of Politics*, 76(2), 415–429.

Bogaards, M. (2007). Electoral systems, party systems, and ethnic conflict management in Africa. In M. Basedau, G. Erdmann, & A. Mehler (Eds.), *Votes, money and violence: Political parties and elections in Africa* (pp. 168–193), Nordiska Afrikainstitutet.

(2009). How to classify hybrid regimes? Defective democracy and electoral authoritarianism. *Democratization*, 16(2), 399–423.

Bollard, A., McKenzie, D., Morten, M., & Rapoport, H. (2011). Remittances and the brain drain revisited: The microdata show that more educated migrants remit more. *The World Bank Economic Review*, 25(1), 132–156, https://doi.org/10.1093/wber/lhr013

Boone, C., & Batsell, J. (2001). Politics and AIDS in Africa: Research agendas in political science and international relations. *Africa Today*, 48(2), 3–33.

Boyle, B. (2022). *Exit, voice, and loyalty in North Korea: What can refugees tell us about Hirschman's theory in the world's longest lasting totalitarian state?* (Doctoral thesis, Johns Hopkins University). https://jscholarship.library.jhu.edu/handle/1774.2/67467

Bracking, S., & Sachikonye, L. (2006). *Remittances, poverty reduction and informalization in Zimbabwe 2005–6: A political economy of dispossession?* (Brooks World Poverty Institute Working Paper No. 28). The University of Manchester. http://economics.ouls.ox.ac.uk/14038

(2010). Migrant remittances and household wellbeing in urban Zimbabwe. *International Migration*, 48(5), 203–227.

Bratton, M. (2011). Violence, partisanship and transitional justice in Zimbabwe. *The Journal of Modern African Studies*, 49(3), 353–380.

Bratton, M., Bhavnani, R., & Chen, T. H. (2012). Voting intentions in Africa: Ethnic, economic or partisan? *Commonwealth & Comparative Politics*, 50(1), 27–52.

Bratton, M., Dulani, B., & Masunungure, E. (2016). Detecting manipulation in authoritarian elections: Survey-based methods in Zimbabwe. *Electoral Studies*, 42, 10–21.

Bratton, M., & Kimenyi, M. S. (2008). Voting in Kenya: Putting ethnicity in perspective. *Journal of Eastern African Studies*, 2(2), 272–289.

Bratton, M., & Masunungure, E. (2012). *Voting intentions in Zimbabwe and the margin of terror* (Paper No. 103). Afrobarometer.

Bratton, M., & Van de Walle, N. (1994). Neopatrimonial regimes and political transitions in Africa. *World Politics*, 46(4), 453–489.

Brinkerhoff, J. M. (2006). Digital diasporas and conflict prevention: The case of Somalinet.com. *Review of International Studies*, 32(1), 25–47.

Brownell, J. (2008). The hole in Rhodesia's bucket: White emigration and the end of settler rule. *Journal of Southern African Studies*, 34(3), 591–610.

Brunet, R. (2017). *Macron camp crushes competition as overseas French voters cast first legislative votes*. French24. www.france24.com/en/20170606-france-legislative-election-2017-macron-camp-crushes-competition-voters-abroad

Brusila, J. (2002). Modern "traditional" music from Zimbabwe: Virginia Mukwesha Mbira record "Matare." In Mai Palmberg & Annemette Kirkegaard (Eds.), *Playing with identities in contemporary music in Africa* (pp. 35–45). Nordika Afrikainsteutet.

Bukari, C., Peprah, J. A., Ayifah, R. N. Y., & Annim, S. K. (2021). Effects of credit "plus" on poverty reduction in Ghana. *The Journal of Development Studies*, 57(2), 343–360. https://doi.org/10.1080/00220388.2020.1797689

Burgess, K. (2016). Organized migrants and accountability from afar. *Latin American Research Review*, 51(2), 150–173.

Campsie, A. (2019). *When Robert Mugabe was stripped of his honorary degree from Edinburgh University*. Scotsman.com. www.scotsman.com/heritage-

and-retro/heritage/when-robert-mugabe-was-stripped-of-his-honorary-degree-from-edinburgh-university-496374

Carlson, E. (2010, April 22). *Great expectations: Ethnicity, performance, and Ugandan voters* (Paper presentation). Working Group on African Political Economy Meeting, Pomona College. www.sscnet.ucla.edu/polisci/wgape/papers/18_Carlson.pdf

Catholic Commission for Justice and Peace & Legal Resources Foundation in Harare. (Eds.). (2008). *Gukurahundi in Zimbabwe: A report on the disturbances in Matebeleland and the Midlands, 1980–1988*. Columbia University Press.

Centers for Disease Control and Prevention. (1990). *Reports on HIV/AIDS*.

Cheeseman, N., & Klaas, B. (2018). *How to rig an election*. Yale University Press.

Chigora, P., & Nciizah, E. (2007). Elections and vote rigging/electoral fraud in Zimbabwe: A critical analysis of the 2000–2008 parliamentary and presidential elections. *SSRN Electronic Journal*. https://doi.org/10.2139/ssrn.1083382

Chigudu, S. (2020). *The political life of an epidemic: Cholera, crisis and citizenship in Zimbabwe*. Cambridge University Press.

Chigwedere, P., Seage, G. R., III, Gruskin, S., Lee, T.-H., & Essex, M. (2008). Estimating the lost benefits of antiretroviral drug use in South Africa. *JAIDS Journal of Acquired Immune Deficiency Syndromes*, 49(4), 410–415.

Chikalipah, S. (2021). Sovereign debt and growth in Zambia: Determining the tipping point. *Social Sciences & Humanities Open*, 4(1), 100188.

Chikanda, A. (2005). Nurse migration from Zimbabwe: Analysis of recent trends and impacts. *Nursing Inquiry*, 12(3), 162–174. https://doi.rog/10.1111/j.1440-1800.2005.00273.x

(2006). Skilled health professionals' migration and its impact on health delivery in Zimbabwe. *Journal of Ethnic and Migration Studies*, 32(4), 667–680.

(2007). Medical migration from Zimbabwe: Magnitude, causes and impact on the poor. *Development Southern Africa*, 24(1), 47–60.

Chinaka, C. (2000). Strike fear in White hearts, urges Mugabe. *IOL News*. www.iol.co.za/news/africa/strike-fear-in-white-hearts-urges-mugabe-56427

Chipato, F., Ncube, C., & Dorman, S. R. (2020). The politics of civil society in Zimbabwe. In M. Tendi, J. McGregor, & J. Alexander (Eds.), *The Oxford handbook of Zimbabwean politics*. Oxford University Press. https://doi.org/10.1093/oxfordhb/9780198805472.013.8

Chirambo, K. (2004). *Impact of HIV/AIDS on electoral processes in Southern Africa*. Electoral Institute of Southern Africa.

Chitura, D., & Chitura, M. (2014). Burnout syndrome in intensive care unit nurses in Zimbabwe. *European Scientific Journal*, 10(10), 436–457.

Chung, R. Y.-N., Liao, T. F., & Fong, E. (2020). Data collection for migrant live-in domestic workers: A three-stage cluster sampling method. *American Behavioral Scientist*, 64(6), 709–721.

Collier, P., & Vicente, P. C. (2012). Violence, bribery, and fraud: The political economy of elections in Sub-Saharan Africa. *Public Choice*, 153, 117–147. https://doi.org/10.1007/s11127-011-9777-z

Compagnon, D. (2000). Zimbabwe: Life after ZANU-PF. *African Affairs*, 99(396), 449–453.

Cowell, A. (1984, August 12). Zimbabwe plans one-party rule but does not seek hasty change. *New York Times.* www.nytimes.com/1984/08/12/world/zimbabwe-plans-one-party-rule-but-does-not-seek-hasty-change.html

Cox, G. (2009). *Authoritarian elections and leadership succession, 1975–2004* (Paper presentation). American Political Science Association Meeting, Toronto, ON. http://papers.ssrn.com/sol3/papers.cfm?abstract_id=1449034

Crush, J., Chikanda, A., & Tawodzera, G. (2015). The third wave: Mixed migration from Zimbabwe to South Africa. *Canadian Journal of African Studies / Revue canadienne des études africaines, 49*(2), 363–382. https://doi.org/10.1080/00083968.2015.1057856

Crush, J., & Tevera, D. (Eds.). (2010). *Zimbabwe's exodus: Crisis, migration, survival.* Institute for Democracy in South Africa.

Daimon, A. (2016). ZANU (PF)'s manipulation of the "alien" vote in Zimbabwean elections: 1980–2013. *South African Historical Journal, 68*(1), 112–131.

Dalton, R. J., McAllister, I., & Wattenberg, M. P. (2000). The consequences of partisan dealignment. In R. J. Dalton & M. P. Wattenberg (Eds.), *Parties without partisans: Political change in advanced industrial democracies* (pp. 37–63). Oxford University Press.

Daniel, S. (2021). *How many orphans are in Zimbabwe?* The Flat. https://theflatbkny.com/africa-and-middle-east/how-many-orphans-are-in-zimbabwe/

Danielson, M. S. (2017). *Emigrants get political: Mexican migrants engage their home towns.* Oxford University Press.

Darboe, K. (2003). New immigrants in Minnesota: The Somali immigration and assimilation. *Journal of Developing Societies, 19*(4), 458–472.

Davenport, C. A., Moore, W. H., & Poe, S. C. (2003). Sometimes you just have to leave: Domestic threats and forced migration, 1964–1989. *International Interactions, 29*(1), 27.

Daxecker, U., & Rauschenbach, M. (2023). Election type and the logic of pre-election violence: Evidence from Zimbabwe. *Electoral Studies, 82,* 102583. https://doi.org/10.1016/j.electstud.2023.102583

Deinla, I. B., Mendoza, G. A. S., Mendoza, R. U., & Yap, J. K. (2022). Emergent political remittances during the pandemic: Evidence from a survey of overseas Filipino workers. *Asian and Pacific Migration Journal, 31*(2), 141–161. https://doi.org/10.1177/01171968221112119

Denaro, C. (2020). Voice through exit: Syrian refugees at the borders of Europe and the struggle to choose where to live. In S. Pasquetti & R. Sanyal (Eds.), *Displacement* (pp. 131–152). Manchester University Press.

Dendere, C. (2019). *Using semi-structured ethnographic interviews to study politically sensitive topics with immigrant populations.* SAGE Publications.

Dendere, C., & Young, L. (2023, April 19). *Understanding voter registration in a hybrid regime: A field experiment in Zimbabwe* (Paper presentation). Boston Area Working Group – African Political Economy Miniconference, Yale University, New Haven, CT.

de Waal, A. (2006). *AIDS and power: Why there is no political crisis – Yet.* Zed Books.

Dionne, K. Y., & Inman, K. L. (2014). *Another resource curse? The impact of remittances on political participation* (Afrobarometer Working Paper No. 45). Afrobarometer.

Docquier, F., Lodigiani, E., Rapoport, H., & Schiff, M. (2011). *Emigration and democracy* (Development Studies Working Paper 307). Centro Studi Luca d'Agliano. https://doi.org/10.2139/ssrn.1926790

Dombo, S. (2019). Zimbabwe's "Capturing a Fading National Memory Project": An evaluation and reconsideration. *Journal for Contemporary History*, 44(2), 55–73.

Donno, D. (2013). Elections and democratization in authoritarian regimes. *American Journal of Political Science*, 57(3), 703–716.

Dorman, S. R. (2002). *Inclusion and exclusion: NGOs and politics in Zimbabwe* (Unpublished doctoral dissertation). University of Oxford.

(2005). "Make sure they count nicely this time": The politics of elections and election observing in Zimbabwe. *Commonwealth and Comparative Politics*, 43(2), 155–177.

(2016). *Understanding Zimbabwe: From liberation to authoritarianism*. Hurst.

Dowding, K., John, P., Mergoupis, T., & Van Vugt, M. (2000). Exit, voice and loyalty: Analytic and empirical developments. *European Journal of Political Research*, 37(4), 469–495.

Downs, A. (1957). An economic theory of political action in a democracy. *The Journal of Political Economy*, 65(2), 135–150.

Duquette-Rury, L. (2020). *Exit and voice: The paradox of cross-border politics in Mexico*. University of California Press.

Dzimiri, C. T., Dzimiri, P., & Batisai, K. (2019). Fighting against HIV and AIDS within a resource constrained rural setting: A case study of the Ruvheneko Programme in Chirumhanzu, Zimbabwe. *SAHARA-J: Journal of Social Aspects of HIV/AIDS*, 16(1), 25–34. https://doi.org/10.1080/17290376.2019.1605537

Edwards, C. (2024, March 17). *Putin extends one man-rule in Russia after stage-managed election devoid of credible opposition*. CNN. www.cnn.com/2024/03/17/europe/putin-wins-russia-presidential-election-intl/index.html

Electoral Institute for Sustainable Democracy in Africa. (2000). *Zimbabwe election update 2000*. www.eisa.org.za/wep/zimresults2000r.htm

Erdmann, G. (2007). *Ethnicity, voter alignment and political party affiliation: An African case – Zambia*. German Institute of Global and Area Studies. http://papers.ssrn.com/sol3/papers.cfm?abstract_id=978175

Escribà-Folch, A., Meseguer, C., & Wright, J. (2015). Remittances and democratization. *International Studies Quarterly*, 59(3), 571–586.

Escribà-Folch, A., Wright, J., & Meseguer, C. (2022). *Migration and democracy: How remittances undermine dictatorships*. Princeton University Press.

Ferdaous, J. (2016). Impact of remittances and FDI on economic growth: A panel data analysis. *Journal of Business Studies Quarterly*, 8(2), 58.

Ferree, K. E. (2006). Explaining South Africa's racial census. *Journal of Politics*, 68(4), 803–815.

Fiorina, M. P. (1978). Economic retrospective voting in American national elections: A micro-analysis. *American Journal of Political Science*, 22(2), 426–443.

Fujii, L. A. (2015). Five stories of accidental ethnography: Turning unplanned moments in the field into data. *Qualitative Research*, 15(4), 525–539.
  (2017). *Interviewing in social science research: A relational approach*. Routledge.
Gandhi, J., & Lust-Okar, E. (2009). Elections under authoritarianism. *Annual Review of Political Science*, 12, 403–422.
Gao, X., Kikkawa, A., & Kang, J. (2021). *Evaluating the impact of remittances on human capital investment in the Kyrgyz Republic* (Economics Working Paper Series No. 637). Asian Development Bank. https://doi.org/10.2139/ssrn.3849991
Geddes, B. (1999). What do we know about democratization after twenty years? *Annual Review of Political Science*, 2(1), 115–144.
  (2005, September 1–3). *Why parties and elections in authoritarian regimes?* (Paper presentation). Annual Meeting of the American Political Science Association, Washington, DC.
Gettleman, J. (2011, March 16). Libya's oil money let Qaddafi buy support in Africa. *The New York Times*. www.nytimes.com/2011/03/16/world/africa/16mali.html
Global Burden of Disease Health Financing Collaborator Network. (2018). Spending on health and HIV/AIDS: Domestic health spending and development assistance in 188 countries, 1995–2015. *The Lancet*, 391(10132), 1799–1829. https://doi.org/10.1016/S0140-6736(18)30698-6
Gonese, E., Musuka, G., Ruangtragool, L., Hakim, A., Parekh, B., Dobbs, T., Duong, Y. T., Patel, H., Mhangara, M., Mugurungi, O., Mapingure, M., Suzue Saito, S., Herman-Roloff, A., Gwanzura, L., Tippett-Barr, B., Kilmarx, P. H., & Justman, J. (2020). Comparison of HIV incidence in the Zimbabwe Population-Based HIV Impact Assessment Survey (2015–2016) with modeled estimates: Progress toward epidemic control. *AIDS Research and Human Retroviruses*, 36(8), 656–662. https://doi.org/10.1089/AID.2020.0046
Gottlieb, S. (2000). UN predicts half the teenagers in Africa will die of AIDS. *BMJ: British Medical Journal*, 321(7253), 72.
Gregson, S., Garnett, G. P., Nyamukapa, C. A., Hallett, T. B., Lewis, J. J. C., Mason, P. R., Chandiwana, S. K., & Anderson, R. M. (2006). HIV decline associated with behavior change in eastern Zimbabwe. *Science*, 311(5761), 664–666.
Habyarimana, J., Humphreys, M., Posner, D., & Weinstein, J. (2007). *Placing and passing: Evidence from Uganda on ethnic identification and ethnic deception* (Paper presentation). Annual Meeting of the American Political Science Association, Chicago.
Hadley, L. H. (1977). The migration of Egyptian human capital to the Arab oil-producing states: A cost-benefit analysis. *International Migration Review*, 11(3), 285–299.
Halkitis, P. N. (2019). The Stonewall riots, the AIDS epidemic, and the public's health. *American Journal of Public Health*, 109(6), 851–852. https://doi.org/10.2105/AJPH.2019.305079
Halperin, D. T., Mugurungi, O., Hallett, T. B., Muchini, B., Campbell, B., Magure, T., Benedikt, C., & Gregson, S. (2011). A surprising prevention

success: Why did the HIV epidemic decline in Zimbabwe? *PLoS Medicine*, 8(2), e1000414.
Hammar, A., McGregor, J., & Landau, L. (2010). Displacing Zimbabwe: Crisis and construction in southern Africa. *Journal of Southern African Studies*, 36(2), 263–283.
Hansen, T. (1994). Local elections and local government performance. *Scandinavian Political Studies*, 17(1), 1–30.
Harris, A. (2008). Discourses of dirt and diseases in Operation Murambatsvina. In M. T. Vambe (Ed.), *The hidden dimensions of Operation Murambatsvina* (pp. 40–52). Weaver.
Hassan, G. M., & Rahman, S. (2015). *Is the democratisation process responsive to remittance flows? Evidence from Bangladesh* (Working paper). University of Waikato. https://repec.its.waikato.ac.nz/wai/econwp/1506_Hassan_Rahman.pdf
Hawker, G. (2002). Zimbabwe, AIDS & President Mbeki. *AQ: Australian Quarterly*, 74(2), 21–40.
Heins, V. M. (2020). Can the refugee speak? Albert Hirschman and the changing meanings of exile. *Thesis Eleven*, 158(1), 42–57.
The Herald. (2004, September 11). *RBZ launches Homelink*. https://allafrica.com/stories/200409130290.html
Higashijima, M. (2022). *The dictator's dilemma at the ballot box: Electoral manipulation, economic maneuvering, and political order in autocracy*. University of Michigan Press.
Hirschman, A. O. (1970). *Exit, voice, and loyalty: Responses to decline in firms, organizations, and states*. Harvard University Press.
  (1978). Exit, voice, and the state. *World Politics*, 31(1), 90–107.
Hlabyago, K. E., & Ogunbanjo, G. A. (2009). The experiences of family caregivers concerning their care of HIV/AIDS orphans. *South African Family Practice*, 51(6), 506–511.
Hlatshwayo, M. (2019). Precarious work and precarious resistance: A case study of Zimbabwean migrant women workers in Johannesburg, South Africa. *Diaspora Studies*, 12(2), 160–178. https://doi.org/10.1080/09739572.2018.1485239
Hodzi, O. (2014). The youth factor in Zimbabwe's 2013 harmonised elections. *Journal of African Elections*, 13(2), 48–70.
Huefner, J. C., & Hunt, H. K. (1994). Extending the Hirschman model: When voice and exit don't tell the whole story. *The Journal of Consumer Satisfaction, Dissatisfaction and Complaining Behavior*, 7, 267–270.
Human Rights Watch. (2003). *South Africa should allow peaceful AIDS protest*. www.hrw.org/news/2003/03/20/south-africa-should-allow-peaceful-aids-protest
Huntington, S. P. (1968). *Political order in changing societies*. Yale University Press.
Islam, M. R., & Lee, K.-K. (2023). Do foreign remittances promote democracy? A dynamic panel study of developing countries. *Hitotsubashi Journal of Economics*, 64(1), 59–85.
Kandeh, J. D. (2003). Sierra Leone's post-conflict elections of 2002. *The Journal of Modern African Studies*, 41(2), 189–216.

Kanyenze, G., Chitambara, P., & Tyson, J. (2017). *The outlook for the Zimbabwean economy*. Supporting Economic Transformation. http://set.odi.org/wp-content/uploads/2017/08/SET-Outlook-for-Zimbabwe-Economy_Sep2017.pdf

Kapur, D. (2010). *Diaspora, development, and democracy: The domestic impact of international migration from India*. Princeton University Press.

Karombo, T. (2022, July 6). *The battle for a share of Zimbabwe's billion dollar remittance industry*. Quartz. https://qz.com/africa/2185437/the-battle-for-a-share-of-zimbabwes-billion-dollar-remittance-industry/

Katedza, R. (2022). *Transactions*. Mai Jai Films.

Kenrick, D. (2016). Kenrick on Charumbira, "Imagining a nation: History and memory in making Zimbabwe". H-Nationalism. https://networks.h-net.org/node/3911/reviews/157394/kenrick-charumbira-imagining-nation-history-and-memory-making-zimbabwe

Kerr, N., Krönke, M., & Wahman, M. (2024). Where are the sore losers? Competitive authoritarianism, incumbent defeat, and electoral trust in Zambia's 2021 election. *Public Opinion Quarterly, 88*(SI), 608–631.

Khan, A. (2021). *Thomas Mapfumo on music, politics and unity*. News24. www.news24.com/channel/music/news/thomas-mapfumo-on-music-politics-and-unity-20211214

Kuhlmann, J. (2010). *Political activism of the Zimbabwean diaspora: Opportunities for, and challenges to, transnational mobilisation*. Leipziger University-Verlag.

Laakso, L. (2002). The politics of international election observation: The case of Zimbabwe in 2000. *The Journal of Modern African Studies, 40*(3), 437–464.

Lafleur, J.-M. (2013). *Transnational politics and the state: The external voting rights of diasporas*. Routledge.

Lazarsfeld, P. F., Berelson, B., & Gaudet, H. (1968). *The people's choice: How the voter makes up his mind in a presidential campaign*. Columbia University Press.

LeBas, A. (2006). Polarization as craft: Party formation and state violence in Zimbabwe. *Comparative Politics, 38*(4), 419–438.

(2013). The urban roots of democracy and political violence in Zimbabwe: Harare and Highfield, 1940–1964 by Timothy Scarnecchia, [Book review]. *The Journal of Modern African Studies, 51*(1), 191–192.

Leck, J. D., & Saunders, D. M. (1992). Hirschman's loyalty: Attitude or behavior? *Employee Responsibilities and Rights Journal, 5*(3), 219–230.

Lee, S. (2021). "Life was a party before AIDS arrived in London." *BBC News*. www.bbc.com/news/uk-england-london-55983269

Levitsky, S., & Way, L. A. (2002). The rise of competitive authoritarianism. *Journal of Democracy, 13*(2), 51–65.

Lewanika, M. (2023). ZANU-PF's bigwig rallies as performative politics during Zimbabwe's 2008 and 2013 elections. *Commonwealth & Comparative Politics, 61*(3), 273–292. https://doi.org/10.1080/14662043.2023.2250064

Lewis-Beck, M. S., & Stegmaier, M. (2007). Economic models of voting. In R. Dalton, & H. D. Klingemann (Eds.), *The Oxford handbook of political behavior* (pp. 518–537). Oxford: Oxford University Press.

Lindberg, S. I. (2006). *Democracy and elections in Africa*. Johns Hopkins University Press.

Lindberg, S., & Morrison, I. (2008). Are African voters really ethnic or clientelistic? Survey evidence from Ghana. *Political Science Quarterly*, 123(1), 95–122.

Lindley, A. (2022). *The early morning phonecall: Somali refugees' remittances*. Berghahn Books.

Lipset, S. M., & Rokkan, S. (1967). *Party systems and voter alignments: Crossnational perspectives*. Free Press.

Lodigiani, E., & Salomone, S. (2012). *Migration-induced transfers of norms: The case of female political empowerment* (Development Studies Working Paper 343). Centro Studi Luca d'Agliano. https://doi.org/10.2139/ssrn.2214978

Lopman, B., & Gregson, S. (2008). When did HIV incidence peak in Harare, Zimbabwe? Back-calculation from mortality statistics. *PLoS ONE*, 3(3), e1711. https://doi.org/10.1371/journal.pone.0001711

Mabweazara, H. M., Muneri, C. T., & Ndlovu, F. (2020). News "media capture," relations of patronage and clientelist practices in Sub-Saharan Africa: An interpretive qualitative analysis. *Journalism Studies*, 21(15), 2154–2175. https://doi.org/10.1080/1461670X.2020.1816489

Magaisa, A. (2019). Zimbabwe: An opportunity lost. *Journal of Democracy* 30(1), 143–157. https://doi.org/10.1353/jod.2019.0011

Magaloni, B. (2006). *Voting for autocracy: Hegemonic party survival and its demise in Mexico*. Cambridge University Press.

Mahomva, A, Greby, S., Dube, S., Mugurungi, O., Hargrove, J., Rosen, D., Dehne, K. L., Gregson, S., St. Louis, M., & Hader, S. (2006). HIV prevalence and trends from data in Zimbabwe, 1997–2004. *Sexually Transmitted Infections*, 82(S1), 42–47.

Mail & Guardian. (2000, May 2). Hundreds back Zim's war veterans leader in fraud trial. https://mg.co.za/article/2000-05-02-hundreds-back-zims-war-veterans-leader-in-fraud-trial/

Makina, D. (2008). A profile of Zimbabwean migrants in Johannesburg. In S. Johnstone, A. Berstein, & R. de Villiers (Eds.), *Migration from Zimbabwe: Numbers, needs and policy options* (pp. 14–28). Centre for Development Enterprise.

(2012). Migration and characteristics of remittance senders in South Africa. *International Migration*, 51(s1), e148–e158. https://doi.org/10.1111/j.1468-2435.2012.00746.x

Makota, R., Birri, B., & Musenge, E. (2023). Estimating HIV incidence over a decade in Zimbabwe: A comparison of the catalytic and Farrington models. *PLOS Global Public Health*, 3(9), 1–13. https://doi.org/10.1371/journal.pgph.0001717

Makumbe, J. M. (2002). Zimbabwe's hijacked election. *Journal of Democracy*, 13(4), 87–101.

Makumbe, J. (2006). Electoral politics in Zimbabwe: Authoritarianism versus the people. *Africa Development*, 31(3), 45–61.

Manby, B. (2019). *Report on citizenship law: Zimbabwe*. European University Institute. https://cadmus.eui.eu/bitstream/handle/1814/60436/RSCAS_GLOBALCIT_CR_2019_01.pdf

Mangongera, C. (2014). A new twilight in Zimbabwe: The military vs. democracy. *Journal of Democracy*, 25(2), 67–76.

Maphosa, F. (2005). *The impact of remittances from Zimbabweans working in South Africa on rural livelihoods in the southern districts of Zimbabwe*. University of the Witwatersrand Forced Migration Studies Programme.

Maringira, G., & Gukurume, S. (2022). Youth political mobilization: Violence, intimidation, and patronage in Zimbabwe. *Political Psychology*, 43(6), 1027–1041.

Maroleng, C. (2004). Malawi general election 2004: Democracy in the firing line. *African Security Review*, 13(2), 77–81 https://doi.org/10.1080/10246029.2004.9627287

Masunungure, E. (2011). Zimbabwe's militarized electoral authoritarianism. *Journal of International Affairs*, 65(1), 47–64.

Mbiba, B. (2004). Zimbabwe's global citizens in "Harare North": Some preliminary observations. In R. Palmberg & M. Primorac (Eds.), *Skinning the Skunk: Facing Zimbabwean futures* (pp. 26–38). Nordic Institute.

McClure, J. (2020). An analysis of Zimbabwean health crises since independence. *The Internationalist: Undergraduate Journal of Foreign Affairs*, 5(1), 32–38.

McGreal, C. (2002, January 16). Analysis: The trail from Lancaster House. *The Guardian*. www.theguardian.com/world/2002/jan/16/zimbabwe.chrismcgreal

McGregor, J., & Primorac, R. (Eds.). (2010). *Zimbabwe's new diaspora: Displacement and the cultural politics of survival*. Berghahn Books.

Meardi, G. (2007). More voice after more exit? Unstable industrial relations in Central Eastern Europe. *Industrial Relations Journal*, 38(6), 503–523. https://doi.org/10.1111/j.1468-2338.2007.00461.x

Melander, E., & Öberg, M. (2006). Time to go? Duration dependence in forced migration. *International Interactions*, 32(2), 129–152.

Meldrum, A. (2006). *Where we have hope: A memoir of Zimbabwe*. Grove Press.

Meldrum, M. (1991). Brave message from a dead Bhundu Boy. *Weekly Mail*. https://pubmed.ncbi.nlm.nih.gov/12295501

Mhanga, F., & Ndebele, H. (2016). Diaspora remittances reach US$830 million. *Zimbabwe Independent*. www.theindependent.co.zw/2016/07/29/diaspora-remittances-reach-us830-million/

Miachel, S. (2013). The silent devastation of AIDS on New York's art and fashion worlds. *Vanity Fair*. www.vanityfair.com/culture/1987/03/devastation-of-aids-1980s

Moore, D. (2008). Coercion, consent, context: Operation Murambatsvina and ZANUPF's illusory quest for hegemony. In M. Vambe (Ed.), *The hidden dimensions of Operation Murambatsvina in Zimbabwe* (pp. 25–39). Weaver Press.

Morley, N. (2016). *Powerful images from HIV epidemic protests in the 1980s and 1990s*. Metro UK. https://metro.co.uk/2016/11/23/powerful-images-from-hiv-epidemic-protests-in-the-1980s-and-1990s-6274896

Morrison, K. M. (2009). Oil, nontax revenue, and the redistributional foundations of regime stability. *International Organization*, 63(1), 107–138.

Moyo, D. (2009). *Dead aid: Why aid is not working and how there is a better way for Africa*. Macmillan.

Moyo, I., & Nicolau, M. D. (2016). Remittances and development: Zimbabwean migrant teachers in South Africa and their impact on their Zimbabwean families. *African Population Studies*, 30(2), 2507–2519.

Moyo-Nyede, S. (2020). *Fear and trust: Explaining professed popular trust in Zimbabwe's presidents*. Africa Portal. www.africaportal.org/publications/fear-and-trust-explaining-professed-popular-trust-zimbabwes-presidents/

Mpofu, S., & Ncube, A. (2023). Religion and the consolidation of the ZANU-PF political ideology. In B. Dube (Ed.), *Regime, religion and the consolidation of ZANU-PFism in Zimbabwe* (pp. 201–220). Springer Nature Switzerland. https://doi.org/10.1007/978-3-031-46084-5_10

Mpondi, D. (2015). The institutionalization of one man rule and the politics of succession and patronage in Zimbabwe. *International Relations and Diplomacy*, 3(8), 511–519.

Mugabe, R. (2001). *Inside the Third Chimurenga*. Department of Information and Publicity Office of the President and Cabinet.

Murithi, T., & Mawadza, A. (2011). *Zimbabwe in transition: A view from within*. Jacana Media.

Mutambasere, T. G. (2022). Diaspora citizenship in practice: Identity, belonging and transnational civic activism amongst Zimbabweans in the UK. *Journal of Ethnic and Migration Studies*, 48(3), 732–749.

Muzondidya, J. (2007). Jambanja: Ideological ambiguities in the politics of land and resource ownership in Zimbabwe. *Journal of Southern African Studies*, 33(2), 325–341.

Mvundura, E. (2020). Zimbabwe's elections: A legitimate ritual of ZANU-PF. *International Journal of Humanities and Social Science*, 10(8), 101–108.

Mwonzora, G., & Mandikwaza, E. (2019). The menu of electoral manipulation in Zimbabwe: Food handouts, violence, memory, and fear – Case of Mwenezi East and Bikita West 2017 by-elections. *Journal of Asian and African Studies*, 54(8), 1128–1144. https://doi.org/10.1177/0021909619862595

Nashed, M. (2024, January 9). "They're targeting us": Sudan's army cracks down on democracy activists." *Al Jazeera*. www.aljazeera.com/features/2024/1/9/sudans-army-is-retaliating-against-activists-amid-the-war-for-their-role-in-bringing-down-their-former-boss-and-president-omar-al-bashir-in-april-2019

Ndakaripa, M. (2020). Zimbabwe's 2018 elections: Funding, public resources and vote buying. *Review of African Political Economy*, 47(164), 301–312.

Ndawana, E. (2020). The military and democratisation in post-Mugabe Zimbabwe. *South African Journal of International Affairs*, 27(2), 193–217.

Ndawana, E., & Hove, M. (2023). ZANU(PF)'s survival strategies and the co-option of civil society, 2000–2018. *Journal of Southern African Studies*, 49(1), 49–66. https://doi.org/10.1080/03057070.2023.2183024

Ndlela, T. (2011). *Evolution of Zimbabwe's economic tragedy: A chronological review of macroeconomic policies and transition to the economic crisis*. Munich Personal RePEc Archive. https://mpra.ub.uni-muenchen.de/id/eprint/32703

Ndoma, S. (2017). *Almost half of Zimbabweans have considered emigrating: Job search is main pull factor*. Afrobarometer. www.afrobarometer.org/publication/ad160-almost-half-zimbabweans-have-considered-emigrating-job-search-main-pull-factor/

New Humanitarian. (2005). *Remittances: Govt hopes they can save economy.* www.thenewhumanitarian.org/feature/2005/05/18/remittances-govt-hopes-they-can-save-economy

New Humanitarian. (2011). *A timeline of HIV/AIDS activism.* www.thenewhumanitarian.org/report/93877/south-africa-timeline-hivaids-activism

News24. (2017). Opposition parties rubbish survey report suggesting Zimbabweans "still trust Mugabe." www.news24.com/news24/africa/zimbabwe/opposition-parties-rubbish-survey-report-suggesting-zimbabweans-still-trust-mugabe-20170513

New York Times. (2008, June 25). Queen Elizabeth II strips Mugabe of knighthood. www.nytimes.com/2008/06/25/world/africa/25iht-25zimbabwe-queen.13987844.html

Noushad, A. P., Parida, J. K., & Raman, R. K. (2022). Low-skilled emigration, remittances and economic development in India. *Migration and Development*, 11(3), 389–419. https://doi.org/10.1080/21632324.2020.1787099

O'Brien, S., & Broom, A. (2010). The prevalence and politics of HIV/AIDS in Zimbabwe: Examining the ideological, political and historical factors behind the "decline." *Politikon*, 37(2–3), 311–330, https://doi.org/10.1080/02589346.2010.530448

Ogunmefun, C., Gilbert, L., & Schatz, E. (2011). Older female caregivers and HIV/AIDS-related secondary stigma in rural South Africa. *Journal of Cross-Cultural Gerontology*, 26(1), 85–102. https://doi.org/10.1007/s10823-010-9129-3

Omotola, J. (2011). A cabalised regime: Neopatrimonialism, President Yar'Adua's health crisis and Nigeria's democracy. *CEU Political Science Journal*, 6(2), 222–253.

Oosterom, M., & Gukurume, S. (2022). Ruling party patronage, brokerage, and contestations at urban markets in Harare. *African Affairs*, 121(484), 371–394.

Opalo, K. O. (2011). *Ethnicity and elite coalitions: The origins of "big man" presidentialism in Africa.* https://papers.ssrn.com/sol3/papers.cfm?abstract_id=1853744

Owczarzak, J. (2009). Defining democracy and the terms of engagement with the postsocialist Polish state: Insights from HIV/AIDS. *East European Politics and Societies*, 23(3), 421–45.

Papic, M., & Noonan, S. (2011). *Social media as a tool for protest.* Stratfor. www.stratfor.com/weekly/20110202-social-media-tool-protest

Pasura, D. M. (2008). *A fractured diaspora: Strategies and identities among Zimbabweans in Britain.* University of Warwick. http://wrap.warwick.ac.uk/id/eprint/2378

Pasura, D. (2010). Zimbabwean transnational diaspora politics in Britain. In J. McGregor & R. Primorac (Eds.), *Zimbabwe's new diaspora: Displacement and the cultural politics of survival* (pp. 103–211). Berghahn.

(2012). A fractured transnational diaspora: The case of Zimbabweans in Britain. *International Migration*, 50(1), 143–161. https://doi.org/10.1111/j.1468-2435.2010.00675.x

Patterson, A. S. (Ed.). (2005). *The African state and the AIDS crisis.* Ashgate Publishing.

(2011). *The church and AIDS in Africa: The politics of ambiguity*. First Forum Press.

(2018). *Africa and global health governance: Domestic politics and international structures*. Johns Hopkins Press.

Patterson, A. S., & Cole, R. (2006). The politics of AIDS in Africa. *Bulletin of the African and African American Studies Program, Grand Valley State University*, *39*. https://citeseerx.ist.psu.edu/document?repid=rep1&type=pdf&doi=074154e9a8ba22689af3772858459d059d480e2d#page=41

Pfutze, T. (2012). Does migration promote democratization? Evidence from the Mexican transition. *Journal of Comparative Economics*, *40*(2), 159–175.

Piot, P., Kazatchkine, M., Dybul, M., & Lob-Levyt, J. (2009). AIDS: Lessons learnt and myths dispelled. *The Lancet*, *374*(9685), 260–263.

Posner, D. N. (2005). *Institutions and ethnic politics in Africa*. Cambridge University Press

(2007). Regime change and ethnic cleavages in Africa. *Comparative Political Studies*, *40*(11), 1302–1327.

Posner, D. N., & Young, D. J. (2007). The institutionalization of political power in Africa. *Journal of Democracy*, *18*(3), 126.

Potts, D. (2006). "Restoring order"? Operation Murambatsvina and the urban crisis in Zimbabwe. *Journal of Southern African Studies*, *32*(2), 273–291.

Price-Smith, A. T. (2004). *Downward spiral: HIV/AIDS, state capacity, and political conflict in Zimbabwe*. United States Institute of Peace.

Raftopoulos, B. (2002). Briefing: Zimbabwe's 2002 presidential election. *African Affairs*, *101*(404), 413–426.

Ratha, D. (2024). *Remittances 2024*. World Bank. www.worldbank.org/en/topic/migration/brief/remittances-knomad

Read, B. L. (2018). Serial interviews: When and why to talk to someone more than once. *International Journal of Qualitative Methods*, *17*(1), 1609406918783452.

Reuter, O. J. (2010). The politics of dominant party formation: United Russia and Russia's governors. *Europe-Asia Studies*, *62*(2), 293–327.

Reuters. (1997, December 10). *World news briefs: Tax to aid war veterans is canceled in Zimbabwe*. www.nytimes.com/1997/12/10/world/world-news-briefs-tax-to-aid-war-veterans-is-canceled-in-zimbabwe.html

Reyntjens, F. (2020). Respecting and circumventing presidential term limits in Sub-Saharan Africa: A comparative survey. *African Affairs*, *119*(475), 275–295.

Riker, W. H. (1976). The number of political parties: A reexamination of Duverger's law. *Comparative Politics*, *9*(1), 93–106.

Robins, S. (2006). From "rights" to "ritual": AIDS activism in South Africa. *American Anthropologist*, *108*(2), 312–323. https://doi.org/10.1525/aa.2006.108.2.312

Sachikonye, L. M. (2012). *Zimbabwe's lost decade: Politics, development and society*. African Books Collective.

Schatz, E. (Ed.). (2013). *Political ethnography: What immersion contributes to the study of power*. University of Chicago Press.

Scheiner, E. (2005). *Democracy without competition in Japan: Opposition failure in a one-party dominant state*. Cambridge University Press.

Scoones, I., Marongwe, N., Mavedzenge, B., Murimbarimba, F., Mahenehene, J., & Sukume, C. (2010, November 11). Zimbabwe's land reform: Myths and realities. *The Zimbabwean*. http://ids.ac.uk/files/dmfile/zimbabwean4pdf.pdf

Seawright, J. (2016). Better multimethod design: The promise of integrative multimethod research. *Security Studies*, 25(1), 42–49.

Shaw, W. H. (1986). Towards the one-party state in Zimbabwe: A study in African political thought. *The Journal of Modern African Studies*, 24(3), 373–394.

Silver, A. (2014). Families across borders: The emotional impacts of migration on origin families. *International Migration*, 52(3), 194–220. https://doi.org/10.1111/j.1468-2435.2010.00672.x

Singhal, A., Cody, M. J., Rogers, E. M., & Sabido, M. (2003). *Entertainment-education and social change: History, research, and practice*. Routledge.

Sithole, M., & Makumbe, J. (1997). Elections in Zimbabwe: The ZANU (PF) hegemony and its incipient decline. *African Journal of Political Science*, 2(1), 122–139.

Skocpol, T. (1979). *States and social revolutions: A comparative analysis of France, Russia and China*. Cambridge University Press.

Song, Y., Paramati, S. R., Ummalla, M., Zakari, A., & Kummitha, H. R. (2021). The effect of remittances and FDI inflows on income distribution in developing economies. *Economic Analysis and Policy*, 72, 255–267. https://doi.org/10.1016/j.eap.2021.08.011

Stanecki, K. A. (2000). *The AIDS pandemic in the 21st century: The demographic impact in developing countries* (Paper presentation). 13th International AIDS Conference, Barcelona.

Stover, J., Glaubius, R., Kassanjee, R., & Dugdale, C. M. (2021). Updates to the Spectrum/AIM model for the UNAIDS 2020 HIV estimates. *Journal of the International AIDS Society*, 24(S5), e25778. https://doi.org/10.1002/jia2.25778

Stover, J., Walker, N., Grassly, N. C., & Marston, M. (2006). Projecting the demographic impact of AIDS and the number of people in need of treatment: Updates to the Spectrum projection package. *Sexually Transmitted Infections*, 82(S3), iii45–iii50.

Syed Zwick, H. (2022). Onward migration aspirations and destination preferences of refugees and migrants in Libya: The role of persecution and protection incidents." *Journal of Ethnic and Migration Studies*, 48(15), 3705–3724. https://doi.org/10.1080/1369183X.2022.2031923

Szent-Ivanyi, B., & Kugiel, P. (2020). The challenge from within: EU development cooperation and the rise of illiberalism in Hungary and Poland. *Journal of Contemporary European Research*, 16(2), 121–138.

Tachibana, T., Goto, R., Sakurai, T., Rayamahji, S., & Adhikari, A. (2019). Do remittances alleviate negative impacts of disaster on mental health? A case of the 2015 Nepal earthquake. *Social Science & Medicine*, 238, 112460. https://doi.org/10.1016/j.socscimed.2019.112460

Tendi, B. M. (2013a). Ideology, civilian authority and the Zimbabwean military. *Journal of Southern African Studies*, 39(4), 829–843. https://doi.org/10.1080/03057070.2013.858543

(2013b). Robert Mugabe's 2013 presidential election campaign. *Journal of Southern African Studies*, 39(4), 963–970. https://doi.org/10.1080/03057070.2013.858537

(2017). Transnationalism, contingency and loyalty in African liberation armies: The case of ZANU's 1974–1975 Nhari mutiny. *Journal of Southern African Studies*, 43(1), 1–18.

Tendi, B.-M. (2020). *The army and politics in Zimbabwe: Mujuru, the liberation fighter and kingmaker*. Cambridge University Press.

Tevera, D., & Chikanda, A. (2009). *Migrant remittances and household survival in Zimbabwe*. Institute for Democracy in South Africa.

Tibaijuka, A. (2005) *Report of the fact-finding mission to Zimbabwe to assess the scope and impact of Operation Murambatsvina by the UN special envoy on human settlements issues in Zimbabwe*. United Nations. www.un.org/News/dh/infocus/zimbabwe/zimbabwe_rpt.pdf

Tonah, S., & Codjoe, E. (2020). Risking it all: Irregular migration from Ghana through Libya to Europe and its impact on the left-behind family members. *Global Processes of Flight and Migration*, 25, 25–37.

Tsourapas, G. (2022). Migration and development in Egypt: A holistic view. *International Development Policy*, 14, 94–370.

Tungwarara, O. (2005). *Case study: Zimbabwe highly restrictive provisions*. IDEA Publications.

Tupy, M. (2008, March 27). *Marian Tupy on BBC World talking about Zimbabwe's elections*. Cato Institute. www.cato.org/multimedia/media-highlights-tv/marian-tupy-bbc-world-talking-about-zimbabwes-elections

Tyburski, M. D. (2014). Curse or cure? Migrant remittances and corruption. *Journal of Politics*, 76(3), 814–824. https://doi.org/10.1017/S0022381614000279

UNAIDS. (2017). *Bringing HIV services to hard-to-reach people in Victoria Falls*. www.unaids.org/en/resources/presscentre/featurestories/2017/march/20170322_zimbabwe

United Nations News Report. (2000). *Zimbabwe: DRC war figures disputed*. Africa News Service, 1008244u2537.

United Nations Refugee Agency. (2024). *Democratic Republic of the Congo*. Retrieved March 26, 2024, from https://reporting.unhcr.org/operational/operations/democratic-republic-congo

United States Census Bureau. (2012). *Selected countries of birth for the United States and 15 metropolitan statistical areas with the largest African-born populations: 2008–2012*. www.census.gov/library/publications/2014/acs/acsbr12-16.html

Van de Walle, N. (2003). Presidentialism and clientelism in Africa's emerging party systems. *The Journal of Modern African Studies*, 41(2), 297–321.

(2007). Meet the new boss, same as the old boss? The evolution of political clientelism in Africa. In H. Kitschelt & S. I. Wilkinson (Eds.), *Patrons, clients and policies: Patterns of democratic accountability and political competition* (pp. 50–67). Cambridge University Press.

van Moorsel, J., & Bonfiglio, A. (2023). *Mixed migration consequences of Sudan's conflict: Round 2*. Mixed Migration Centre. https://mixedmigration.org/mixed-migration-consequences-sudan-conflict-june-2023

Vanyoro, K. (2023). The political work of migration governance binaries: Responses to Zimbabwean "survival migration" at the Zimbabwe–South Africa border. *Refugee Survey Quarterly*, 42(3), 286–312. https://doi.org/10.1093/rsq/hdad006

Venter, D. (2002). Malawi: The transition to multi-party politics. In J. A. Wiseman (Ed.), *Democracy and political change in Sub-Saharan Africa* (pp. 164–204). Routledge.

Vicente, P. C., & Wantchekon, L. (2009). Clientelism and vote buying: Lessons from field experiments in African elections. *Oxford Review of Economic Policy*, 25(2), 292–305.

Voice of America Zimbabwe. (2012). *Zimbabwe president urge MPs to reveal HIV status to fight stigma.* www.voanews.com/a/article–zimbabwe-president-urge-mps-to-reveal-hiv-status-to-fight-stigma-141064773/179915.html

Wamsley, L. (2023, June 28). Nearly 2,000 migrants have died crossing the Mediterranean this year. Here's why. *NPR.* www.npr.org/2023/06/28/1184581187/migrant-deaths-mediterranean-crossing

Wantchekon, L. (2003). Clientelism and voting behavior: Evidence from a field experiment in Benin. *World Politics*, 55(3), 399–422.

Warren, M. E. (2011). Voting with your feet: Exit-based empowerment in democratic theory. *American Political Science Review*, 105(4), 683–701.

Way, L, & Levitsky, S. (2002). The rise of competitive authoritarianism. *Journal of Democracy*, 13(2), 51–65. https://doi.org/10.1353/jod.2002.0026

Weinel, M. (2009). *Thabo Mbeki, HIV/AIDS and bogus scientific controversies.* Online Research @ Cardiff. https://orca.cardiff.ac.uk/id/eprint/73738/

Wellman, E. I. (2021). Emigrant inclusion in home country elections: Theory and evidence from Sub-Saharan Africa. *American Political Science Review*, 115(1), 82–96.

(2023). Refugee status as a patronage good? The interaction of transnational party mobilization and migration policy in the Global South. *Journal of Ethnic and Migration Studies*, 49(10), 2500–2520.

Williams, K. (2017). Do remittances improve political institutions? Evidence from Sub-Saharan Africa. *Economic Modelling*, 61, 65–75. https://doi.org/10.1016/j.econmod.2016.12.004

Wong, S. H.-W., Ho, K., Clarke, H. D., & Chan, K. C.-M. (2023). Does loyalty discourage exit? Evidence from post-2020 Hong Kong. *Journal of Asian & African Studies*, 58(1), 101–119.

World Bank. (2022). *Death rate, crude (per 1,000 people).* https://data.worldbank.org/indicator/SP.DYN.CDRT.IN?locations=ZW

World Bank. (2023). *Remittance flows continue to grow in 2023 albeit at slower pace* (Migration and Development Brief 39). www.worldbank.org/en/news/press-release/2023/12/18/remittance-flows-grow-2023-slower-pace-migration-development-brief

World Bank Group. (n.d.). *GDP growth (annual %): Zimbabwe.* https://data.worldbank.org/indicator/NY.GDP.MKTP.KD.ZG?locations=ZW

Wu, A., & McWilliam, A. (2023). Remittances for marriage: Quality of life changes among seasonal worker households in Timor-Leste. *Australian Geographer*, 54(2), 193–212.

Young, D. J. (2009). *Is clientelism at work in African elections? A study of voting behavior in Kenya and Zambia* (Working paper). Afrobarometer.

Young, L. E. (2019). The psychology of state repression: Fear and dissent decisions in Zimbabwe. *American Political Science Review*, 113(1), 140–155.

(2020). Who dissents? Self-efficacy and opposition action after state-sponsored election violence. *Journal of Peace Research*, 57(1), 62–76.

Zakaria, F. (1997). The rise of illiberal democracy. *Foreign Affairs*, 76, 22.

Zanamwe, L., & Devillard, A. (2009). *Migration in Zimbabwe: A country profile.* Zimbabwe National Statistical Agency; International Organisation for Migration, Harare.

(2018). *Migration in Zimbabwe: A country profile 2014–2016.* Zimbabwe National Statistics Agency: International Organization for Migration.

Zeldin, W. (2008). *Zimbabwe: Indigenization and Empowerment Act.* Global Legal Monitor. www.loc.gov/lawweb/servlet/lloc_news?disp3_l20540383_text

Zerihun, M. F. (2020). Remittances and economic growth: Evidence from Ethiopia, Kenya, and Uganda. *African Human Mobility Review*, 6(3), 6–27.

Zewdu, G. A. (2014). *The impact of migration and remittances on home communities in Ethiopia* (Doctoral thesis, University of Adelaide). Adelaide Research & Scholarship. https://digital.library.adelaide.edu.au/dspace/handle/2440/106785

Zimbabwe Election Support Network. (2013, August 10). *Zimbabwe: 2013 harmonised elections preliminary statement.* www.shabka.org/2013/08/10/zimbabwe-election-support-network-2013-harmonised-elections-preliminary-statement

The Zimbabwean. (2011). *Restore the diaspora vote.* www.thezimbabwean.co/2011/05/restore-the-diaspora-vote/

Index

Afrobarometer, 34, 46, 56, 73, 152
   HIV, 51, 114
   migration, 52, 54, 126, 128, 143, 196
   political preferences, 9, 47–49, 125, 196
   remittances, 53, 154–155, 166–170, 173, 192
Algeria, 23
antiretroviral therapy (ART), 12, 51, 79, 81, 84, 86–87, 89, 99
Arab Spring, 118, 156
Australia, 116
authoritarianism, electoral, 5–6, 11, 13–14, 33, 37, 39–41, 44–45, 73, 118
avoiding bias, 71–73

Bangladesh, 203
Bhebhe, Abedenico, 132
Bhundu Boys, 104
Biafra, 55
Biti, Tendai, 151
Bono, 79
Botswana, 11, 15, 23, 82, 137, 139, 201
Bulawayo, 18, 84, 90, 94, 96, 111, 121, 128–129, 137–139, 151, 179–180
Burundi, 22

Cameroon, 23
caregiver fatigue, 111–112
Chad, 23
Chamisa, Nelson, 107, 109
chimurenga music, 104
Chimurenga, First, 15
Chimurenga, Second, 16
Chimurenga, Third, 17, 28

China, 4, 16, 116, 201
Chitepo, Herbert, 15–16
constitution, 21, 26, 106, 131–133, 135
   Rwanda, 40
   Uganda, 40
Cuba, 4

Dangarebga, Tsitsi, 71
democracy, illiberal, 4–7, 11, 33, 37–39, 44–45, 73
Democratic Republic of Congo (DRC), 22, 24, 77, 202
diaspora vote, 31, 130–132, 197
   citizenship, 133–136
   fear, 136–138
   financial pressure, 140–141
   lack of time, 141–142
   organizing, 138–140
Djibouti, 23
Dongo, Margaret, 23

Egypt, 39, 44
election, combined
   2008, 130, 200
   2013, 99–102, 145, 200
election, constitutional referendum, 121
election, parliamentary
   1980, 17–18
   1985, 20
   1990, 21
   1996, 91
   2000, 1, 91–94, 145, 198

election, parliamentary (cont.)
  2005, 91–94, 145, 198
  2008, 91–99
  by-elections, 96, 102, 107–109, 195
election, presidential
  2002, 88, 91–94, 130, 145, 198
  2008, 30, 85, 88, 91–96, 145
  all, 45
Eritrea, 4, 201
Ethiopia, 11, 203
European Union (EU), 36, 116
exit–voice–loyalty (EVL),
  3, 33–37, 119
  extensions, 3–4, 30, 37–44, 117, 154, 194

foreign direct investment (FDI),
  155, 158
France, 5, 36
fraud
  credit card, 71
  electoral, 14, 29, 41, 90, 99, 145

Gabon, 23
Gambia, 13, 32, 116
Ghana, 19, 22, 32, 155, 202
Gonda, Violet, 116
Gono, Gedion, 160
government of national unity, 99, 132, 140,
  151, 200
Guinea, 22–23
Gukurahundi genocide, 3, 18–20, 63, 83,
  103, 129
Guni, Frank, 81

Harare, 58, 62, 74, 84, 193
  constitutional referendum, 121
  diaspora, 120, 128–129, 177
  elections, 1, 94, 96
  HIV, 78, 90, 96
  migration, 12, 67, 143
  remittances, 160, 164, 176, 179, 190
  strikes, 24
historical legacies, 14–17
HomeLink, 160–161
Hong Kong, 43
human rights, 38, 131, 139
Hungary, 39
Hunzvi, Chenjerai, 26

India, 15, 201, 203
Indigenization and Empowerment Act, 28, 162

inflation, 55, 198
  hyperinflation, 11, 25, 49, 122, 153,
    159–160, 198, 201
  migration, 130
  remittances, 158, 161, 166
International Organization for Migration, 9,
  52, 143
Italy, 201

Japan, 23, 121, 201
Jongwe, Learnmore, 108–109

Kagone, Rise, 104
Katedza, Rumbi, 179
Kenya, 13, 19, 22, 76, 80, 131
Kuti, Fela, 104
Kyrgyz Republic, 189

Lancaster House Agreement, 16, 26
land reform, 2, 19, 26–28, 68, 96, 108, 121,
  129
Lesotho, 63
LGBTQI, 75, 80, 84
Libya, 202
Limpopo River, 2, 12, 180
Lovemore, France, 83

maintaining elite unity, 14, 20–23
Malawi, 13, 21–22, 24, 76, 80, 107,
  133–134
  Banda, Hastings Kamuzu, 10, 13,
    121
  change in ruling party, 122
Malaysia, 23
Manicaland, 17, 94
manipulation, 4–6, 14, 18, 22, 29–31,
  39–40, 80, 85, 88, 102, 111, 130, 133,
  194, 197–198
  remittances, 44
Mankaba, 104
Mano, Rebecca, 164
Mapfumo, Thomas, 71, 102–103, 105–106
Marley, Bob, 103
Mashonaland, 16
  elections, 121
Mashonaland Central, 187
  elections, 17, 90–91
Mashonaland East
  elections, 17, 91, 94
Mashonaland West
  elections, 17, 94

Masvingo, 17, 28, 94
Matambanadzo, Bella, 111
Matebeleland, 16, 18–19, 28, 83–84, 129
    elections, 18
Matebeleland North
    elections, 90, 94
Matebeleland South
    elections, 94
Mbeki, Thabo, 12, 81
Mercury, Freddie, 104
Mexico, 20, 30, 121, 189, 203
Midlands, 18, 94, 143
Mnangagwa, Emmerson, 16, 18, 122
MoneyGram, 159
Movement for Democratic Change (MDC), 1, 17, 26, 28, 47, 56, 70, 126, 128, 137, 151, 194, 196
    diaspora, 119–121, 125, 130, 132, 136, 138–142, 151, 161–162
    elections, 1, 45, 91, 94, 99, 107, 121–122, 130
    factions, 99, 139–140
    founding, 2, 23, 27, 88, 121, 193–194
    leaders HIV deaths, 96, 107–109
    remittances, 179
Moyo, Jonathan, 105
Mozambique, 10, 23, 133
Mtetwa, Beatrice, 131
Mthwakazi, 129
Mtukudzi, Oliver, 71, 104–106, 110
Mtwakhazi, 140
Mugabe, Robert, 1, 10, 19, 23, 25–26, 81, 83, 106, 108, 137, 201
    coup, 16–17, 70, 122, 141, 187
    elite unity, 20
    independence, 14, 16–17
    one-party state, 20–22
    ZANU-PF founding, 16
Mukoko, Jestina, 106
Mupandwa, Proud, 108
music activists, 102–107
Mutongi, Amos, 109
Muzorewa, Abel, 16–17

Namibia, 80, 82
Ndebele, 10, 16, 18–19, 63, 72, 83, 128, 154
    diaspora, 140, 142
Ndhlovu, Jabulani, 108
Nehanda Radio, 139
Nepal, 189

Nicaragua, 13
Niger, 23
Nigeria, 5, 13, 55, 203
Nkomo, Joshua, 15–18, 20, 23
    unity, 21
North Korea, 4, 16, 36–37

Operation Murambatsvina, 2, 81, 87, 108, 140, 142, 195, 200
orphaned children, 3, 51, 71, 74, 76, 84, 86, 111–114, 164, 195

pandemic, cholera, 99
pandemic, COVID-19, 11, 61, 85, 125, 176, 179, 203
patronage, 3, 14, 22, 25–29, 40, 137, 156, 203
performance legitimacy, 14, 23–25
Philippines, 44, 203
Poland, 36, 84, 116

Qatar, 54

recruiting participants, 61–71
Rhodes, Cecil, 15
Rhodesia, 15–16, 103, 105
Romania, 36
Russia, 16, 30, 32, 39, 54–55, 116, 201–202
    dominant party, 39–40
    Ukraine War, 11, 55
Rwanda, 22–23, 30, 39
    dominant party, 40–41

sampling strategy, 60–61, 123–125
Scotland, 33, 56, 65, 71, 120–121, 141–142, 165, 179
    Edinburgh, 57, 71
    Glasgow, 71, 141
    Stirling, 60, 124
Senegal, 121
Shona, 10, 18–19, 58, 63, 72, 103, 128, 154
Sibanda, Gibson, 140
Singapore, 23
Sithole, Ndabaningi, 15–16, 20
Smith, Ian, 16
Somalia, 63
South Africa, 11, 80, 201
    African National Congress (ANC), 11, 15, 20
    apartheid, 23, 80

South Africa (cont.)
  Cape Town, 59, 67–69, 137–138, 165, 179
  cross-border traders, 143
  diaspora, 60–61, 116, 123, 136, 138, 140, 191
  ethnography, 9, 61, 63, 67–69, 124, 152
  HIV, 11, 75–77, 81, 84, 107, 109
  Johannesburg, 61, 67, 123, 129, 138
  migration, 2, 12–13, 116, 126, 136, 138, 143, 176, 180
  Pretoria, 67
  remittances, 53, 161, 168, 189
South Sudan, 22
Southern Migration Project, 51–52
spectrum model, 9, 49, 52, 85–86, 143
Sudan, 5, 11, 201
Swaziland, 82
Syria, 4, 32, 37

Taiwan, 23
Tanzania, 22, 69, 76, 107
Tekere, Edgar, 16, 21
Tembo, Biggie, 104
Togo, 23
Tsvangirai, Morgan, 99, 107, 122, 140, 191
  diaspora, 132, 139
  elections, 1, 85, 94, 96, 99, 130, 145
  MDC founding, 196
  MDC leadership, 1
  trade union, 24, 121
Tunisia, 23
Turkey, 39

Uganda, 11, 23, 39, 77, 81
  dominant party, 40
Ukraine, 5, 11, 55, 202
UNAIDS
  migration data, 34, 114, 143, 152
  Spectrum HIV data, 9, 34, 49, 51, 73, 78–79, 85, 114, 152
United Kingdom, 36, *See* Scotland
  Birmingham, 65
  diaspora, 52, 55, 57, 61–63, 72, 74, 77, 123, 131, 136, 139, 141, 151, 175, 177, 179, 190
  ethnography, 9, 61, 65–67, 152
  Herefordshire, 65
  High Wycombe, 134, 137
  Leeds, 65
  London, 17, 57, 61, 65–66, 110, 115, 123, 142, 159, 175

  migration, 2, 12–13, 115, 136, 176, 179, 190, 196
  remittances, 159, 173, 177, 180, 183, 190
  Slough, 65
United National African Council (UANC), 17, 20
United Nations Refugee Agency, 9, 53, 136, 202
United States
  Atlanta, 62–63, 134
  diaspora, 61, 123, 135–136, 139–140, 142, 180, 184, 187
  ethnography, 9, 61–65, 152
  HIV, 77
  Indiana, 62–63
  migration, 115, 134, 136, 189
  New York City, 64
  Oregon, 55, 62–63
  remittances, 161, 164–165, 181, 185
  Texas, 62
  Washington, 120
  Washington DC, 57, 62, 64, 69, 72, 81, 135, 140
United States Achievers Program (USAP), 161, 164

Venezuela, 32
Victoria. *See* Masvingo
Victoria Falls, 83, 111, 166, 192
Vietnam, 4, 201
violence, 3, 11, 13, 18, 38, 41, 43, 48, 68, 90, 109, 130, 151, 154, 171, 185, 192–193, 197, 200, 203
  activists, 12
  electoral, 96, 99, 118, 145
  leading to migration, 2, 10, 64, 72, 119–120, 136–137

war veterans, 17, 24–26, 68, 121
weaponization of identity, 14, 17–20
Western Union, 153, 159–162
White Zimbabweans
  diaspora, 60, 67–69, 124, 129, 134
  independence, 15–17, 21, 26
  land reform violence, 2, 67, 137
  migration, 2–3, 12, 17, 65, 128, 136
  politics, 1, 19–20, 25–27, 132–133, 137
World Remit, 160
Wright, Eric Lynn (Eazy-E), 104

Index

Zambia, 11, 13, 16, 21–24, 55, 76, 121, 135, 161
coethnic voting, 19
HIV, 77, 80, 107
Kaunda, Kenneth, 11, 24, 121
Zimbabwe African National Union – Patriotic Front (ZANU-PF), 2–3, 5, 10, 13–14, 20–21, 26, 41, 47–49, 51, 53, 56, 59, 70, 73, 75–76, 88, 102, 108–110, 112–113, 117, 120, 122, 125–126, 157, 162, 176, 187, 193
diaspora, 61, 64, 72, 116, 120, 123, 128, 131–132, 138–139, 142, 151–152, 196
economy, 24, 159, 197
elections, 1, 9, 17, 21, 23, 30, 45, 76, 85–86, 90–91, 94, 96, 99, 102, 107, 109, 114, 116–117, 121–122, 130, 145, 152, 154, 193, 198, 200
independence, 14–17, 105
land reform, 137
leaders HIV deaths, 96, 102, 108, 195
patronage, 4, 27, 29, 193
remittances, 4, 154, 158–159, 170
rigging, 27, 29, 102, 105, 132, 193, 195
violence, 4, 12, 14, 19–20, 138, 142, 193, 197
Zimbabwe African People's Union (ZAPU), 15–16
elections, 17, 20
leaders, 16, 18
unification with ZANU, 19
Zimbabwe Associations in the United Kingdom/United States, 139
Zimbabwe Election Support Network (ZESN), 91
Zimbabwe Electoral Commission (ZEC), 29–30, 70, 91
Zimbabwe Population-Based HIV Impact Assessment, 51, 86
Zimbabweans in the United States (ZUSA), 142
ZimVigil, 139

For EU product safety concerns, contact us at Calle de José Abascal, 56–1º, 28003 Madrid, Spain or eugpsr@cambridge.org.

www.ingramcontent.com/pod-product-compliance
Ingram Content Group UK Ltd.
Pitfield, Milton Keynes, MK11 3LW, UK
UKHW041732130126
466887UK00012B/211